12

A Theology *for* Christian Education

James R. Estep Jr.

Michael J. Anthony

& Gregg R. Allison

ACADEMIC

Nashville, Tennessee

To

Dr. Dennis E. Williams

Professor, Scholar,

Leader, Author, Colleague, and Friend

A Theology for Christian Education
Copyright © 2008 by James R. Estep Jr., Michael J. Anthony, and Gregg R. Allison
All rights reserved.

Published by B & H Publishing Group
Nashville, Tennessee

ISBN: 978-0-8054-4457-5

Dewey Decimal Classification: 268
Subject Heading: CHRISTIAN EDUCATION/
DOCTRINAL THEOLOGY

Printed in the United States of America

1 2 3 4 5 6 7 8 9 10 11 12 • 16 15 14 13 12 11 10 09 08
LB

CONTENTS

CHAPTER 6

Michael J. Anthony

CHAPTER 7

Michael J. Anthony

CHAPTER 8

Gregg R. Allison

CHAPTER 9

Gregg R. Allison

CHAPTER 10

James Riley Estep Jr.

CHAPTER 11

James Riley Estep Jr.

James Riley Estep Jr.

Introduction

C hristian education must be more than simply using existing approaches to education in the service of the church and ministry. Becoming a Christian educator is more than simply attending a Christian college or seminary to receive biblical and theological training and then attending a state university to receive a degree in education. This approach to education would just keep the ministry's Christian content in one hand and the ministry's approach to education in the other—totally separated. Such an approach also assumes that educational approaches are philosophically or theologically neutral. What if an educational approach maintained that truth was relative, that students were incapable of changing, that teaching could only be done by lecture, or that memorization was all education sought to accomplish? Can you imagine how the Bible would be taught if any of these premises were used in Christian education? Christian education is more than just its content, and education itself is more than just methods, materials, and resources.

WHAT IS CHRISTIAN ABOUT EDUCATION?

Christian is both a noun and an adjective. Christian education refers to the content of instruction (noun), but it should also be an approach toward education that is distinctively Christian (adjective), one that reflects our theological beliefs and convictions. While content is important, this book will focus on

1

Christian education as an adjective by endeavoring to develop a distinctively Christian approach to educational ministries in the church. How can the church's approach to educational ministry be distinctively Christian?

The guiding premise of this book is that Christian education is *Christian* because what we believe theologically should inform and influence not only the content of education in the church but also the overall approach to education in the church. As Figure 0.1 indicates, we have certain theological convictions that instruct the rudimentary elements in forming an approach to education, resulting in a distinctively *Christian* education.

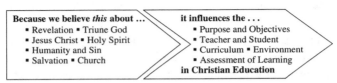

Because we believe *this* about ...	it influences the . . .
▪ Revelation ▪ Triune God	▪ Purpose and Objectives
▪ Jesus Christ ▪ Holy Spirit	▪ Teacher and Student
▪ Humanity and Sin	▪ Curriculum ▪ Environment
▪ Salvation ▪ Church	▪ Assessment of Learning
	in Christian Education

Figure 0.1: Premise of the Book

ABOUT THIS BOOK

Chapters 1–3 lay the foundations for a theology for Christian education. Chapter 1 endeavors to define *theology* and *education* as two fields of study, while chapter 2 asserts the necessity of integrating them into a single approach toward Christian education. Both of these chapters itemize the issues implicit in writing a theology of Christian education. Chapter 3 provides an overview of biblical principles of education, asking, "What does the Bible say about education in the church?"

Chapters 4–10 provide a systematic theology for Christian educators. Each of these chapters is generally divided into two sections. The first section is a presentation of evangelical theological affirmations, forming the "what we believe" section. The second section gives a general educational reflection on the specific doctrine addressed in the chapter, forming the "so we educate" section. The doctrines addressed—revelation, the

Trinity, Christology, pneumatology, humanity and sin, salvation, and ecclesiology—provide a basic systematic theology for the Christian educator.

Chapter 11 is the final chapter and provides more than just a summary. In effect, it is the third section. It provides a brief sketch of how a theologically informed approach to education in the church should appear. It contains the practical educational insights drawn collectively from the preceding chapters. Figure 0.2 illustrates the book's contents, continuity, and design.

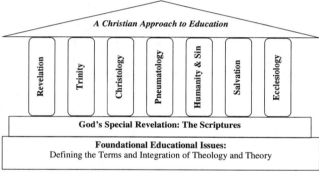

Figure 0.2: Graphic of the Book

Chapters 1–2 provide the introductory educational issues, including a rubric for formulating an approach to education. Chapter 3 expresses the importance of Scripture as the basis of theology as well as identifying the biblical insights into education in the church. Chapters 4–10 then serve as the pillars, the individual doctrines that compose the desired systematic theology. Finally, chapter 11 provides a basic sketch of education that is theologically informed, utilizing the rubric introduced in chapter 1.

ABOUT THE AUTHORS

This book is a reflection of its authors. Michael Anthony and I are Christian educators, students of theology, and scholars in the field of education. Gregg Allison is a theologian, a scholar of theology, and a student of education. We are all professors, so we are all practitioners in Christian education. While each chapter was written by one primary author, it was the task of the others to review and offer changes to each of the chapters. Gregg contributed significantly to this book not only by writing three chapters but also by providing significant theological insight and attention to the chapters written by Michael and me. Gregg engaged us in theological scholarship and facilitated further practical reflection on our part. Together, we believe this book reflects the integration of theological and educational scholarship into a theologically informed approach to Christian education. As the book's editor, I greatly appreciate the efforts of my cocontributors and their contributions not only to this book but also to the work of the ministry. Our hope as authors is that you, the readers, find great spiritual benefit from our endeavor and that this book helps you to "take captive every thought to make it obedient to Christ" (1 Cor 10:5 NIV).

James Riley Estep Jr., Ph.D.
Professor of Christian Education
Lincoln Christian Seminary
Lincoln, Illinois

Chapter 1

The Nature of
Theology and Education

Michael J. Anthony

DEFINITIONS AND
CATEGORIES OF THEOLOGY

We begin our rather daunting task of understanding the nature of God with an honest confession: we cannot say that we can actually understand the eternal God with our finite minds. Indeed, we proclaim that God is incomprehensible and too vast to be known. We recite the words of Job's friend Zophar, who declared, "Can you fathom the mysteries of God? Can you probe the limits of the Almighty?" (Job 11:7). We feel inept trying to answer Isaiah's question, "Who will you compare God with? What likeness will you compare him to?" (Isa 40:18). It seems a rather unlikely task actually to understand everything there is to know about God. Even the apostle Paul, to whom the Lord personally appeared, could not conceive of fully understanding Him: "Oh, the depth of the riches both of the wisdom and the knowledge of God! How unsearchable His judgments and untraceable His ways!" (Rom 11:33).

Yet God can be known by us. In Jer 9:23–24 the prophet exclaimed:

> This is what the Lord says: "Let not the wise man boast
> of his wisdom or the strong man boast of his strength
> or the rich man boast of his riches, but let him who

boasts boast about this: that he understands and knows
me, that I am the Lord, who exercises kindness, justice
and righteousness on earth, for in these I delight."

Accordingly, while confessing that God is incomprehensible, the church has affirmed that God reveals himself and can
therefore be known by the community of faith—at least to some
degree. In fact, God wants us to come into a relationship with
him and worship him for who he is and for all that he has done.
The more we come to know about God, the more we will worship him and come to appreciate all that he has done on our
behalf. It helps to know that our inquiry into the nature and
character of God is desired on his part and, as a result, he will
assist us along the way. In fact, Jesus said that one of the ministries of the Holy Spirit would be to lead and guide us into
all truth (John 16:13). So we embark on this journey with the
assurance that we have his presence and provision for what lies
ahead.

Coming to Terms

Defining terms is critical to having a meaningful dialogue.
In fact, without agreeing on some basic definitions, two people
may be involved in a rather intense debate and be talking about
two entirely different concepts. J. Macquarrie stated:

Definitions can be misleading, but they are not unimportant, for our approach to any study or investigation
whatsoever is guided by our initial assumptions about
what we are seeking and how we are to seek it, and it
is an advantage to make these assumptions explicit in
a definition.[1]

Definitions must always be the starting point for interaction
between two people entering into meaningful discussion.

Theology has been defined as "that discipline that strives to
give a coherent statement of the doctrines of the Christian faith,
based primarily on the Scriptures, placed in the context of cul-

ture in general, worded in a contemporary idiom, and related to the issues of life."[2] That is, theology seeks to study and express the key tenets or beliefs of Christianity. Its authoritative source is Scripture, while a secondary resource is other truth about God. Theology is always carried out in a particular context—for this book American evangelicalism at the beginning of the third millennium—and expressed in a contemporary and relevant manner. As it examines all the relevant doctrines, theology seeks to bring them together cohesively and coherently in such a manner as not to contradict or mislead. For this reason we must first get a handle on what the major tenets are in order to organize our investigation. These doctrinal categories help us bring together a vast amount of material into a more manageable conversation.

Categories of Theology

Our approach is to follow the categories of systematic theology: revelation, God, Jesus Christ, the Holy Spirit, humanity and sin, salvation, and the church. These categories allow for a more objective yet comprehensive discussion. They don't require knowledge in other areas or allow for as much bias. We also start from the point of view that God is the center of our discussion. It is not about humanity or creation. Theology has as its focal point the study of God and only branches out into other areas after that groundwork has been established. Though it may seem obvious to you to take this approach, theology hasn't always been done this way across history.

> Up to the beginning of the nineteenth century it was common practice to begin the study of Dogmatics with the doctrine of God, but a change came about under the influence of Schleiermacher, who sought to safeguard the scientific character of theology by the introduction of a new method. The religious consciousness of man was substituted for the Word of God as the source of

theology. Faith in Scripture as an authoritative revelation of God was discredited, and human insight based on man's own emotional or rational apprehension became the standard of religious thought.[3]

Eventually this approach was discredited, and people returned to the more traditional methodology of starting the investigation with God rather than with man.

The categories of theology that we use in this book are common to those who have studied or are currently studying theology at a Christian college or seminary. What's in a name? Apparently quite a bit to the many who have gone down this academic journey before us. Sometimes the broad range that has been used to delineate parameters has led to an overload of terms and theological concepts. For example, if you pick up a dozen texts on theology, you'll come across a plethora of terms used to set theological boundaries. These categories include dogmatic theology, apologetic theology, historical theology, biblical theology, philosophical theology, pastoral theology, moral theology, applied theology, and the list goes on and on. The point is that many people call categories of theology by a variety of names. What follows is a brief description of the more prominent categories.

Natural Theology. This form of theological investigation starts with the premise that God has revealed something about himself in nature (Rom 1:18–25; Ps 19:1–6), his providential care of the creation (Acts 14:15–17), the human conscience (Rom 2:12–16), and an innate sense of God (Acts 17:22–31). The assertion of natural theology is that this general revelation of God manifests his existence, something about his attributes (such as his power and his care), and a basic notion of right and wrong. Such revelation is enough to point people to God since human beings are also given a mind to reason and to form a consciousness about God. Catholic and Protestant theologians have differed in the degree to which they accept general revelation as a basis for knowing God.

In keeping with Thomas Aquinas (1225–1274), Catholics hold to a view that natural theology can construct a definable body of knowledge about God with its own sources, principles, and methods based on the application of reason to general revelation. Specifically, natural theology has developed several proofs for the existence of God: cosmological arguments (from the existence of the world), ontological arguments (from the idea of God), teleological arguments (from the complex design and order evident in the world), and anthropological arguments (from the purpose for humanity). Catholics do not negate the priority of special revelation from God through Scripture, but they tend to see revelation on a continuum between general revelation (that which can be known about God through creation and natural reason) and special revelation (that which is known about God through Christ and the Scriptures).[4]

Though Protestant theologians acknowledge the contributions of natural theology, they believe that it is deficient in specificity about God. Historically, Protestants have been cautious about this line of philosophical reasoning and have preferred to elevate the role of special revelation—particularly Jesus Christ and Scripture—as being a far superior source of revelation about God. Certainly, they agree that general revelation provides knowledge about God, but they also believe that once sin entered into the world, creation was marred and became an insufficient source of revelation for "what is necessary for salvation."[5] Experience, rational thought, and philosophical speculations may have their roles to play; but they are far below the supremacy of Christ, the message brought to us through his prophets, and the written Word of God.

Historical Theology. This theological endeavor focuses its attention on the biblical interpretations and theological formulations contributed by the church in time periods previous to the contemporary era. For example, historical theology studies

Augustine's theology of sin and grace in the early church, the theological and philosophical underpinnings of the sacraments offered by Aquinas in the medieval period, the doctrines of justification and biblical authority articulated by Martin Luther and John Calvin in the Reformation, and the defense of the inspiration of Scripture offered by B. B. Warfield in the modern era. Such exegetical findings and doctrinal statements form, in a certain sense, the tradition of the church. In terms of a healthy perspective on this, Kenneth Kantzer said: "While tradition is not infallible, it must be acknowledged as God's guidance of his people in accordance with his promise to the church of all ages."[6]

Historical theology makes an important contribution to the overall theological endeavor. It provides theologians today with insights from the past; such wise interpretive and doctrinal discoveries are neglected to our demise. It also provides theologians today with doctrinal truths—such as the trinitarian formula of God as three Persons in one essence and the Christological affirmation of the full deity and the full humanity of the Son of God incarnate—that have withstood the test of time. These consensus formulations help define the parameters of orthodoxy and heresy, saving us from having to reinvent the proverbial wheel while warning us not to transgress these established boundaries. Moreover, historical theology benefits the church today by highlighting what constitutes the essentials—and encouraging a focus on these—while reminding it that secondary and tertiary issues should not be points of bitter division.

Even though the contemporary church is largely ahistorical in orientation, historical theology does exert an influence on it. The church today studies and interprets the Bible, affirms and teaches various doctrinal beliefs, engages in numerous practices, and worships in a certain manner, but it does not carry out these activities in a vacuum. Whether acknowledged or not, tradition influences the present. Historical theology can ensure that the tradition that exerts the greatest influence on the contemporary church—the tradition of biblical interpretations and doctrinal formulations—is a sound tradition.

Apologetical Theology. The word *apology* used here refers to a defense; thus the emphasis of apologetical theology is the defense of the Christian faith. The task of this form of theological study is to answer two questions: (1) Does God exist, and, if so, (2) has God spoken? "Whether such a being as God exists needs to be ascertained, and if such a being exists, whether he is knowable; whether such creatures as men are capable of knowing him, and, if so, what sources of information concerning him are accessible. This is the tack of apologetical theology."[7] As we have already seen, God has spoken through general revelation. Examining this as a means of understanding God is the essence of natural theology that we discussed earlier. Moreover, beyond this general form of communication are other more specialized forms of communication. This is called special revelation and includes the revelation of God in Jesus Christ and the Bible, the written communication between God and humanity.

Exegetical Theology. The study of exegetical theology concerns itself with examining Scripture to determine the message that God has provided for us. It is concerned with three primary questions: (1) What books form the canon of Scripture? (2) What is the proper text of Scripture? (3) What does the text of Scripture mean? The canon of the Protestant Bible is composed of 66 books, and this canon is closed or fixed. The proper text of Scripture is determined by the science of textual criticism, and most Protestant Bibles are excellent translations. Determining what the text means is dependent on the method of interpretation. Hermeneutics provides the general principles of biblical interpretation while exegesis applies those principles in determining the meaning of particular texts. Exegesis is grammatical in that it focuses on the words and sentence structure of the text. It is also historical in that it interprets the text in the context of the historical setting of the author. This grammatical-

historical approach to exegetical interpretation is the foundation
for all theology.

Biblical Theology. Biblical theology is an intermediate or
bridge discipline between exegetical theology and systematic
theology, growing out of the first and leading to the second.[8] It
is based on the observable fact that God's revelation of himself
and his ways with his people is progressive in nature; that is, it
has changed in its arrangements (such as the difference between
the old covenant and the new covenant), its emphases (such as
the difference between the ministry of the Holy Spirit before
Pentecost and afterwards), its focal points (such as the difference between sanctification following purity laws and sanctification that has been freed from these ceremonial laws), and so
forth. Biblical theology seeks to study and describe this progressive divine revelation by focusing on the various groupings
of Scripture and by collecting and arranging the many themes
of these biblical groupings.

> This is done in three steps: first, we study the theo-
> logical themes in terms of individual books, then we
> explore the theology of an author, and finally we trace
> the progress of revelation that unites a Testament and
> even the Bible as a whole (that is, historical develop-
> ment of these themes throughout the biblical period).
> In this way biblical theology collates the results of
> exegesis and provides the data for the systematic theo-
> logian to contextualize in developing theological dog-
> mas for the church today.[9]

Specifically, this means that we may engage in a biblical theology of Joel or Jude (a single book by a single author), a biblical theology of the Pentateuch or the Johannine letters (multiple
volumes by one author), a biblical theology of the eighth-century
BC writing prophets (Amos, Micah, Isaiah, Hosea, and Jonah;
chronological similarity), a biblical theology of the Synoptic
Gospels (Matthew, Mark, Luke; a similarity of subject matter

and approach), an Old Testament theology, a New Testament theology, and other such combinations.

Though biblical theology is different from the other theological disciplines discussed in this section, their similarities should not be overlooked. For example, both biblical and systematic theology rely on exegetical theology for their interpretation of Scriptural texts. Indeed, though one is called biblical and the other systematic theology, this does not mean that systematic theology does not have the Bible as its source; neither does it mean that biblical theology is not systematic, that is, random or chaotic. Rather, biblical theology takes a portion of the Bible as its source (such as the Old Testament prophets, the letters of Paul), whereas systematic theology considers what the entire Bible affirms about a particular topic. And biblical theology organizes its material according to biblical themes (such as the presence of God in the tabernacle/temple) while systematic theology's organizing principle is topical (such as the doctrine of God).

Practical Theology. Practical theology is concerned with the application and communication of the other theological studies to the practice of how Christians live their daily lives. The way that the message of God's Word is communicated is of supreme importance to those in the field of practical theology. As the name implies, this form of theology is practiced and displayed in the world and in the local church. It includes such activities as homiletics (both preaching and teaching), "church organization and administration, worship, Christian education, pastoral theology, and the work of missions."[10]

Systematic Theology. Sometimes referred to as dogmatic theology because of its insistence on authoritative sources, it has also come to be known as Christian theology. We prefer the more contemporary designation of systematic theology. We have already provided some degree of explanation regarding this form of theological inquiry while comparing and contrasting it to other forms mentioned thus far. Suffice it to say

here that systematic theology gathers together the truths that
the other forms of theological inquiry discover (listed above)
and develops a well-ordered presentation of these truths into a
coherent whole.

> Systematic theology thus begins with divine revela-
> tion in its entirety, applies the Spirit-illumined mind to
> comprehend the revelation, draws out the teachings of
> Scripture via sound grammatical-historical exegesis,
> provisionally respects the development of the doctrine
> in the church, orders the results in a coherent whole,
> and applies the results to the full scope of human
> endeavor.[11]

Why Systematic Theology?

A reasonable question to ask is, Why study the nature and
meaning of God through the lens of systematic theology when
there are so many other lenses to use? What makes systematic
theology more beneficial as a foundation for Christian education than one of the other forms we have identified? Were we to
be honest, we would have to admit that the Bible is no more a
system of theology than any other form of scientific inquiry. So
why rely at all on a theological discipline that is systematic?

As we have defined it, systematic theology focuses on certain
broad subjects such as Jesus Christ, the Holy Spirit, the church,
and salvation; this discipline studies and expresses what Scripture teaches about these subjects throughout its entirety. Thus
the finished product is a well-ordered and coherent presentation
of the major doctrines of the Christian faith. This becomes an
excellent and sufficient resource for drawing out implications
for Christian education. On the foundation of systematic theology, we construct our theology of education.

Divisions of Systematic Theology

History has put forth a list of essential subjects to be included
in the field of systematic theology. Generally speaking, the sub-

ject matter to be included in a systematic study of theology includes ten subjects: bibliology, theology proper, Christology, pneumatology, angelology, anthropology, hamartiology, soteriology, ecclesiology, and eschatology (see Figure 1.1)

Doctrinal Division	Definition
Angelology	The nature and ministry of angels
Anthropology	The origin, nature, and purpose of humanity
Bibliology	The nature and function of the Scriptures
Christology	The person and work of Christ
Ecclesiology	The identity, purpose, and structure of the church
Eschatology	The end and consummation of all creation
Hamartiology	The origin, nature, and consequences of sin
Pneumatology	The person and work of the Holy Spirit
Soteriology	The nature and application of salvation
Theology Proper	The person and work of God (Trinity)

Figure 1.1: Theological Subjects

Means or Ends?

You might well ask at this point in our discussion if systematic theology is an end or a means to an end. You are not alone in asking since so much effort has gone into its development. Eminent theologian B. B. Warfield said that "the systematic theologian is preeminently a preacher of the gospel; and the end of his work is obviously not merely the logical arrangement of the truths which come under his hand, but the moving of men, through their power, to love God with all their hearts and their neighbors as themselves; to choose their portion with the Savior of their souls."[12] So then it must be concluded that the study of systematic theology is a means to an end and not the end itself. The end should be viewed as presenting every person complete in Christ (Col. 1:28) by bringing together the discovery of biblical truths (theology) and the communication of those truths (education) to people who in turn live out those truths in daily practice (discipleship). Viewed this way, theology and education become the means to accomplishing the Great Commission of Matthew 28:18–20.

THE NATURE OF EDUCATION

Perhaps the best place to start this leg of our journey is to again come back to the basics of definition. Education can be a complex process, or it can be relatively simple to explain. Education has been generically described as follows:

1. The activity of parents, teachers, and schools with children, adolescents, and adults
2. The learning process that occurs in the learner
3. The product of learning, that is, an education
4. The discipline of education, that is, the formal study of the above three items

The common thread in all these descriptions is the notion of learning. In its most basic form, education can be understood as the intentional process of facilitating preferred learning. As such, education is a systematic approach to intentional learning that combines the activity of educating students, the process of students becoming educated, and the educational result of this approach. In this section we focus both on educational formats and on the formation of educational systems, and we introduce the idea of education's practical place in the church. Having done this, the reader will be prepared to enter the integrative discussion in chapter 2.

Three Education Formats

Learning occurs in three formats, and hence education has three general formats (Figure 1.2). The first and perhaps most recognizable is formal educational settings such as schooling. In this setting, learning is intentional, structured, and institutionalized by a set of predetermined learning objectives and methods primarily in a classroom environment. Application is not immediate, but instruction is given to prepare the student for adult life after graduation from high school or to enter a chosen profession from college. A second form of educational setting is nonformal, such as seminars or training sessions. In this setting, learning is intentional but not necessarily institutionalized like a school. Learning has objectives, but it is typically related to the performance of a task or to a piece of content. The United States military is perhaps the most recognized provider of non-formal education. When one goes through basic training for any branch of service, the instruction is intentional and application immediate. For example, the army does not discuss the history and philosophy of grenades, but it does teach someone how to use one. However, businesses that use seminar or in-service training for employees would also employ nonformal educational formats. The third and least recognized or acknowledged setting is informal or socialization. One learns by living in and experiencing a culture or society. Learning may or may not be regarded as intentional, but it does take place. In fact, socialization is often the most life-changing learning format in any setting. A person may study a foreign culture or language in either a formal or nonformal setting—even studying the history and culture of that society. But when he actually relocates to the country speaking that language and lives in that culture, learning not only occurs but is immediately applicable.

	Formal	Nonformal	Socialization
Institutional	⇧	⇔	⇩
Intentional	⇧	⇧	⇔
Application	⇩	⇧	⇧

Figure 1.2: Educational Formats

Education in the church occurs on all three levels. For example, when an adolescent walks into the church building, sees the architecture and artistic expressions, hears the music, engages in dialogue with others, and even gets a "glare" from a parent because of her hairstyle, this is socialization. The adolescent is taught through the engagement of the congregation's culture. When the adolescent finds her way to a Sunday school class or youth group, where a lesson is taught, this is nonformal education; intentional instruction intends to produce immediate life application. The following morning, the young lady attends a Christian high school where she experiences Christian education in a formal setting. Christian education is not restricted to any one learning environment, and all these learning environments can contribute to the spiritual growth of the individual when they are intentionally used to guide and direct someone toward Christ.

Formation of Educational Theory

The most recognizable elements in an educational system are its means and methods. We all have our favored means of providing education. In the church alone we have Sunday school, small groups, discipleship programs, new members classes, library and media services. This variety is a means of providing instruction that avoids monotony. Many times students discuss education in terms of methodological preferences: "I like Professor Smith because she uses discussions, while Professor Tyler just lectures." While this may be the visual, outer portion of an educational system, it is only the surface component of it (see Figure 1.4 on page 20).

At its core, its innermost component, education is based primarily on a worldview, a philosophical or theological system of understanding reality, truth, and values. As such, education is ultimately a practical expression of one's philosophical convictions. For example, note these two opposing views of education commonly held among contemporary educators in Figure 1.3:

What would account for such a difference in educational theory? How could the fundamental assumptions of the educa-

Two Opposing Views of Education	
The transmission of knowledge and culture has been the prevailing concept of education throughout history. The purpose of education is that the learners acquire whatever the society and culture regard as important for them to receive. The teacher is the conveyer of cultural content, and the student is to absorb it. Hence, the test of the educational effectiveness is the ability of students to recall information and the conformity of their behavior to cultural expectations.	Education is the process of the guided growth of learners toward their complete potential as human beings. The purpose of education is to aid individuals to develop their abilities and capacities to become cultural change agents, not merely to affirm the prevailing culture. The teacher's role is best described as a guide or facilitator of informed dialogue among students, e.g., problem solving. Educational effectiveness is measured by the student's ability to think, question, produce, and act.

Figure 1.3: Two Opposing Views of Education

tional process be so divergent? It is because they are based on a different view of reality, truth, and values—a different worldview. At the core of any educational system is a worldview that influences the formation of educational paradigms. However, the leap from worldview to means and methods of education is not immediate, for two more components comprise one's approach to education.

The social sciences likewise have a voice in forming an approach to education. What are social sciences? They are commonly referred too as a "soft science," since they use humans as their subjects. Unlike biology, which studies the physical aspect of humans and human development, the social sciences study the psychological and sociological development of humans.

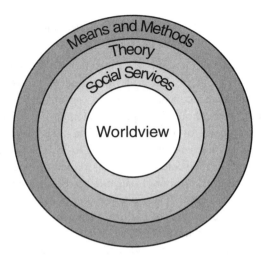

Figure 1.4: Education System Paradigm[13]

These insights are then applied to various fields of study and inquiry such as education or counseling. Studies such as cognitive development (Piaget and Vygotsky), socioemotional development (Brunfenbrenner and Erikson), learning styles (Gardner), students with disabilities, moral development theories (Kohlberg and Gilligan), and even faith/religious development (Fowler and Goldman) are all social science theories relevant to education.[14] The social sciences alone are insufficient as a core for education; rather one's worldview in concert with the social sciences provides an adequate core for the formation of education theory. The necessity of integrating a theologically informed worldview (Christian) and insights gleaned from the social sciences to form a distinctively Christian education theory is discussed in chapter 2.

Educational theory, the next ring on Figure 1.4, involves the implications of one's worldview integrated with social science theories. Such expressions usually include the following:

- Purpose and objectives of education: Why are we educating? What do we hope to produce?
- Role of the instructor: What is expected of a teacher?
- Role of the student: What is expected of a student?
- Relationship of teacher and student: How do students and teachers interact?
- Curriculum content: What is the scope and sequence of the topics to be studied?
- Learning environment and methods: What about classroom management? In what environment do students learn best? What methods best facilitate learning?
- Means of evaluation: How do we know if the purposes and objectives were fulfilled?

From this theory the educational means and methods are derived. When one lectures, it is more than just a simple choice based on personal preference. Rather, lectures reflect the instructor's educational theory, and that theory is derived from one's worldview and the social sciences (see chapter 2). However, to those who see the means and methods of ministry as being unrelated to theology, we would reply that they are ultimately a reflection of our theological assumptions about education ministry; they are not separate from it.

Education in the Service of the Church

In endeavoring to define education, we have done so based on learning formats, as well as the components comprising educational theory, but education can and must be understood as a ministry of the church. As such, Christian education is far more than the transmission of content from one person to another, and it must be if it is to accomplish its goal. Christian education is distinct from other kinds of education in that its goal is the transformation of the whole person into the likeness of Christ (Col. 1:28). Christian education is the process of accomplishing this goal.

Educators can learn the basic principles and methods of education, but God ultimately convicts and guides people to change a thought pattern or behavior. True spiritual transformation is far more than delivering content or measuring behavior. Students need knowledge, but it is more a means rather than an end. The end is discipleship, which requires the ability to understand a lesson and apply it to daily living.

> Education is based upon an assumption that what is learned in the classroom can and should be applied outside the classroom. By definition, learning requires that the student be able to meaningfully transfer a concept from one setting to another. But the transfer of truth is not automatic. Effective teachers know this. They know that there is a difference between parroting answers and transferring those facts into life scenarios.[15]

Theology, defined as the study of the nature of God, is a prerequisite for developing a relationship with God. We cannot worship what we do not know and understand. In fact, the more we know about God and what he has done on our behalf, the more we are motivated and led to worship him for who he is and for his goodness to us. So the end of theology is not the acquisition of mere head knowledge. The goal rather is heart transformation. Our knowledge of God leads us to faith and repentance, motivates us to adore and worship him, and prompts us to serve him out of love and devotion. This is the heart of discipleship. Each of the chapters that follow begins with a survey of a category of theology followed by a discussion of the implications of that category for Christian education. In essence, educational methods should follow out of theory based on the social sciences but ultimately grounded in our theology.

PRACTICAL IMPLICATIONS

- Christian educators should identify their theological assumptions and tradition before assuming the role of education.
- Christian educators must develop or accept a distinctive approach to education for the church that is integrated with a theologically aligned worldview.

QUESTIONS FOR REFLECTION

1. How did this chapter change your definition and understanding of theology?
2. Similarly, how did this chapter change your definition and understanding of education?
3. Can you begin to speculate how theology and education are related? How might you describe that relationship?
4. Why would a Christian educator value theology? Is it just for content or much more? Speculate!

---

1   J. Macquarrie, *Principles of Christian Theology* (New York: Scribner's, 1977), 1.1.
2   M. J. Erickson, *Christian Theology* (Grand Rapids: Baker, 1983), 21.
3   L. Berkhof, *Systematic Theology* (Grand Rapids: Eerdmans, 1963), 20.
4   J. Van Engen, "Natural Theology," in *The Evangelical Dictionary of Theology,* ed. W. A. Elwell (Grand Rapids: Eerdmans, 1984), 752–53.
5   C. Hodge, *Systematic Theology* (Grand Rapids: Eerdmans, 1995), 25.
6   Kenneth S. Kantzer, "A Systematic Biblical Dogmatics: What Is It and How Is It to Be Done?" in *Doing Theology in Today's World,* ed. John D. Woodbridge and Thomas Edward McComiskey (Grand Rapids: Zondervan, 1991), 466.
7   B. B. Warfield, *Studies in Theology* (Edinburgh: Banner of Truth, 1932), 91.
8   This presentation of biblical theology reflects the influence of several scholars and their writings on the discipline. Cf. C. H. H. Scobie, *The Ways of God: An Approach to Biblical Theology* (Grand Rapids: Eerdmans, 2003); G. Osborne, *The Hermeneutical Spiral: A Comprehensive Introduction to Biblical Interpretation,* rev. and exp. ed. (Downers Grove: IVP Academic, 2006).
9   Osborne, *Hermeneutical Spiral,* 347.

10   F. H. Barackman, *Practical Christian Theology* (Grand Rapids: Kregel, 2001), 15.

11   B. A. Demarest, "Systematic Theology," in *The Evangelical Dictionary of Theology,* 1064.

12   Warfield, *Studies in Theology,* 86.

13   J. R. Estep Jr., CE662: Theology of Christian Education—Course Packet (Lincoln, IL: Lincoln Christian Seminary, 2005).

14   See J. W. Santrock, *Educational Psychology* (Boston: McGraw-Hill, 2006); J. L. Elias, *Psychology and Religious Education* (Malabar, FL: Krieger, 1990).

15   L. O. Richards and G. Bredfeldt, *Creative Bible Teaching,* rev. ed. (Chicago: Moody, 1998), 113.

Chapter 2

"What Makes Education Christian?"[1]

James Riley Estep Jr.

W hat makes anything Christian? Books, music, television programs, radio stations, and movies are often described as being Christian or inversely non-Christian. The use of the word *Christian* as an adjective requires a judgment or assessment to be made about the subject in question. As expected, such assessments imply that certain criteria are used to determine if something is Christian or not. No one criterion can ensure that something is Christian, hence there is the need for requiring a number of criteria to provide further orientation to Christianity. Such criteria may require biblical or theological content, invoking Christian metaphors or images such as the cross or water baptism, advocating moral standards or spiritual practices such as self-sacrifice or prayer in solitude, or affirming a God-glorifying purpose.

All of these items, if they are to be distinctively Christian, must be theologically informed; that is, they arise from Christian theology, are defined by it, or directly refer to the content of Christian theology. As such, each criterion's definition and conceptualization must be informed by Scripture, Christian tradition, and theology so as to reflect a distinctively Christian quality. For example, some may consider a song *spiritual*, but is it consistent with Christian spirituality? What would distinguish it from a Buddhist melody? Immediately, its content would certainly not be Christian, nor would it affirm and glorify the God of Scripture. Further, the spiritual and moral implications would not necessarily be Christian. In short, something is Christian if it reflects the theological convictions of the Christian community in its content, purpose, message, and life implications; all of these rest on theologically informed criteria.

What makes education Christian? The same conviction about the necessity of theologically informed criteria must be affirmed for education as well. If education is to be *Christian*, it must be theologically informed on a variety of levels.

> Theology is more than the content of Christian education; it is a process of instruction and discernment by which persons are educated in their identity, interpret the realities of their lives, and are sent into the world. . . . [This is] the task and vocation of practical theologians of education.[2]

For education to be *Christian*, the presence of theology beyond the basic level of content is essential.

This chapter will affirm three conclusions that address the question, "What makes education Christian?" (1) Education in the church insists that both theology and social science theories be used in concert to provide an adequate base for Christian education. (2) The level of integration between theology and social science theory determines the degree of Christian distinctiveness in church education, as introduced in chapter 1. (3) There is a need for itemizing the benefits of integration for Christian education and educators.

THE NECESSITY OF THEOLOGY
IN CHRISTIAN EDUCATION

The Christian education community, particularly among Evangelicals, frequently affirms that "Christian education is a theological discipline that draws upon the behavioral sciences."[3] As such, Christian education draws from the integration of the study of God's special revelation (theology) and the study of his general revelation through nature (science).[4] However, the matter of integrating theology and the social sciences into a *distinctively* Christian education is difficult to define, and the manner in which they are to be integrated is even more problematic to explain. Ted Ward satirically quipped, "Christian education is *neither*. . . . In far too many cases Christian education is neither thoroughly Christian nor soundly educational."[5] Similarly, John Hull described the "Theology of Education" as "a field of applied or practical theology" and more generally as "a relatively *underdeveloped* inter-disciplinary field."[6] Similarly, H. Norman Wright bemoaned the "cleavage between Christian education and theology" in the church due to the diminished appreciation of theology in many churches, the shift in definition of education away from a theological discipline, and the demise of theological content in Christian instruction.[7] The critique of Christian education's integrative challenge is not simply voiced from the theological or social science communities but from within the Christian education community itself as a candid means of self-assessment.

Insufficient theological integration in Christian education has led to a state of crisis in the field. John Westerhoff wrote an article entitled "Discipline in Crisis" in 1979 to assess the status of Christian education.[8] In this article he identified current issues that shape the discipline of Christian education, the first two being "What will the discipline be named?" and "What is the relationship between theology and education?" He then offered three possible responses to the second question. (1) "Education is primarily the servant of theology," that is, it is the means of theological instruction. (2) "Theology and education are two independent and distinct disciplines in dialog, each informing the other." (3) "The theological disciplines . . . provide the norm, the point of reference for both the what and the how of education."

This crisis was later acknowledged by Charles Melchert who asserted that "it has become a cliché to suggest that we are in the midst of a crisis in religious education" and posed the question, "Does the church really want religious education?"[9] Such confusion on this issue raises the question, *How Christian is education in the church?*

Worldview and Social Sciences

As expressed in chapter 1, education is a systematic approach to intentional learning that combines the activity of educating students, the process of students becoming educated, and the educational result of this approach. Education theory is the product of the integration of worldview and social science theories. Education theory is not merely a philosophical expression, nor is it equal to the arbitrary utilization of social science theories. Rather, it is the integration of social science theories (such as learning, learning methods, developmental stages, and behavioral studies) informed by a set of prescriptive philosophical assumptions (such as metaphysics, epistemology, axiology, and the purposes and outcomes of education). As the social sciences are used in concert with a particular philosophy that contributes to the development of an approach to education, various forms of educational paradigms result, as the following demonstrates.[10]

- Pragmatism + Social Science → Progressive Education
- Realism + Social Science → Perennialism's Education
- Idealism + Social Science → Essentialism's Education
- Existentialism + Social Science → Deschooling Education

By replacing philosophy with theology, a new educational paradigm results:

- Theology + Social Science → Education in the Church

This can be described further as different theologies combined with the social sciences yield different kinds of Christian education, as demonstrated in the following:[11]

- Process Theology + Social Science →Miller's Process Education

- Liberation Theology + Social Sciences →Freire's *Conscientization*[12]
- Classical Liberal Theology + Social Sciences → Religious Education
- Evangelical Theology + Social Sciences → Christian Education

Our worldview, whether it be philosophically or theologically based, provides the grid that determines the use of the social sciences, forming a distinctive educational paradigm. Figure 2.1 illustrates the idea of education as a combination of philosophy or theology and social sciences as follows:

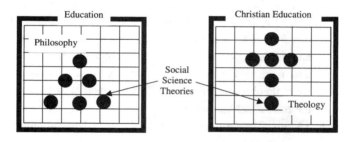

Figure 2.1: Philosophy or Theology and the Social Sciences

In the case of Christian education, the integration of evangelical theology and the social sciences produces a distinctively Christian education. What are the possible ways theology can relate to education, specifically the social sciences? The classic expression of this concern is Sara P. Little's five hypothetical roles that theology can have in Christian education.[13]

1. *Theology as Source:* "Theology provides the content to be taught and education works on settings, processes, and the like, critically reflecting on utilization of policies and procedures from secular disciplines." This means that theology is limited to the content of instruction.

2. *Theology as Resource:* "Education [as a social science]
   has implicit goals and learning theories that are deter-
   minative for both structure and content. Where theology
   helps meet goals or provide perspective and interpretation for the meaning of present experiences, it is a worthy resource." This means that theology is in a supportive
   role of the social sciences.

3. *Theology as Norm:* "Subject areas to be included in the
   teaching ministries are selected and interpreted in relationship to theological formulations." This means theology is the filter through which other subjects are taught in
   the curriculum.

4. *"Doing Theology" as Educating:* "When one engages in
   critical reflection on the meaning of experience and on
   discussions to be made in relationship to God's presence
   and purpose, one may be said to be 'theologizing,' using
   a term devised in the twentieth century to reflect an activity of theological reflection." This means that theology is
   the product of education.

5. *Theology and Education in Dialogue:* "Three assumptions characterize this alternative. Theology and education are separate but related disciplines, each with its
   special contribution and functions. Each draws on a clus-
   ter of related disciplines from which it utilizes appropriate contributions. And the educative processes not only
   educate, but also make a substantive contribution to the
   ongoing development of the theological formulations of
   the church."

A final addition to Little's list could be entitled *Theology
as Irrelevant.* This sixth position raises the issue of the sufficiency or adequacy and legitimacy of theology as a basis for
developing a theory of Christian education. This approach has
been proposed but has been generally rejected by the Christian
education community.[14]

What possible value may be placed on theology's role in education? Whereas Little identified the possible roles of theology in education theory ("theology as . . ."), John Hull assessed more precisely the possible value an educator may place on theology in education theory. He indicated that the Christian education community must decide if theology is necessary (essential, not an option, theology must be present if education is to be Christian) or sufficient (that theology alone can sustain education theory in the church). Hull presents five possible values of theology in education theory, all of which are combinations of the necessity and sufficiency of theology in Christian education theory.[15]

1. Christian theology might be both necessary and sufficient for an understanding of education (that is, there is no need for the social sciences).
2. Christian theology might provide a necessary but not sufficient understanding of education. Theology in this case needs assistance from philosophy or psychology (that is, the social sciences are necessary).
3. Christian theology might provide a sufficient but not a necessary understanding of education. Other belief systems, including nonreligious ones, might also be able to offer sufficient accounts of education (that is, theology is not necessary but optional).
4. Christian theology might provide a possible and legitimate understanding of education, but one which is neither sufficient nor necessary (that is, the presence of theology in Christian education should be minimal).
5. Christian theology might be impossible and illegitimate as a way of understanding education. It would have no contribution to offer (that is, theology is irrelevant, and possibly even misleading, for Christian education).

His categories raise for the Christian educator the concern for appropriately valuing theology in Christian education, not undermining or overinflating its function in forming a cohesive theory of Christian education. Thus, the relationship of theology and the social sciences is diverse, and the various forms of integration produce different educational paradigms in the church—some more theologically aligned than others.

LEVEL OF THEOLOGICAL INFLUENCE ON EDUCATION

Can education be made Christian by using a few passages of Scripture to illustrate educational practices? Or does the rejection of the social sciences equate education and theology? To what degree can and should theology be integrated with the social sciences? By its very nature Christian education is a practical expression of the evangelical concern for faith-learning integration.[16] The issue at hand is the quality of integration shared between theology and the social sciences so as to formulate a distinctively Christian approach to education suitable for the church. A five-tiered progression of the integration of theology and the social sciences can be proposed, each with a different way of describing the *Christian* presence in Christian education. This conceptual framework can be used to describe the scope of the integrative process for the integration of theology and the social sciences, and to assess the status of one's conceptualization on the subject of theology's place and role in Christian education. While it may parallel the previously referenced works of Little and Hull, Christian education is actually designed to serve as a taxonomy for the integration of theology and the social sciences (that is, progressive levels of integration) and to indicate the process of moving from the absence of integration (which is undesirable to Christian educators) toward a thorough integration of theology and the social sciences. Ultimately, it aids us in responding to the impending question of what makes education Christian.

Levels of Integration in Christian Education

Level 1—Disintegration: At this level education is not Christian. It is not Christian because it is a level of nonintegration due to being unaware of theology or regarding it to be irrelevant to the subject of education. At this level education is based on the social sciences. When the issue of theological integration is raised, one's attitude may be, "Integrate what?"—a reflection of being unaware or not valuing the significance of theology. In this instance education is *not* Christian due to the absence of theology. As such, Christian educators cannot accept this approach to education in the church, and in all probability such an education would not adapt to the needs and ministry of the church.

Level 2—Segregation: Education is considered Christian because of its rejection of what some regard as the secular influences of social science. In effect, it is a level of anti-integration wherein there is an awareness of the social sciences' existence but a devalued and unfavorable disposition toward them. At this level one's attitude toward integration may be, "We *cannot* integrate! It is a theological compromise!" As such, one would eliminate the influence and place of the social sciences as being incompatible with Christian theology. Education would be Christian because it is wholly theological but probably not educational; in fact, education could barely be distinguished from theology.

Level 3—Paradoxical: At this level education may be considered Christian because it discriminately uses both theology and the social sciences. A student is exposed to both the social sciences and theology since the acknowledgement and the relative value of both is given but no attempt is made to synthesize them, only to combine them. Thus one's attitude toward integration may be, "Both have some valid points and observations, so I use both, sometimes theology and other times social science." The educator acknowledges the validity of both but selectively determines which one has primary voice and relevance. Education is Christian because it utilizes theology *and* is educational because of the inclusion of the social sciences, but the lack of integration makes their respective voices sporadic and potentially inconsistent.

Level 4—Synthetic: At this level education is Christian because it is a social science in the service of the church. Such an approach provides a theological description of social sciences, endeavoring to move social science insights into a closer, even correlative, relation with theology. The social sciences provide the substance and theology provides the form of education in the church. A common attitude toward this integration may be, "We should integrate them, but education is education . . . theology can provide the veneer." This level represents an initial attempt at integration but an insufficient attempt at it.

Level 5—Paradigmatic: At this level education is Christian because it is an integrated field of theology with the social sciences in the service of the church. Integration endeavors to be a holistic endeavor, transformative, and based on a worldview informed by evangelical theology. Theology and social science cooperatively validate one another's insights and influence on education. A common attitude toward this integration may be, "Both theology and social sciences are insufficient on their own, so we *must* integrate them to have education that is Christian." Acknowledging human fallibility and finitude when exploring God's special and natural revelations requires both knowledge and imagination with the integration process. Education is indeed simultaneously Christian and educational in nature due to the thorough integration of the two.

These five levels of integration may be illustrated by a student's term paper on a Christian educator's view of human development. If she has Paul's theology of humanity (as in the Epistle to the Romans) and Jean Piaget's *The Psychology of the Child* (1966),[17] how does she integrate them? Picture this student at a desk armed with her copy of Piaget's work, a Bible opened to Romans, and her laptop. How does she proceed to address an educational question from a Christian perspective?

- *Level 1:* The student uses Piaget, *unaware* of Paul's possible voice on the subject, or she regards him as irrelevant to the subject; hence neglected, Paul is *removed* from the table, and she and Piaget interact. The paper is a summary and application of Piaget, due to her unawareness of Paul.
- *Level 2:* She uses Paul, but though *aware* of Piaget, she *rejects* him as being incompatible with Scripture and subsequently removes him from the table. So then she and Paul interact. The paper is a summary and application of Paul due to her rejection of Piaget.
- *Level 3:* The student uses both Paul and Piaget *independently*, selecting one or the other depending on the situation. Hence, part of the paper is from Paul and other parts from Piaget but with no integrative component.
- *Level 4:* She uses both Paul and Piaget, but she gives Piaget priority by placing Piaget's theory over Paul's theology. She uses Paul sparingly, simply as theological form for the social science substance. Hence, she uses Piaget for the substance and tosses in an occasional Scripture citation, biblical image, or theological vocabulary from Paul to illustrate it, but no significant engagement of Scripture is attempted.
- *Level 5:* The student uses both Paul and Piaget in the formation of a conceived conceptualization of human nature. At this level both the form and substance of education are derived from theology and the social sciences. She endeavors to use Paul and Piaget simultaneously. All the advantages of the previous levels are present without the limitations or inadequacies. Hence, the student's paper reflects Paul and Piaget together in terms of both analysis and application.

Figure 2.2 illustrates the progression of integrative levels described above.

Achieving a Level of Integration

In this model six factors contribute to the individual's ability to engage in the process of integration.

1. *The Individual's Expertise with the Various Components:* How well do they know both theology and the social sciences? Which is better known? In which field can they more readily converse?

2. *The Individual's Valuing of the Various Components:* Is their primary allegiance to theology or the social sciences? Which one receives greater voice in the integrative process?

3. *The Individual's Acceptance of an Integrative Paradigm:* Does the individual have a schema by which integration can occur or be accomplished? Is the idea of integration considered a purely theoretical and/or a practical exercise to the individual?

4. *The Individual's Ability to Deal with Apparent Contradictions and Paradoxes That Occur in the Process of Integration:* How does the individual deal with ambiguity? Can the individual maintain a conceptual balance in the midst of discontinuity?

5. *The Individual's Level of Commitment to the Process and Product of Theological Integration:* Does the individual genuinely value faith-learning integration?

6. *The Individual's Ability to Analyze, Synthesize, and Decide on Matters of Integration:* Does the individual possess the necessary cognitive abilities to significantly integrate theology and the social sciences?

Without any of these factors the likelihood of achieving a paradigmatic level of integration is impeded.

Level 1:
Disintegration
Use of social sciences,
theology unknown or
regarded as irrelevant

Level 2: *Segregation*
Use of theology, social
sciences known and
rejected

Level 3: *Paradoxical*
Social Sciences and
theology used
independently.

Level 4: *Synthetic*
Primary and
substantial use of
social sciences,
theology used
sparingly and
marginalized, an
appendix for
appearances.

Level 5: *Paradigmatic*
The social sciences
and theology are both
valued as necessary
and legitimate, both
are used
simultaneously and
interactively.

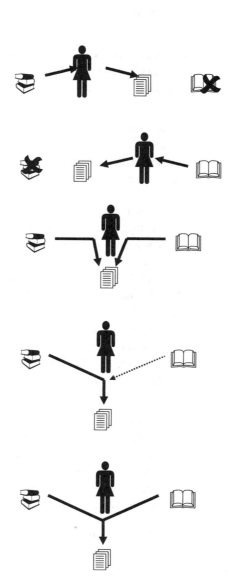

*Figure 2.2: Student Integrative
Endeavor*

WHAT MAKES EDUCATION CHRISTIAN?

We now return to our fundamental question: What makes education Christian? As one reflects on the previous three paradigms by Little, Hull, and Estep, certain convictions emerge about the kind of education that makes it Christian education such as the following:

1. Education should have a theologically informed and constructive use of social science theories. Education should understand that the nature of the student is both developmental in nature and is innately the *imago dei*, the image of God.
2. Education has a theologically informed purpose. This means that education is for the glory of God, maturity in the Christian faith, and the advancement of the kingdom.
3. Education features a theologically informed selection of content. This means that education starts with Scripture but includes theological tradition, church history, Christian living, and ministry preparation.
4. Education evidences a theologically informed design. This means that education develops relevant theological assumptions for educational theory, such as teacher-student roles and relationships, educational environment, and instructional methods.

Education can be Christian, suitable for the Christian community of faith, if the educational theory and methodologies of instruction directly reflect a theologically informed worldview. As illustrated by the levels of integration paradigm, the more significant the level of integration (that is, the paradigm), the more it is distinctively Christian.

THEOLOGY'S CONTRIBUTION
TO CHRISTIAN EDUCATORS

What can theology provide for education and the Christian educator? What benefit is there for an integrated approach to Christian education? The following serves as a summary of the contributions of theology to the field of Christian education and to the work of Christian educators.

Integrity: Theological integration provides consistency between our convictions as Christians and our convictions as educators. It provides a means through which our faith may be consistently expressed not only by our life and words but also in the theory and practice of the education ministry in which we serve. Theology governs both our lives and our ministries as Christian educators. It requires us to align our personal, pastoral, and professional lives to God.

Distinction: As practitioners we share much in common with our neighbors in the education field. However, the value we place on theological integration distinguishes us from other educators. Theology provides the substance of our ministries. Christian education is qualitatively distinct from other forms of education because of its theological integration.

Direction: Curricular or learning objectives are ultimately derived from our philosophical convictions. While sharing some common learning objectives with the general educational community, many of our objectives reflect the theological assumptions of Christian educators, such as outcomes regarding Christlikeness, Bible knowledge, and skills in evangelism. In addition to curricular matters, the policies and procedures of Christian education are informed by our theological convictions.

Content: Biblical and theological instruction is not unique to Christian educators since most major universities and even some high schools offer courses in the Bible as literature. But Christian education is characterized by our commitment to the Bible as education's primary content. While Christian education is not limited to biblical instruction, the Bible does have a central role in the curriculum, primarily due to the theological conviction regarding its origin (divinely revealed and inspired), nature (inerrant, sufficient, authoritative), and function (infallible, powerful).

Parameters: Theology imposes limitations. A natural implication of providing distinctions is the exclusion of elements not sharing these distinctions. Hence, theology informs not only the substance of Christian education but also the form and shape of it. For example, its purpose, objectives, and teacher-student relationships make Christian education distinct from the broader educational community in which it exists. Theology provides Christian educators with limitations to identify what can be considered *Christian* in education.

Conviction: The motivation and fervor of a Christian educator is one that is based not only on personal commitments to an educational system or institution but also to a spiritual commitment to fulfill Christ's calling in the Great Commission to make disciples by "teaching them to observe everything I have commanded you" (Matt 28:20). Theology provides the Christian educator with a motive beyond the current circumstances or even the current educational venue, stemming from a relationship with an immanent yet transcendent God through Christ in the community of his body. Our commitment as educators is based on the life-transforming promises contained in Scripture and expressed in our theological beliefs.

Pastoral Focus: Christian education is not simply education for education's sake, nor is it merely driven by pragmatic necessities; rather it is a *ministry* of the church. Our theological convictions as Christian educators serve as a constant reminder that education in the church is not a program or department but a ministry. Education that seeks simply to impart knowledge or raise levels of cognition or awareness falls short of education as a calling to pastoral service within the community of faith. Christian educators must never forget that we are first pastors and then educators and that education serves the pastoral function of nurturing faith within the community of the church.

Process: As previously mentioned, parallels do exist between our understanding of the nature of theology and education. We tend to shape our approach to Christian education much the same way we approach the task of doing theology. Theology underlies our hermeneutic, and our hermeneutic is not limited to the pages of Scripture; rather, theology extends to our comprehension of life and the integration of belief into experience.

In short, theology informs and shapes our conceptualization of more than just education.

Cohesive Filter: Theology provides the glue for the Christian educator since it serves as the philosophy of education. As such, it provides a filter through which to interpret the social sciences and hence adds perspective to the formation of a distinctively Christian approach to education.

CONCLUSION

For education to be Christian in its fullest sense, it must become an integrated field of theology and social science that understands itself to be in the service of the church. This chapter has endeavored to demonstrate that for education to be Christian it must be a theologically informed discipline. If anything, this chapter signals one warning: it is the lack of theological attention and intentionality in the formation of Christian education that has raised the question of its legitimacy for the church, as Westerhoff and Melchert explained. Christian educators must become theologians as well as educational theorists if we are to ensure the integrity of our ministry and discipline.

Since all truth is God's truth, Christian educators must avoid building walls between themselves and either the theological community or the social science community. As Robert Frost penned in "Mending Walls" (*North of Boston* 1915, Lines 33–35):

> Before I built a wall I'd ask to know;
> What I was walling in or walling out,
> And to whom I was like to give offence.
> Something there is that doesn't love a wall.

If Christian education is to preserve its Christian distinctiveness, then it must be a theological discipline; and if it is to be educational, it must be a social science discipline. It is through the thorough integration of theology and the social sciences on a paradigmatic level that a consistently Christian theory of education will be achieved and the benefits of such a union realized.

PRACTICAL IMPLICATIONS FOR
CHRISTIAN EDUCATORS

- Christian educators must be well read in both educational theory and theology.
- Christian educators must think *theologically* about their ministry beyond the level of content.
- Christian educators must write their own theological approach to education so they can intentionally continue to more thoroughly refine and express a Christian education.
- Christian educators must share their theological convictions within an educational context so they can orient and motivate others in the task of teaching.
- Christian educators must dialogue with other professionals to glean further insights into both the theology and theory of their ministry.

REFLECTION QUESTIONS

1. How would you have defined Christian education prior to reading this chapter? What about now?
2. Which do you value more or know better: theology or the social sciences? Why?
3. On a scale of 1 to 5, how well do you currently fulfill the above stated practical implications?
4. What areas of improvement did this chapter evoke for you?

---

1   This chapter was originally presented as a paper at the Stone-Campbell Journal Conference in Florissant, Missouri (2003) and the North American Professors of Christian Education in Boston, Massachusetts (2003) as well as published in part as "How Christian is Christian Education? The Relation of Theology and Education in the Church," *Stone-Campbell Journal* 10.1 (Spring 2007): 63–76.

2   J. L. Seymour, "The Clue to Christian Religious Education: Uniting Theology and Education," *Religious Education* 99.3 (Summer 2004): 279, 284.

3   D. C. Wyckoff, "Theology and Education in the Twentieth Century," *Christian Education Journal* 15.3 (Spring 1959): 12.

4   In educational circles this model is frequently attributed to T. Ward. See
     P. G. Downs, *Teaching for Spiritual Growth* (Grand Rapids: Zondervan,
     1994), 14–16; and C. Stonehouse, *Joining Children on the Spiritual Journey*
     (Grand Rapids: Baker, 1998), 14–16.

5   T. Ward, "Facing Educational Issues," in *Reader in Christian Education
     Foundations and Basic Perspectives*, ed. Eugene Gibbs (Grand Rapids:
     Baker, 1992), 333.

6   J. M. Hull, "What Is Theology of Education?" *Scottish Journal of The-
     ology* 30 (1977): 3 [emphasis added].

7   H. N. Wright, "Theology as the Basis for Christian Education," *Bib-
     liotheca Sacra* 119.510 (1971): 142–47.

8   J. Westerhoff, "Discipline in Crisis," *Religious Education* 74.1 (1979):
     7–15.

9   C. F. Melchert, "Does the Church Really Want Religious Education?"
     Religious Education 69.1 (1974): 12.

10   See G. R. Knight, *Philosophy and Education*, 3rd ed. (Berrien Springs,
     MI: Andrews University Press, 1998), 97–136; and M. J. Anthony and
     W. S. Benson, *Exploring the History and Philosophy of Christian Edu-
     cation* (Grand Rapids: Kregel, 2003), 381–409.

11   See H. W. Burgess, *An Invitation to Religious Education* (Birmingham,
     AL: Religious Education Press, 1975) and idem., *Models of Religious
     Education* (Nappanee, IN: Evangel, 1996); M. C. Boys, *Educating in
     Faith* (New York: Harper & Row, 1989).

12   P. Freire, *Pedagogy of the Oppressed* (New York: Continuum, 1995).

13   S. Little, "Theology and Education," *Harper's Encyclopedia of Reli-
     gious Education*, ed. I. V. Cully and K. B. Cully (San Francisco: Harper
     & Row, 1990), 649–51.

14   See E. J. Newell, *"Education Has Nothing to Do with Theology"*
     (Eugene, OR: Pickwick Publishers, 2006) for a critical analysis of the
     social science approach to education proposed by J. M. Lee.

15   J. M. Hull, "Christian Theology and Educational Theory: Can There
     be Connections?" *British Journal of Educational Studies* 24.2 (1976):
     128–29; see M. Boys, "The Role of Theology in Religious Education,"
     Horizons 11.1 (1984): 81–85 for similar materials.

16   See J. R. Estep Jr., "The Church and College in Culture: A Paradigm
     for Faith-Learning in the Bible College Curriculum," *Stone-Campbell
     Journal* 2.2 (1999): 191–208; and idem., "Faith as the Transformer of
     Learning," *Christian Education Journal* 2 NS, no. 2 (1998): 59–76.

17   J. Piaget and B. Inhelder, *The Psychology of the Child* (New York: Basic
     Books, 1996).

CHAPTER 3

Biblical Principles for a Theology for Christian Education

James Riley Estep Jr.

J esus loves me this I know, *for the Bible tells me so."* This is a simple yet profound lyric. The Bible is the epistemo-logical center of the Christian faith. Without Scripture theology would become undirected speculation about an elusive God who does not want to be known. Although we do not worship the Bible, Christian educators must acknowledge that it is through the Bible that we know whom to worship (see 2 Tim 3:13–15).[1] As for every aspect of the evangelical tradition, the witness of Scripture is of paramount importance.

WHY ARE BIBLICAL PRINCIPLES CRITICAL FOR CHRISTIAN EDUCATION?

The Bible serves as the primary textbook of Christian education. Not only does it supply the content of Christian instruction, but it also provides direction, models of education, methodology, and a rationale for Christian education. It serves as the cornerstone of theological foundations and the prolegomena of the historical foundations for Christian education. As such, Scripture is the primary lens through which the Christian educator perceives and prescribes the character of education in the church.

The primary reason for regarding Scripture as foundational to Christian education is its claims of revelation and inspiration.[2] Because of this special revelation from God, the Christian

educator is compelled to formulate a model of Christian education that is consistent with God's expressed design. The apostle
Paul contends that the Scriptures "were given for our *instruction*" (Rom 15:4; see 1 Cor 10:5–11; 2 Tim 3:15–17).[3] Likewise, D. C. Wyckoff comments that "the theological enterprise
[in Christian education] is necessary because of the fact of revelation."[4] As with all other endeavors of Christian thought, we
must "take captive every thought to make it obedient to Christ"
(2 Cor 10:5), including those on the educational ministry of the
congregation.

Bible versus Theology

Why did we include a chapter on biblical principles? Chapter 4 will address Scripture as God's special revelation and the
educational implications associated with the fact that *God has
spoken*. This chapter addresses a different question. What does
the Bible itself, as a narrative of God's people in community,
imply about the nature of education among God's people? This
chapter makes observations of the biblical narrative in regard to
the nature of education in the church and from it draws implications for contemporary Christian education in the church.
Unlike many biblical foundation pieces, this one does not
endeavor simply to catalog passages from the Old and New Testaments that reflect educational approaches or methods. Rather,
it seeks to provide general observations and biblically based
imperatives for Christian educators.[5] The imperatives provide
a biblically informed rubric for education that theology further
informs throughout this text.

What Kind of Biblical Principles?

It is a daunting task to assume that the Bible's witness to education among the Hebrew-Jews of the Old Testament and the
early Christians of the New Testament can somehow be encap-
sulated into a single document. In fact, if one were to review the
different biblical foundation pieces produced by the Christian

education community the variety would become rather obvious. Some approach the issue of foundations from a literary or historical perspective, such as articles in the *Evangelical Dictionary of Christian Education* on "Education in the Epistles" or "Education in the Monarchy and the Prophets." Others take a more topical approach such as the "Biblical Foundations for Education" in the *Evangelical Dictionary of Christian Education* or E. A. Daniel's and J. W. Wade's *Foundations for Christian Education.* Others have sought to provide a biblical basis for Christian education through the study of educational practices of key individuals, such as R. Zuck's *Teaching as Jesus Taught* and his *Teaching as Paul Taught.* Hence the question arises, What kind of biblical foundation does a theology of Christian education require?

Theologically, the biblical narratives provides us with a scaffolding, a structure, upon which to build our theology of Christian education. Whatever theology is eventually constructed must rest upon the existing structure in Scripture, echoing its educational mandate and convictions. Therefore, a theology of Christian education requires a biblical foundation that is not merely descriptive of what the Bible says about education but prescriptive of what the Bible mandates about education—both in terms of theory and practice. Practically, the biblical principles of education serve as reference points for the Christian educator as they navigate through decision-making about curriculum, programming, and ministry direction. Hence, the Bible is the foundation for Christian education's theory and practice.

EDUCATIONAL PRINCIPLES
FROM THE SCRIPTURES

The Scriptures are saturated with educational imperatives and implications. Throughout the Scriptures there is an emphasis on the promotion and preservation of both personal and community faith, but the specific nature and means utilized to complete this aim are distinctive between the Old and New Testaments. *What the Bible provides is a glimpse into the educational convictions and practices of God's people millennia ago, with relevant principles for today.* However, within this lies a caution: some models of education in the Scriptures are by nature culture-specific models that *cannot* simply be mimicked or transplanted into the contemporary era. While the biblical principles are undeniably essential to Christian education, the specific methods must be assessed in light of their relevance and effectiveness. Hence, it is the realization of the mandate that is essential for Christian education, not the preservation of specific methods as being "divinely established."

1. *Education in church is God-centered.* Such an assertion is almost self-evident, since faith always requires an object, something in which to place one's faith. Hence, for Christians all of life is centered on God, including Christian education. This is evident since the culture and educational endeavors of ancient Israel are centered on one central Identity: *God.* For example, in light of the educational mandate of Deut 6:1–9, where Moses instructs parents to provide faithful instruction to their children, McKay concluded: "To him [the author of Deuteronomy] Israel is the son/pupil of Yahweh, the father/teacher, and the only proper attitude that can be adopted by Israel in this relation is that of filial obedience, reverential love, or *pietas* [virtue]."[6] God himself was Israel's prime teacher. David said, "Make Your ways known to me, LORD; teach me Your paths. Guide me in Your truth and teach me, for You are the God of my salvation; I wait for You all day long" (Ps 25:4–5 HCSB). In Genesis, the first interaction between God and humanity was instruction regarding our role in the creation (Gen 1:28–30; 2:16–17).[7] Elihu stated, "Look, God shows Himself exalted by His power. Who is a teacher like Him? Who has appointed His way for Him, or who has declared, 'You have done wrong'?" (Job 36:22–23 HCSB). This suggests that God's instructions are both prescriptive and corrective. Throughout the Old Testament God's revealing acts, both in deed and word, demonstrate his place as the teacher of the faith

community. Perhaps the most significant act of verbal revelation was the giving of the law (Heb. *torah*, which can be translated "instruction") to Moses, which was used by all the Old Testament's teachers. The aim of education was belief and behavior, both tied directly to the nature of God.

As in the Old Testament, the triune *God* is described as teaching the New Testament's community of faith (Titus 2:11–12; 1 John 2:27). Through his acts of grace and revelation, God instructs the Christian community. Christ is central to the community, its worldview and educational endeavors, as demonstrated in Col 1:15–29. In this passage Paul's ministry of "admonishing and teaching everyone with all wisdom, so that we may present everyone perfect in Christ" (v. 28) is contingent on Christ's being the fullness of God (vv. 15,19), Creator (vv. 16–17), supreme Head of the Church (v. 18), and Savior (vv. 19–20). In short, instruction in the faith communities of the Old and New Testaments was centered on God.

A God-centered approach to education is one of Christian education's distinctives. For example, James Pluddeman's seminal article "Do We Teach the Bible or Do We Teach Students?" raises the ever present issue in education as to the center of our endeavors.[8] Are we content centered? teacher centered? student centered? society centered? Christian educators avoid such matters by understanding something more worthy of being considered central than any of these—God (see Figure 3.1).

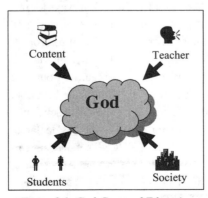

Figure 3.1: God-Centered Education

All of these items are necessary components and considerations in developing an approach to education, but education is not *centered* on them. Rather it is centered on the one who provided the truth, who is the prime Teacher of the faith community, who created students in his image, and who forms the faith community.

2. *Education is obligatory upon the Christian community.* Put quite simply, education is not an *option*; it is a necessity. In fact, it is a divine imperative, a command. At every level of the faith community, in both Testaments, from the family unit to the congregation to the nation and then to whole world, the essential task of instruction is impressed upon the faithful (Deut 6:6–9; Matt 28:16–20; Acts 1:8). This commitment to Christian education is demonstrated through the lives of the faithful men and women of the Old Testament period, particularly during and after the Babylonian exile, when they had to preserve their faith in a hostile social context and reestablish the nation's faith after returning to Judah (2 Chr 17:7–9; 34:29–30). The practice of the New Testament community likewise denotes a commitment to instruction, as described in Acts 2:42: "They devoted themselves to the apostles teaching." Christian education is the fulfillment of a divine imperative. The church that fails to accept the task of educational ministry is neither functioning by the pattern of a New Testament congregation nor fulfilling the Great Commission to "make disciples" (Matt 28:19).

3. *Faith is learned in and through the church.* Can the faith be learned? Yes, in terms of the content of the faith, practices of the faith, and appropriate faith experiences. This is why education in the faith community is considered an essential for the Christian educator. Learning requires an appropriate context, and in turn that context influences learning. The socialization of the faithful is accomplished through intentional instruction by, exposure to, and involvement in the faith community. Through the church we become aware of the teachings and traditions of the faith. This is particularly relevant to the education of children. A child who sees adults participating in worship may ask what is being done and why—a contemporary parallel to Deut 6:1–9. Christian educators must address the issue of how one's exposure and encounter with

a congregation shapes and influences the faith of the individual. Christian education becomes a communal endeavor, with every aspect of its ministry designed to facilitate spiritual formation in the lives of its members, including the content, disciplines, and ministries of the Christian faith.

4. *Education is provided in a variety of formats.* Education is not homogenous. As a matter of fact, as mentioned in chapter 1, education occurs in three formats. First, *formal* education is intentional instruction where students study to advance through an institutional curriculum with life applications made later, as in a school. Second, *nonformal* education includes intentional instruction, but it is not part of a school setting and is typically designed to make immediate application, such as in training sessions or apprenticeships. Third, *informal* education (or *socialization*) is the learning that occurs through one's life experiences in a community and through cultural encounters that include adopting social norms. These three formats lie on a spectrum that transitions from one to the other. For example, it may be possible to be in a *formal* academic setting, but included in its curriculum is a *nonformal* element, such as an internship; and learning may also be expected to occur through your experience as a student, which is *informal* or socialization (Figure 3.2).

Church School or	*Ministry Training*	*Life Experience in*
Christian College	*Internship*	*the Faith-Community*
Formal	**Non-formal**	**Informal**

Intentional, overt, structured curriculum increases toward the left

Figure 3.2: Education Formats

In the Scriptures all three formats are present although socialization and nonformal educational formats are far more prevalent. For example, Charles Melchert identified Old Testament "settings" in which wisdom literature, specifically Proverbs, might have been learned.[9] In his list of settings or learning contexts, he identified formal education (instruction provided in scribal schools and royal courts), nonformal education (conversation in informal gatherings), and informal education (family), explaining that instruction would be given "as everyday life gives occasion."[10] While other examples could be given—such as the formal instruction of priests, the nonformal training of musicians, and the socialization process implicit in Deut 6:1–9—Melchert's observations are quite sufficient.

In the New Testament the narrative of the earliest Christian community (Acts 2:42–47) demonstrates this to some degree. This passage speaks of the nonformal ("apostles' teaching") as well as the informal socialization of Christians in community with one another ("fellowship," "the breaking of bread," and "prayers"). What about formal education in the New Testament? Acts 19:9 indicates that Paul taught in a "school" (KVJ, NASB) or "lecture hall" (NIV), which was a Roman *schole* or secondary school. Paul was not a member of its faculty, and the New Testament does not indicate that first-century Christians established schools. However, soon after the first-century the Christian community did in fact establish schools as a means of providing education, adopting the schooling tradition of the Romans.[11]

5. *Teachers are heterogeneous within the church.* In both the Old and New Testaments, no one group or individual was *the* instructor—except God himself. While all teachers may have accepted the educational imperative of the Scriptures, they were by no means identical. A plurality of teaching contexts, emphases, and styles was maintained because of the heterogeneous nature of God's people. Hence, teachers were a diverse element designed to reach the diverse constituents in the faith community.

Who were Israel's teachers? As previously noted, God was Israel's principle teacher. But God also bestowed upon others the ability to teach (Exod 35:34), as is evident throughout the history of Israel. Early in Israel's history as a nation, educational responsibility was placed primarily on the family.[12] Both parents were to be involved in the instruction of their children (Prov 1:8), as well as other family members, making education in the family an intergenerational matter (Deut 4:9–11; 11:19–20; Exod 12:26–27). Perhaps the most telling passage in this regard is Ps 78, where God's interventions on Israel's behalf are recounted with the exhortation for parents to recount these events to the children. Christian education has always included the passing down of the history and traditions of the faith community, so our faith becomes an intergenerational affair.

However, parents alone were not the teachers of the faith community. Priests received formal education and provided instruction to the community (Deut 22; Ps 27:31; 40:8; Hag 2:11; Mal 2:6–9; 3:11). The priests used the law in their instruction (Ps 37:31; 40:8; Hag 2:11; Mal 2:6–9). In fact, Deut 31:9–13 indicates that the priests were to read the law for the instruction of the Hebrew nation, including "foreigners living within your gates" (v. 12). The priesthood represented the establishment of the first permanent group of teachers in Israel *outside* the family.

The prophets constituted perhaps the most vocal and obvious teachers of the Old Testament (Isa 8:3–16; 42:21–24; Jer 8:8; 9:13; 16:11; Hos 1:3–9; Mic 6:8; Zech 7:12). Moses served as a paradigm for future prophets (Exod 18:20; 24:12; Deut 4:14; 6:1; 31:19). The prophets, like the priests, made use of the law in their instruction (Isa 8:16; 42:21,24; Jer 9:13; 16:11; Zech 7:12). What might look like a school for prophets (1 Sam 10:10; 19:20; 2 Kgs 2:3–5; 4:38; 6:1) should not be understood as a contemporary formal educational institution. The actual phrase in 2 Kings is "sons [Heb. is plural of *ben*] of the prophets," but in the ancient Near East it was not uncommon to express instructional relationships in schools with family terms.

While always present in Israel, additional groups of teachers began to take prominence during the monarchical and exilic periods of the Old Testament. Sages or wise men, not to be confused with the eastern magi (Matt 2:1), constitute another body of teachers in the Old Testament (1 Kgs 4:32–34; Prov 1:6; 13:20; 15:7; Eccl 12:9). These men were knowledgeable of the law and able to make practical application of its instruction (Prov 9:12; 13:14). Similarly, scribes emerged near the close of the Old Testament era, both before (1 Chr 27:32; Jer 8:8) and after (Neh 8:1–8) the exile. They are mentioned frequently in the New Testament as experts in the law. Ezra is described as a teacher-scribe and serves as a model for this category of teacher (Ezra 7:6,10).[13]

Often neglected as an instructor of Israel and Judah is the community itself as a means of socialization. As a theocracy the nation reflected in its culture a sense of spirituality and religious devotion. The community itself was a teacher. The reason for festivals, worship sites, and activities in public assemblies all had educational significance.[14] For example, the Passover reminded adults and instructed children of the exodus from Egypt (Exod 12:1–30; Deut 16:1–8). The feasts and festivals usually coincided with the celebration of historic events in the national life of Israel, serving as a memorial for God's relationship with his people and the history of the nation.

What about rabbis? They are not mentioned in the Old Testament, and their origins are not mentioned in the New Testament since rabbinical studies and sectarian Judaism are a development of the fourth and third centuries BC. In the Apocrypha, 1 Maccabees 2:42 describes them as "mighty men of Israel . . . such as were voluntarily devoted unto the law." The Pharisees, a sect composed almost entirely of rabbis, were the most influential education reform voice in Judaism. They were the authors of rabbinical literature and numerous advanced educational agendas in Judaism, including mandatory elementary education and the establishment of secondary schools.[15]

Who are the teachers in the new covenant? As in the Old Testament, the New Testament describes God as teaching the community of faith. Through his acts of grace and revelation, God instructs the Christian community. The Holy Spirit is a teacher to the disciples of Jesus Christ.[16] In Acts, the Holy Spirit is further described as a "guide" in the Christian life (see Rom 8:1–27; Gal 5:16–26). "The Holy Spirit was the major teacher (Acts 1:1), but teaching was done by both the apostles (the leadership: Acts 4) and laity (Acts 18:24–28)."[17]

While he was addressed by many titles, Jesus was frequently called "teacher." Mark 10:1 states that it was Jesus' "custom" to teach. The Gospels use a variety of titles to describe Jesus' instructional activity: "Teacher" (Gk. *didaskalos*), "Rabbi" (Heb. for "teacher"), "Rabouni" (Aram. for "honored teacher")—as well as the more generic "Master" (Gk. *kurios*) and "Leader" (Gk. *kathēgētēs*)—are used in regard to Jesus' educational endeavors.[18]

The term *disciple* is used 142 times in the Synoptic Gospels, which implies that they in turn were learning how to teach (see Matt 28:20; Mark 6:30; Luke 12:12). Disciples adhered their lives to the instruction of their teacher, requiring a distinctive approach to instruction and relationship with the teacher's followers. As a teacher, Jesus did bear some similarity to his contemporaries. For example, the metaphor of the "yoke" in Matt 11:29–30 was used to describe the relation of a teacher to his pupil in rabbinic Judaism (see Sirach 6:30; 51:25–26). Similarly, the phrase "follow me" (see Mark 1:17) was frequently employed by both Greek philosophers and Hebrew sages to their pupils. Discipleship was their instructional context and method, and their followers learned through socialization and nonformal teaching.[19]

Eleven of Jesus' disciples became the apostles who assumed the task of teaching believers through instruction, preaching, and writing. Acts depicts the apostles as completing Jesus' mission (Acts 1:1) by making disciples for Christ (Acts 14:21). Doctrine assumes a crucial role in the church through their instruction (Acts 2:42; 5:28; 13:2; 17:19). The apostle Paul was perhaps the most prolific educator among the apostles, particularly through his correspondences and established missionary endeavors, such as in Corinth and Ephesus.[20]

As in the Old Testament, the community of faith was instructional. The church's community life introduced and reinforced the formation of faith through exposure and involvement in the community (Acts 2:42–27). In both place and function the teacher is regarded as a gift from God to the church (Rom 12:3–8; 1 Cor 12:27–31; Eph 4:7–13,29; 5:15–20; 1 Pet 4:10–11).

Similarly, in the early years of the church, elders were appointed by the apostles in the congregations and assumed teaching roles. Elders were obviously more than teachers since being "able to teach" (1 Tim 3:2; Titus 1:9) was only one of their qualifications. Teaching is an essential aspect of leadership and hence a qualification for being an elder. The pastor-teacher of Eph 4:11 would exemplify this task. The ability to teach sound doctrine had three immediate applications to the early Christian community as contained in the qualifications for elders (see 1 Tim 3:1–13; Titus 1:5–16): (1) advancing personal faithfulness of the individual; (2) preserving the sanctity of the Christian family; and (3) guarding the Church against false teaching. All of these aspects of instruction place a high value on the teaching ministry of elders.

6. *Diverse learning methodologies were utilized to match diverse learning outcomes, based on the individual and situation.* Instruction in the Bible takes place in many forms. Recent interest on instructional methodologies in the ancient Near East, and especially Israel, has yielded a wealth of insight. D. Estes, J. Crenshaw, C. Melchert, and D. Morgan have identified the broad spectrum of learning methods utilized by the instructors of wisdom literature in ancient Israel.[21] At one end of the spectrum are learning methods resembling teacher-centered indoctrination of students, the presentation of prearranged clusters of content. At the other end are learning methods resembling teachers as facilitators, wherein instructors provide students with materials

(as in Job, Proverbs, and Ecclesiastes) and encourage students to wrestle individually with the text. N. Shupak commented:

> The ancient Hebrew educators perceived knowledge first and foremost as traditional, exemplary material, to be passed down from generation to generation. . . . The dominant teaching method was learning by heart [memorization]. . . . The Hebrew educator, however, was also aware of another way of learning, one based on the pupil's creative flair. This sort of learning, which departed from the tradition, was an attempt to expand transmitted, dogmatic knowledge. It was the autodidactic study, through experimentation and personal learning, without the mediation of an educational authority.[22]

The prophets likewise employed a variety of teaching methods. In addition to the oral and written messages from the prophets, their methods included proverbs (Jer 31:29; Ezek 12:22–23; 16:44; 18:2–3), parables (Ezek 17:1–24; 24:1–14), symbolic acts (1 Kgs 11:29–39; Isa 20:1–6; Jer 19:10–13; 51:63–64; Ezek 4:1–5:17; 12:1–28; 24:15–27), and allegories (Isa 5:1–7; Ezek 16:1–17:24; 23:1–49)—all designed to facilitate learning in a variety of ways.[23]

The New Testament is likewise replete with examples of diverse learning methodologies, as reflected in the vocabulary used to describe the educational endeavors of the early Christian community.[24] While some are rather generic (such as terms for "teacher," "teaching," "knowledge," and "learning"), others are more insightful as to the depth of learning or type of teaching. For example, Paul used the term *paideia* ("training") about parent-child relationships: "Fathers, do not exasperate your children; instead, bring them up in the training and instruction of the Lord" (Eph 6:4).[25] *Katecheo* means "to be informed" in the case of Apollos who had a basic knowledge but required further instruction by Priscilla and Aquila

(Acts 18:25).[26] Similarly, *noutheteo*, meaning "to shape the mind," carries with it the notion of developing a mind-set: "Now these things happened to them as a warning, but they were written down for our *instruction*, upon whom the end of the ages has come" (1 Cor 10:11).[27] A final example is *suniemi* ("to understand, comprehend"): "Therefore do not be foolish, but understand what the will of the Lord is" (Eph 5:17).[28] The variety of terms that indicate various dimensions of learning may be used to further define the type of teaching-learning taking place.

One of the most descriptive vignettes of Jesus' teaching is Luke 24:13–25, the Emmaus road dialogue. In his encounter with the two disciples, he uses discussion (v. 14), question/inquiry (v. 17), correction (vv. 25–27), modeling of desired outcome (vv. 30–31), and direct response to questions/inquiry (vv. 33–35). Teachers must challenge their students to think and reflect, not merely to mimic the teacher's methods or conclusions.

Similarly, in Titus 2:1–15, various demographic groups comprising the church in Crete are identified, with each given its own set of instructional objectives. Such examples as these require Christian education to have a variety of facets and are not simply given for one reason, one format, or one particular group in the church. Rather, the teaching ministry of the congregation is multidimensional, able to respond to the needs ranging from those of the individual to those of the Christian community. Instruction must be tailored to the needs of the specific group or age level. Hence, instruction must take into account the learner and the context in which the instruction will occur.

7. *Education is based on, but not limited to, content transmission.* E. Peterson's *Eat This Book* serves as a reminder that Scripture was meant to be *consumed*, as the apostle John was instructed (Rev 10:9–10). We should not merely "take it and eat it" but digest it as well ("my stomach turned sour").[29] Virtually every educational context in the Scriptures regards education to be based on the content of the Bible, as God's

covenant with his people. Reflection, application, obedience, implications, and life transformation are based on it. Scripture is the content of Christian instruction. Without scriptural content such life-changing outcomes do not occur. In Deut 6:1–9 parents were expected to know the content of their tradition so as to teach their children. Deuteronomy 31:9–13 records that the priests read the law to the assembly of the people (both the Hebrews and the non-Hebrews living among them), including children, so they could know and obey the law. Similarly, in Neh 8:1–9, Nehemiah has Ezra read the Mosaic law to an assembly of the people with the Levites providing commentary and further instruction on the meaning of the text. Memorization was the main method of instruction and the main level of learning to be achieved (Deut 6:1–8; 11:18–19; Prov 3:1–3; 6:20–21; 7:1–3). Christian education must be concerned with communicating the contents of the Bible, but it must also provide commentary that helps students understand the meaning of the Scriptures.

The content emphasis in both the Old and New Testaments assumed at least a partially literate faith community, one that could read and write. Numerous individuals and groups (such as parents, priests, prophets, military personnel) in Israel's history are described as being able to write and/or read, some passages even dating prior to the monarchical period.[30] Archaeologist Allen Millard concluded correctly:

> Ancient Hebrew written documents, recovered by archaeology, demonstrate both that there were readers and writers in ancient Israel, and that they were by no means rare. Few places will have been without someone who could write, and few Israelites will have been unaware of writing.[31]

Similarly, in the New Testament era, the writing of epistles demonstrates that at least a portion of the early Christian communities was literate, and hence Christian authors provided texts in written form as an efficient means of propagating the message of Christ, teaching doctrine, providing guidance for Christian living, and correcting error. For example, Paul assumed the presence of literate members of the early Christian community, at least on an elementary level, who were capable not only of reading his letters (1 Thess 5:27; 1 Tim 4:13) and corresponding with him (1 Cor 7:1) but also of procuring copies of other letters (Col 4:16). This is significant since it meant that Christian education presupposed that individuals had received previous instruction in literacy provided by non-Christian means, such as Greco-Roman schools. Similarly, even today most Christian educators assume that a system of public education to provide literacy and basic skills for Christian instruction is available. Hence, Paul recognized that education in general was necessary and valuable in addition to a distinctively Christian education.

However, Christian education is not limited to content mastery. Knowing the content, such as through rote memorization, is the basis for *wisdom*. The opening verses of Proverbs serve as an introduction to the book and demonstrate the importance of wisdom (1:1–7):

> The proverbs of Solomon son of David, king of Israel: for attaining wisdom and discipline; for understanding words of insight; for acquiring a disciplined and prudent life, doing what is right and just and fair; for giving prudence to the simple, knowledge and discretion to the young—let the wise listen and add to their learning, and let the discerning get guidance—for understanding proverbs and parables, the sayings and riddles of the wise. The fear of the LORD is the beginning of knowledge, but fools despise wisdom and discipline.

Wisdom literature in the Old Testament, particularly Proverbs and Ecclesiastes, uses a variety of "verbs, phrases, and idioms relating to learning" that seem to provide insight into "stages in the learning process" as understood by the Israelites.[32] Nili Shupak of the University of Haifa (Israel) "tries to reconstruct the progressive stages of learning, from the first, passive step to the last, more active and creative step," based on the usage of such vocabulary in Hebrew wisdom literature (see Figure 3.3).[33]

Passive Learning		
	Listening, Obedience	*šmʿ, šyt, lēb,* and synonyms (first meaning)
	Observance	*šmr, nṣr, ṣpn* + objects relating to *ḥokmâ*
	Assimilation	*qnh* + objects relating to *ḥokmâ, bqš* + objects relating to *ḥokmâ* (first meaning)
	Understanding	*šyt lēb* and synonyms (second meaning), *lqḥ mûsār, lmd*
	Mastery	*byn, , śkl (hiphʿil)*
	Searching, Pondering	*leqaḥ* (noun), *ḥqr* (verb, noun), *bqš* (second meaning), *ntn ʾel lēb, ntn ʾet lēb lĕ*
Active Learning		

Figure 3.3: Learning in Old Testament Wisdom Literature

The Old Testament's wisdom literature, most of which was produced during the monarchical period, moves the learner from the mastery of the content toward higher levels of learning and living. Paralleling this progressive teaching strategy in the wisdom literature of the Old Testament was an equally progressive approach to behavioral discipline.[34] In regard to the use of wisdom literature in Hebrew education, E. M. Curtis wrote:

> The Old Testament sages regularly taught in ways that involved ambiguity and created tension in the minds of

their students. Such teaching methods were intended to stimulate thought and reflection on the part of their students as they sought to answer the questions raised by these dilemmas. These intellectual and applicational struggles played a significant role in moving students toward the goal of developing skill in living according to Yahweh's order.[35]

While the New Testament has no such collection or corpus of "wisdom literature" from which to provide a systematic study of such vocabulary, it does utilize a variety of terms associated with the learning process, demonstrating a similar progression from memorization to assessment or decision-making.[36] The author of Heb 5:11–6:3 attests to the idea that spiritual formation is the result of Christian instruction, employing the metaphor of growth from infancy to maturity as an illustration. Similarly, Peter wrote: "Like newborn babies, crave pure spiritual milk, so that by it you may grow up in your salvation" (1 Pet 2:2). Christian education must provide instruction for those of different ages of spiritual maturity and for children at different developmental levels. However, all the higher level processes of learning are directly contingent on the presence of a mastery of content in the mind of the student. This endeavor to provide mastery of content in Christian education is sorely lacking in contemporary Christian education, which must seek to maintain the tradition of "wisdom" as the ability to make suitable applications of the biblical text to life and not merely as the accumulation of knowledge.

Learning beyond the mere mastery of content requires outcomes not only in the cognitive (thinking) but also in the affective (valuing) and active (performance, skills) domains. W. Brueggemann noted that education had at least two dimensions in Scripture, "passion" (affective) and "perspective" (cognitive), and that the two were interrelated.[37] T. Ward presented a biblical model of spirituality in the faith community.[38] In this model Ward identified three aspects of biblical spiritual-ity: thinking like a Christian, experiencing like a Christian, and serving like a Christian—all centered on our relationship with God. Each of these aspects parallels learning objectives present in contemporary Christian education: cognitive, affective, and behavioral.

Jesus identified the greatest commandment as "to love [God] with all your heart, with all your understanding and with all your strength" (Mark 12:33a; see Matt 22:37).[39] Jesus identified the second greatest commandment as having both a communal objective, "love your neighbor," and an individ-ual objective, "as yourself" (Mark 12:33b; see Matt. 23:39). Similarly, the reaction of the audience on the day of Pente-cost reflects this: "When the people *heard* this [cognitive], they were cut to the *heart* [affective] and said to Peter and the other apostles, 'Brothers, what shall we *do* [active]?'" (Acts 2:37–38).[40] Faith is not only expressed in these three ways, but it is also facilitated or learned through these three means.[41] Christian education is not simply concerned with thinking that develops exegetical geniuses. Rather, learning is holistic, engaging every aspect of human learning.

8. *Educational venues are to be expanded to address the necessities of the church.* As the community changes, the edu-cational system in it expands to adapt to these changes so as to remain relevant to the needs of the community, not stagnant and irrelevant. This is most readily observed in the Old Tes-tament, with its over two millennia of history, wherein Israel began as a nomadic family, became a subjugated ethnic group, a confederacy of tribes, a monarchy, and ultimately a vassal state under foreign rule. Figure 3.4 on the next page demon-strates the adaptation of education in the Old Testament to the various periods of the community's history, with new develop-ments identified in italics and abandoned endeavors in strike through.

Period	Dates	Scriptures	Educational Format
Patriarchs	2200–1885 BC	Gen 12–50	*Socialization* *Family Education* *Tribal Elders*
Slavery/ Exodus	1885–1400 BC	Exod, Lev, Num, and Deut	Socialization Familial Education Tribal Elders
Conquest of Canaan	1400–1385 BC	Josh	*Prophets or Seers* *Priests*
Judges	1385–1075 BC	Judg and Ruth	*Judges* *Wisemen/Sages*
United Monarchy	1075–931 BC	1–2 Sam, 1 Kgs 1–11, 1 Chr, 2 Chr 1–9	Socialization Familial Education Tribal Elders Prophets/Seers (writings)
Divided Monarchy	931–722 BC	1 Kgs 12–22, 2 Kgs 1–20, 2 Chr 10–29	Priests ~~Judges~~
Judah Alone	722–586 B.C.	2 Kgs 20–25, 2 Chr 29–36	Wisemen/Sages *Wisdom Literature* *Royal Court* *Education* *Scribal Schools?*
Exilic and Postexilic	586–c.400 BC	Ezra, Neh, Esth	Socialization Familial Education Tribal Elders Prophets/Seers (writings) Priests ~~Judges~~ Wisemen/Sages Wisdom Literature Royal Court Education Scribal Schools? *Origins of the* *Synagogue?*

Figure 3.4: Old Testament Educational Endeavors

Israel could not simply keep its educational system stagnant, so new approaches were adapted into the educational practices while others were abandoned. The synagogue is a prime example of educational innovation. It apparently originated in the sociocultural situation of the Babylonian captivity, which gave rise to its establishment during the intertestamental period.[42] Throughout the New Testament the synagogue is the center for Jewish religious education and worship, yet we have *no* record or reference to its inception or formation in the Old Testament.[43] *Was the synagogue initiated by God or by human design?* The Old Testament contains no mandate as to its formation. By all indications the synagogue was a human innovation designed to accomplish the educational mandate of the Old Testament, one in which Jesus himself even participated.[44] Hence, the synagogue may be an illustration of a human innovation designed to fulfill God's instructional mandates.

Even in the New Testament we observe this principle of adaptation, only on a lesser scale. Early in the book of Acts, the apostles were the only teachers of the church, with no additional leaders or teachers mentioned (Acts 1–5). However, as the Christian community grew, leadership was required, particularly those who also assumed the teaching role. For example, pastor-teachers (Eph 4:11) and elders (1 Tim 3:2; Titus 1:9; 1 Pet 5:1–4) apparently were widely accepted leaders in the early church, but they are not mentioned by name until Acts 11:30; 13:1. Such adaptation enabled the further growth of the faith community and avoided the stagnation of institutionalization.

9. *Educational practices were adopted from neighboring cultures.* In light of the previous observation, a related observation in this regard is that the community of faith has learned to *adopt* educational approaches and practices from the cultural setting. In the Old Testament this practice of adoption is perhaps best demonstrated by the presence of wisdom literature and the possible establishment of scribal schools, both during the rise of the Israelite monarchy. "The acceptance of practical responsibility

for the instruction of youth characterized the wisdom tradition in the Near East long before the emergence of Israel."[45] J. W. Hilbur acknowledged that the

> actual incorporation of ancient Near-Eastern wisdom traditions within the Book of Proverbs underscores this point. . . . The Old Testament wisdom writers shared a common intellectual tradition with current Near Eastern culture, from which they gleaned wisdom and which they adapted to their faith in Yahweh.[46]

For example, passages such as Prov 22:17–24:22; 30:1–33; 31:1–9 find significant parallels in the wisdom literature of the ancient near eastern cultures surrounding Israel. Wisdom literature throughout the Near East may have been used in school settings, including Israel, as indicated by the parallels between the book of Proverbs and the Egyptian book of Instructions or the Teaching of Amenemope.[47]

Similarly, a growing body of archaeological information seems to indicate that the establishment of scribal schools in ancient Israel started with the rise of the Hebrew monarchy.[48] Some biblical passages seem to indicate the presence of a formal setting for religious and scribal training (2 Kgs 6:1; Isa 8:16; 28:10; 1 Chr 25:8; Prov 4:7; 5:13). For example, Davies said that Prov 22:29 and Prov 25–27 may suggest that "schools would have been, at least in part, associated with the training of government officials."[49] The advancement of education in ancient Israel may have risen when formal diplomatic relations with Egypt were established during the time or David or Solomon, requiring a parallel bureaucratic system (2 Sam 8:16–18; 20:23–25; 1 Kgs 4:1–6). This would also explain the advent of wisdom literature as a by-product of formal education in Mesopotamia and Egypt adapted by the Hebrew culture. R. J. Williams concluded: "We must assume the existence of scribal schools as in the neighboring nations. The products of such schools would be known as 'ready scribes' (Ps 45:1)."[50] More recently, Jamieson-Drake— based on textual data, epigraphic remains, and cross-cultural analogy—concluded that the noted increase in public works and luxury items (many with inscriptions) that occurred during the eighth and seventh centuries BC would have necessitated a formal schooling to facilitate such advances.[51]

In the New Testament, Paul engaged the educational community of his era, sometimes critically (1 Cor 1:20; 2:4,8) but other times favorably.[52] Paul demonstrated a basic knowledge of Greek literature (Acts 17:28; 1 Cor 15:33; Titus 1:12) and adapted it for Christian use. Paul likewise employed familiar educational images common to Greco-Roman culture. For example, the term *paidagogos*, a tutor-slave who served in aristocratic Greek and Roman households, is used in Gal 3:24–25 and 1 Cor 4:15 to describe the law, using it appropriately in a Greco-Roman educational context.[53] Similarly, Paul utilized familiar terminology and phraseology of the contemporary educational system in addressing Christian education. R. L. Tyler suggested that the phrase *to me huper a gegraptai* (literally "the 'not beyond what is written'") in 1 Cor 4:6 could reflect pedagogy of writing skills in Hellenistic elementary schools.[54] He further explained:

> Paul refers to a pedagogical conception which his hearers would recognize from their early education. . . . The reference is to the instruction given to children learning to write letters of the alphabet. . . . Throughout the process [of learning to write letters] the pupil had to be careful not to go above the line with some letters or to go below the line with others. One was neither to fall short of the model given nor to go beyond it.[55]

The point to be made is that the early Christian community, Paul in particular, adapted accepted educational practices for the service of the church. As previously noted, though not mentioned in the New Testament, early Christians did adopt a schooling model of education within the first few centuries AD, a model familiar to Greco-Roman culture but not the New Testament.

10. *Education is for conversion and spiritual formation, both personally and corporately.* The purpose of biblical instruction

is the spiritual formation of the individual and the faith community, though it may be expressed in devotion, knowledge, relationship, service, obedience. A holistic faith is the primary goal of Christian education. This goal is intended not only for the individual Christian but also for the maturing of the Christian community as the bride and body of Christ.

The purpose of instruction was also to lead someone to make a personal commitment and greater maturity. In the Old Testament the nation of Israel received instruction and then had to choose between faithfulness and rejection of God (Deut 30:11–20). Even the resident "alien" was to participate regularly in the community's instruction (Deut 31:12; 1 Kgs 8:41–43). It should be noted that the writings of the prophets indicate that they called the nation to accountability to God—not only as individuals but as a nation—and often identified the nation's societal failures.

Perhaps even more evident is the Great Commission of the New Testament (Matt 28:18–20). Jesus' commission to his disciples to continue his disciple-making endeavors explicitly included teaching. Christian education must maintain the focus on making disciples of Christ, which does not simply end with conversion but requires continual instruction for maturing in the faith. Additionally, Paul's instructions to the Corinthian congregation call for spiritual engagement. In 1 Cor 2:6–16 the activity of the Holy Spirit in applying the truth of Scripture to the believer's life is emphasized. The spiritually mature are better able to discern spiritual truth. Teaching must allow for the activity of the Holy Spirit and encourage reflection of the Bible on life.

Christian education is meant for those inside and outside the community of faith. All are called to acknowledge God and live in faithfulness to him. This is true not only personally but corporately as a community of faith. God's sovereignty applies to every aspect of life. The beginning of spiritual formation is conversion, and the educational imperative of the church is fulfilled by evangelism and education toward discipleship.

11. *Teaching and leading are virtually inseparable.* Paul
listed the qualifying characteristics for elders, the leaders of the
congregation, in 1 Tim 3:1–7 and Titus 1:5–9. An elder must
be blameless, among a list of other qualities, and must *not be*
several other less desirable qualities; to function as a leader
he must be able to teach (1 Tim 3:2; Titus 1:9). Paul further
asserted, "The elders who direct the affairs of the church well
are worthy of double honor, especially those whose work is
preaching and teaching" (1 Tim 5:17), denoting that while there
is more to leadership than teaching, teaching (and preaching)
is nonetheless vital. How could someone lead if he could not
teach? Teachers were leaders in the faith community. This is
exemplified in the New Testament, where Paul described the
role of pastor-teacher as being one of Christ's gifts to the church
(Eph 4:7–16). Their purpose is the completion and maturity of
the church, individually and corporately.

> Leaders within the Christian community were expected
> to teach. That ability commended them along with
> other qualifying factors to their office. In Christian
> education, teachers' attitudes and behaviors validate
> the truth of their teaching. Teaching was so crucial to
> the Christian community that the Holy Spirit gave that
> gift as one of the four foundational gifts. . . . Teach-
> ers were the most respected people in the community.
> Therefore, warning about more severe judgment must
> have caught everyone's attention (1 Tim 3:2; 2 Tim
> 2:2; Titus 2:3; Eph 4:11–12; Jas 3:1).[56]

Christian education must teach for personal edification, and
it must also include the skills and talents necessary for the
maturing of the congregation.

A FINAL NOTE

Principles are just that, principles. They are the scaffolding
for a structure and the fixed points of navigation. However, they
do not constitute the entire structure, nor do they set the course

for the Christian educator. Merely *mimicking* the educational endeavors and practices of the ancient community of faith reflected in Scripture, without innovation or developing more culturally relevant models, does not serve the faith community of today. The 11 principles above call us as Christian educators to innovate within the heritage of education, demonstrating our faithfulness to his Word and the faith community.

PRACTICAL IMPLICATIONS FOR CHRISTIAN EDUCATORS

- Christian educators should possess a passion for the teaching ministry of the church based on the biblical precedent for Christian education.
- Christian educators should endeavor to build a biblical rationale for education in the church based on the educational principles reflected in the biblical narrative.
- Christian educators must endeavor to be innovative in their ministry, following the example of their biblical predecessors.

REFLECTION QUESTIONS

1. Which principle seems the most easy to accept?
2. Which principle seemed most difficult to accept?
3. How would you rate the practice of each of the principles in your congregation?
4. What ideas about education in your congregation were spurred on by this chapter?

---

1   See K. Gangel and C. Sullivan, "Evangelical Theology and Religious Education," *Theologies of Religious Education*, ed. R. C. Miller (Birmingham, AL: Religious Education Press, 1995), 59–60.
2   See 1 Cor 2:10–13; 2 Tim 3:15–17; 1 Pet 1:10–12,21; 2 Pet 1:20–21; 3:2,15–16.
3   See G. W. Knight, "The Scriptures Were Written for Our Instruction," *Journal of the Evangelical Theological Society* 39.1 (1996): 31–42.

4   D. C. Wyckoff, "Theology and Education in the Twentieth Century," *Christian Education Journal* 15.3 (1995): 12.

5   See J. R. Estep Jr., "Biblical Foundations of Christian Education," *Evangelical Dictionary of Christian Education* (Grand Rapids: Baker, 2001), 82–85; idem., "Biblical-Theological Foundations of Christian Education," *Foundations for Christian Education*, ed. E. A. Daniel and J. W. Wade (Joplin, MO: College Press, 1999), 13–33.

6   J. W. McKay, "Man's Love for God in Deuteronomy and the Father/ Teacher—Son/Pupil Relationship," *Vetus Testamentum* 22.4 (1972): 435.

7   W. H. Norvell, "Biblical Foundations for the Teaching Ministry of the Church," *Midwest Journal of Theology* 1.1–2 (2003): 85.

8   J. E. Plueddemann, "Do We Teach the Bible or Do We Teach Students?" *Christian Education Journal* 10.1 (1994): 73–81.

9   C. Melchert, *Wise Teaching: Biblical Wisdom and Educational Ministry* (Harrisburg, PA: Trinity Press International, 1998), 24–29.

10 Ibid, 24.

11 See J. R. Estep Jr., "Philosophers, Scribes, Rhetors . . . and Paul? The Educational Background of the New Testament," *Christian Education Journal,* Series 3, 2.1 (2005): 30–47.

12 See Exod 12:26–27; 20:4–12; Deut 4:9–10; 6:6–9; 11:19–20; 29:9; Ps 78:3–6; Prov 6:20.

13 E. Simon, "Hebrew Education in Palestine," *Journal of Educational Psychology* 22.3 (1948): 190.

14 Deut 4:14; 6:1; 26:1–3; 31:39; Josh 8:30–35; 2 Kgs 2:3; 4:38; 5:22; 2 Chr 17:7–19.

15 See J. Estep Jr., *CE: The Heritage of Christian Education* (Joplin, MO: College Press, 2003), 3.5–3.8; 3.12.

16 G. C. Newton, "Holy Spirit," in *Evangelical Dictionary of Christian Education*, 340–41.

17 C. H. Nichols, "Education in the Gospels and Acts," in *Evangelical Dictionary of Christian Education*, 231.

18 R. B. Zuck, *Teaching as Jesus Taught* (Grand Rapids: Baker, 1995), 25.

19 See Zuck, *Teaching as Jesus Taught*; R. Calkins, *How Jesus Dealt with Men* (New York: Abingdon-Cokesbury, 1962); H. H. Horne, *Jesus—the Master Teacher* (New York: Association Press, 1922), and *Teaching Techniques of Jesus* (Grand Rapids: Kregel, 1982); P. Perkins, *Jesus as Teacher* (New York: Cambridge University Press, 1991); Melchert, *Wise Teaching,* 205–71.

20 R. B. Zuck, *Teaching as Paul Taught.*

21 D. J. Estes, *Hear My Son: Teaching and Learning in Proverbs* (Downers Grove, IL: InterVarsity, 1997), particularly 101–24; J. A. Crenshaw, *Education in Ancient Israel* (New York: Doubleday, 1998), 115–38; Melchert, *Wise Teaching*, particularly 47–58, 91–101, 134–38; D. Morgan, *The Making of the Sage: Biblical Wisdom and Contemporary Culture* (Harrisburg, PA: Trinity Press International, 2002).

22   N. Shupak, "Learning Methods in Ancient Israel," *Vetus Testamentum* 53.3 (2003): 424, 426.

23   R. B. Zuck, "Education in the Monarchy and the Prophets," in *Evangelical Dictionary of Christian Education*, 232.

24   E. L. Hayes, "Establishing Biblical Foundations," in *Christian Education: Foundations for the Future*, ed. R. E. Clark et. al., (Chicago: Moody, 1991), 39; J. Estep and B. Johnson, "Paul's Concept of Education in the Church: Paul's Use of *Paralambano* and *Paradidomi*," paper presented at the North American Professors of Christian Education (Rochester, MN), October 2005; R. B. Zuck, "Greek Words for Teach," *Bibliotheca Sacra* 122.486 (1965): 158–68.

25   See 2 Tim 3:16; Heb 12:5,7,11.

26   See Luke 1:4; Acts 21:21; Rom 2:18; 1 Cor 14:19; Gal 6:6.

27   See 1 Cor 4:14; 10:11; Eph. 6:4; Col 3:16.

28   See Matt 13:19,23,51; 16:11–12; 17:11–13; Luke 18:34; 24:45.

29   E. H. Peterson, *Eat This Book* (Grand Rapids: Eerdmans, 2006), 9.

30   See Exod 17:14; 24:7; 34:1; Num 5:23; Deut 6:9; 11:20; 17:18–19; 24:1–3; 31:11; Josh 8:14,32,34; 18:4; 1 Sam 10:25; 2 Sam 11:14; 1 Chr 24:6; 2 Chr 21:12; 34:24; 35:4; 1 Kgs 21:8; 2 Kgs 5:7; 10:1; 19:14; 22:8–10; 23:2; Neh 8:3–8; 9:3; Esth 8:8–9; Prov 3:3; 7:3; Isa 8:1; 10:1,19; 38:9; Jer 8:8; 22:30; 29:29; 36:2–6; 51:61; Ezek 4:18,23; 24:2; Dan 5:17; 7:1; Hab 2:2.

31   A. R. Millard, "An Assessment of the Evidence for Writing in Ancient Israel," *Biblical Archaeology Today* (Jerusalem: Israel Exploration Society/Israel Academy of Science and Humanities, 1985), 308.

32   Shupak, "Learning Methods," 416–26.

33   Ibid, 424; see R. B. Zuck, "Hebrew Words for 'Teach,'" *Bibliotheca Sacra* 121.483 (1964): 228–35.

34   P. D. Wegner, "Discipline in the Book of Proverbs: 'To Spank or Not to Spank?'" *Journal of the Evangelical Theological Society* 48.4 (2005): 715–32.

35   E. M. Curtis, "Learning Truth from the Sages," *Christian Education Journal,* Series 3, 2.1 (2005): 113.

36   See M. Wilson with J. Oden, *Mastering New Testament Greek Vocabulary through Semantic Domains* (Grand Rapids: Baker, 2003), for a complete listing of terms related to human psychological faculties, including those related to learning. Examples are: "be prepared to learn, pay attention" (*prosecho,* Acts 8:6; 16:14; 1 Tim 4:1; Heb 2;1; and *epecho*, 1 Tim 4:16); "know" (*ginosko*, Acts 8:30–31; 17:20; 1 Cor 2:12) or "known" (*gnostos*); "memory" (*mnemoneuo*, 2 Tim. 2:8); "to think, comprehend, understand" (*noeo*, 2 Tim 2:7; and *logizomai*, 2 Cor 10:11); "to decide, conclude" (*krino*, Rom 14:5); and "to evaluate, judge" (*krisis*, John 7:24; and *krima*, Heb 6:2).

37   W. Brueggemann, "Passion and Perspective: Two Dimensions of Education in the Bible," *Theology Today* 42.2 (1985): 172–80.

38   T. Ward's model of spirituality is most thoroughly presented in K. Botton, C. King, and J. Verungopal, "Educating for Spirituality," *Christian Education Journal* NS1.1 (1997): 33–48.

39   Jesus cited Deut 6:5, "Love the Lord your God with all your heart and with all your soul and with all your strength." The parallel passage in Matthew reads slightly differently, which has been the subject of much debate among commentators.

40   R. Pazmino, *By What Authority Do We Teach?* (Grand Rapids: Baker Book House, 1994), 90.

41   See R. Yount, *Created to Learn* (Nashville: B&H, 1996), 249–74.

42   E. Ebner, *Elementary Education in Ancient Israel* (New York: Bloch, 1956), 17n30.

43   See Acts 6:9; 9:20; 13:5,14–15; 14:1; 15:21; 17:1–17; 18:4–26; 24:12.

44   For Jesus' participation in the synagogue see Matt 12:9; 13:54; Mark 1:21; 3:1; 6:2; Luke 4:16; 6:6; John 6:59.

45   G. Cornfeld and D. N. Freedman, *Archaeology of the Bible: Book by Book* (San Francisco: Harper & Row, 1976), 216.

46   J. W. Hilbur, "Old Testament Wisdom and the Integration Debate in Christian Counseling," *Bibliotheca Sacra* 155 (1998): 416–17. See E. M. Curtis, "Old Testament Wisdom: A Model for Faith-Learning Integration," *Christian Scholar's Review* 15.3 (1986): 213–27.

47   Crenshaw, *Education in Ancient Israel,* 94–95, 231–33; G. I. Davies, "Were There Schools in Ancient Israel?" *Wisdom in Ancient Israel* (New York: Cambridge University Press, 1995), 202–3.

48   See J. R. Estep Jr., "The Case for Schools in Monarchical Israel," paper delivered at Evangelical Theological Society Annual Meeting (San Diego, CA), November 14, 2007, for an assessment of the case for scribal schools during the monarchy.

49   Davies, "Were There Schools," 204. See W. Brickman, "Education (Jewish)," *Encyclopedia Judaica* 1996, vol. 6, 383.

50   R. J. Williams, "Writing and Writing Materials," *Interpreter's Dictionary of the Bible* 1962, vol. 4, 915.

51   D. W. Jamieson-Drake, *Scribes and Schools in Monarchic Israel* (Sheffield, England: University of Sheffield, 1991). More recently C. A. Rollston, "Scribal Education in Ancient Israel," paper presented at Stone-Campbell Journal Conference (Cincinnati, OH, 2005).

52   See Estep, "Philosophers, Scribes, Rhetors . . . and Paul?" 32–33, 42–43.

53   Ibid, 36–37.

54   R. L. Tyler, "First Corinthians 4:6 and Hellenistic Pedagogy," *Catholic Bible Quarterly* 60.1 (1998): 97–103.

55   Ibid, 101.

56   M. S. Lawson, "Education in the Epistles," in *Evangelical Dictionary of Christian Education*, 229.

CHAPTER 4

Revelation, Scripture, and Christian Education

Gregg R. Allison with Michael J. Anthony

THE DOCTRINE OF REVELATION

A rchbishop William Temple put his finger on several important questions about revelation that are just as relevant today as when he wrote them in 1937:

> The dominant problem of contemporary religious thought is the problem of revelation. Is there such a thing at all? If there is, what is its mode and form? Is it discoverable in all existing things, or only in some? If in some, then in which? And by which principles are these selected as its vehicle? Where is it found? Or believed to be found? What is its authority?[1]

Historically speaking, the church has affirmed that God does indeed reveal himself and truth about himself and his ways to humanity. Specifically, this divine communication comes in two forms: general revelation and special revelation. General revelation is God's communication to all people at all times and in all places. This revelation occurs through the created order, God's providential care, a basic moral sense of right and wrong (conscience), and an innate sense that deity exists. Special revelation is God's communication to particular people at particular times and in particular places. This revelation takes places especially through God's mighty acts, the person and work of Jesus Christ, and Scripture.

The idea of revelation is that of uncovering or unveiling so that something which was hidden is brought to light. As for what is revealed, a major controversy that was stirred up in the middle of the last century continues today among evangelicals. Neoorthodox theologians claimed that God himself—not truth or facts about God—is revealed. But many evangelicals dissented from this reductionistic idea, noting that Scripture itself indicates that divine revelation certainly is about God himself, but it is not and cannot be limited to this divine self-disclosure. Revelation includes the identity of the Son of God (Matt 16:17), the content of the gospel (Gal 1:12), the disclosure of divine mystery (Eph 3:3–5), specific instructions (Gal 2:2), the future (the book of Revelation), prophetic messages for the growth of the church (1 Cor 14:30), and so on. On the basis of more thorough study, then, the division that had been erected between personal revelation (revelation is the self-disclosure of God) and propositional revelation (revelation is truth about God) was overcome. Sadly some evangelicals are still plagued by this dichotomy while most acknowledge the richness of divine revelation as both personal and propositional. God reveals himself as well as truth about himself and his ways to humanity.

One important ramification of neo-orthodoxy's insistence on personal revelation over against propositional revelation was its disassociation of the Bible from revelation. Though the church had historically equated the Bible with (one form of) revelation, neoorthodox theologians insisted that because the object of revelation is God himself, then the method of revelation is by God's mighty acts, not by means of propositions or truths about God. This led to the idea that the process of revelation was the combination of some mighty act of God (such as the liberation of Israel from Egypt through the plagues, the Passover, and the crossing of the Red Sea) with the interpretation of that event by the divinely illumined mind of the biblical author (such as

Moses as a participant in and divinely inspired interpreter of the exodus event). Sometime afterwards—weeks, months, maybe years later—the biblical author composed what could be considered the "witness" to that revelation, the divine self-disclosure. Thus, the Bible becomes a "witness" to revelation but is itself not revelation (Figure 4.1):

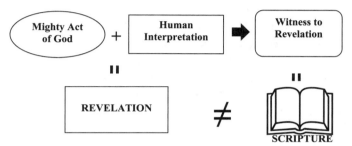

Figure 4.1: Neo-Orthodoxy and Revelation

This notion that the Bible is not revelation flew in the face of the historical position of the church and was rejected by most evangelicals. Evangelicals combined the biblical idea of revelation as both personal and propositional, insisted that revelation consists both of process and product, and maintained the historical view of Scripture as revelation itself. These factors allowed Evangelicals to develop a robust doctrine of revelation, which includes both general and special revelation.

General Revelation

God reveals himself to all people at all times and in all places and through various means. One of the means of this general revelation is the created order or nature. Scripture teaches that "the heavens declare the glory of God" (Ps 19:1), and the apostle Paul, speaking of "what can be known about God" (Rom 1:19), indicates that "his invisible attributes, namely, his eternal power and divine nature, have been clearly perceived, ever since the creation of the world, in the things that have been made" (1:20). This general revelation of the existence and (some of the) attributes of God is intended to lead people to worship and thank the One who created it all and to render honor to him. The actual result, however, is that people "suppress the truth" through ungodliness and unrighteousness (1:18) and engage in idolatry: "They exchanged the truth about God for a lie and worshipped and served the creature rather than the Creator" (1:25). Thus, all people at all times and in all places "are without excuse" (1:20); no one can ever claim that they did not or could not know that God exists.

A second area of general revelation is God's providential care. God created the universe and all that it contains, but he also sustains it and provides for its ongoing needs. As Paul noted when addressing the peasant farmers of Lystra (Acts 14:15–17), God "did not leave himself without witness, for he did good by giving you rains from heaven and fruitful seasons, satisfying your hearts with food and gladness" (v. 17). God reveals his goodness and care for all people at all times and in all places by providentially providing nourishment and other needs that they require.

The third area of general revelation is that God provides his human creatures with a sense of right and wrong. Again, the apostle Paul addressed this (Rom 2:12–16), denying that the Jews, who have the written law of God, have an advantage over the Gentiles who do not have the Mosaic law. Indeed, the Gentiles "show that the work of the law is written on their hearts, while their conscience also bears witness, and their conflicting thoughts accuse or even excuse them" (v 15). God has placed his moral law in the hearts of all people at all times and in all places; thus, they have a basic sense of right and wrong. Moreover, the conscience, which is also a part of the divinely designed human constitution, works in conjunction with this moral sense by causing pangs of guilt when the moral law is violated and by approving situations in which God's standards of right and wrong are upheld. Through this kind of general revelation, people know what they should do and what they should not do because they are accountable to God, the Lawgiver of the moral law.

A fourth and final area of general revelation is an innate sense of deity. God has hardwired all people at all times and in all places with a sense of his existence; everyone just knows that God exists. This was one of Paul's points when addressing the sophisticated, elite philosophers of Athens (Acts 17:22–31). While obliquely chiding them for their rampant idolatry (vv. 22–23), the apostle parlayed their common engagement in religious worship and practice into an opportunity to explain the true worship that is due the one and only true God (vv. 24–27). Indeed, two Athenian poets—Epimenides wrote, "In him we live and move and have our being;" Aratus said, "For we are indeed his offspring" (v. 28)—acknowledged what is true of all people: they possess an innate sense of God. The intended result of this general revelation is that all people "should seek God, in the hope that they might feel their way toward him and find him" (v. 27); they should rely on him and worship him alone. Because of sin, however, people like the Athenians fall into idolatry and engage in ignorant religion. This desperate situation can only be resolved by repentance (v. 30), turning from idols to God's established judge of the entire world, the "man whom he has appointed," Jesus Christ (v. 31).

In summary, general revelation is God's communication to all people at all times and in all places. This revelation functions in such a way that people realize that God exists, know something of his divine attributes, and possess a basic sense of right and wrong. The intended outcome of this revelation is that people would worship this God, give him thanks and depend on him, and do what is right and avoid what is wrong. The actual outcome of general revelation, however, is idolatry, ignorant religion, self-dependence, ungodliness and unrighteousness in the suppression of the truth, and disobedience (with some obedience). As a result of this, all people at all times and in all places fall under the judgment of God and are without excuse before his just condemnation.

Because of this failure of general revelation—which is not a failure on its own part or God's but because sinful human beings consistently draw the wrong conclusions from this revelation—another type of divine revelation is needed to rescue fallen humanity.

Special Revelation

God reveals himself to particular people at particular times and in particular places through various means. One is his mighty acts: the deliverance of his people Israel from slavery in Egypt through the plagues, the Passover, and the crossing of the Red Sea; the conquest of the promised land; the captivity of his rebellious, disobedient people in Assyria and Babylon; the postexilic return to Palestine; the birth of the church on Pentecost; and a host of other such events. Another means of special revelation is dreams and visions by which God communicated with people, foretold future events, provided specific instruction, and so forth. These often were associated with angelic visitations by which God delivered some kind of message. Direct divine speech is another means of special revelation such as God's call of Abraham and his promises to the patriarch, God's speaking with Moses in the burning bush, and his giving of the Ten Commandments. Theophanies were appearances of God or the preincarnate Son as human beings (Gen 16:7–14; Exod 3:2; Josh 5:13–15; 2 Sam 24:16); through such theophanies God communicated with particular people. All of this reached its pinnacle (Heb 1:1–2) in the incarnation of the Son of God; through him God revealed not only his mighty acts (the miracles Jesus performed) and divine speech (the teachings of Jesus), but his very nature as well (the visible, incarnate Son of God who made known the invisible Father; Col 1:15; Heb 1:3; John 14:8–9).

The particular people who were the beneficiaries of these revelations were, of course, those who were eyewitnesses of the mighty acts, the recipients of dreams and visions, the hearers of divine speech, and the disciples and acquaintances of Jesus Christ during his earthly life and ministry. These were the immediate beneficiaries of these modes of special revelation. But other beneficiaries exist as well, such as all those who hear or read in Scripture about the mighty acts of God, his direct speech, and the incarnation of his Son. The Bible is the final means of special revelation. Through the writings of both the prophets (what Christians call the Old Testament) and the apostles (the New Testament), God has provided everything that people need to know about him for salvation and godly living.

In summary, special revelation is God's communication to particular people at particular times and in particular places. This revelation functioned in such a way that people were able to know how to experience salvation and to live lives that pleased God. Such revelation is not confined to the past, however, since Scripture continues to make available—wherever it is read verbally or heard orally—the self-revelation of God and the truth about God and his ways to an ever-expanding number of people. This is so because Scripture—which is itself special revelation—is the inspired, truthful, authoritative, clear, sufficient, necessary, and powerful Word of God. It is to this doctrine of Scripture that we now turn.

THE DOCTRINE OF SCRIPTURE

It is common to describe people by listing and talking about their attributes or characteristics—outgoing, intelligent, vivacious, reflective, beautiful, conscientious, loyal, merciful. Similarly, we may approach the doctrine of Scripture by focusing on its attributes or characteristics—inspiration, truthfulness (or inerrancy), authority, sufficiency, necessity, clarity, and power (effectiveness, profitability). Doing so does not treat Scripture as if it were a person. Nor do we confuse the Word of God with God himself, elevating Scripture to the fourth member of the Trinity. Evangelicals emphasize and rely on the Bible.

They study and meditate on Scripture. But they don't worship it. Moreover, when Evangelicals interact with Scripture, they interact with God himself because the Bible is divine revelation intended as communication from God to people. If, as Martin Luther insisted, the Bible is "our adversary," it is so because we live in the presence of God (*coram Deo*; 2 Cor. 2:17) and he confronts us through his Word.

The Inspiration of the Bible

The apostle Paul explained that "all scripture is inspired by God" (2 Tim 3:16). When Paul made this statement, he was referring to the Tanak, the Bible of the Jewish people that Christians now call the Old Testament. This is clear since the word *Scripture (graphe)* refers to the Old Testament in each of the 51 times it occurs in the New Testament. Paul described all of this (every section and the entirety of Scripture as well) as God-breathed—not so much inspired, breathed in, as expired, breathed out—indicating that Scripture is the product of the creative breath of God. Scripture—the very words themselves—are God-breathed.

The apostle Peter added to our understanding of the process of the inspiration of Scripture: "Knowing this first of all, that no prophecy of Scripture comes from someone's own interpretation. For no prophecy was ever produced by the will of man, but men spoke from God as they were carried along by the Holy Spirit" (2 Pet 1:20–21 ESV). Like Paul's statement above, Peter's comment about "prophecy of Scripture" refers to the Jewish Bible or Old Testament, and it refers to the whole of it, not just the prophetic sections. Peter underscored that the biblical authors did not invent what they wrote; they did not merely give us their interpretations of God's powerful work of salvation. This means, for example, that Moses did not just sit down one day and decide to write a five-volume work called the Pentateuch. Nor did Moses just possess intensified human insight into God and his ways, which he decided to write down as he gave an account of the exodus of his people from Egypt by the mighty hand of God; rather, the Holy Spirit guided Moses as he wrote Scripture. And this was true of all the biblical authors: they were "carried along" by the Holy Spirit, moved by him so that they wrote the Word of God and not just their own words.

The inspiration of Scripture can be defined as the special work of the Holy Spirit in which he superintended the human authors of Scripture in such a manner that, employing their different theological perspectives, writings styles, grammatical abilities, and personalities, he ensured that what they wrote was precisely what he wanted them to write: the very Word of God. The biblical authors did indeed write Scripture. This human aspect is easily detectable by noting the vast difference between, say, the impassioned and at times chiding pleas of the apostle Paul in his letters; the lofty, complex arguments of the letter to the Hebrews; and the simple, unadorned propositions of the apostle John's writings. Luke explained (Luke 1:1–4; Acts 1:1) that he engaged in careful research in the crafting of his Gospel and his story of the early church (Acts), and Paul indicated that he applied sound judgment in offering his counsel to the first Christians (1 Cor 7:25–26,40). Given this evidence, we must dismiss as incorrect the mechanical dictation theory of inspiration, which maintains that the biblical authors were only passive secretaries, writing down by dictation whatever God spoke or whispered into their ears. Certainly the Holy Spirit was actively moving these authors as they wrote, but they were engaged thoroughly in the process of conceiving, arranging, researching, and writing their compositions.

Broadly speaking, Evangelicals hold to the verbal, plenary inspiration of Scripture. *Plenary* means that *all* of Scripture is God-breathed. Not just its important matters—truths about God and salvation, matters of faith and practice, moral commands and prohibitions—are inspired; all of Scripture is. *Verbal* (based on the Latin word *verba* meaning "word") emphasizes that divine inspiration extends to the very *words* of the Bible. The work of the Holy Spirit was not just an influence of providential care or guidance resulting only in a heightened religious consciousness or extending only to the thoughts or ideas in the human authors' minds; rather, the superintendence of the Spirit extended to the words of Scripture so that God's intended truth was communicated. Such inspiration could also be termed "confluent" or "concursive." If the confluence of two rivers is where they flow together so as to combine to form one new body of water, then confluence as applied to inspiration refers to the coming together of the Holy Spirit and the biblical authors so that their written product—Scripture—was a collaborative effort. Similarly, concursive inspiration indicates that the Holy Spirit and the biblical authors wrote together in the production of the Word of God (Figure 4.2). "In short, inspiration is characteristically neither natural, partial, nor mechanical, but supernatural, plenary, and dynamic."[2] One important caveat is that inspiration is affirmed only in regards to the original autographs of Scripture themselves, not to any versions or subsequent translations that have come along during the past 20 centuries.

The Truthfulness (or Inerrancy) of the Bible

An important corollary of the inspiration of Scripture is its truthfulness or inerrancy. The truthfulness of Scripture means that whatever

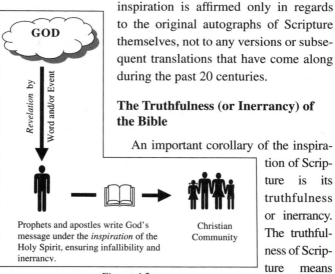

Figure 4.2:
Evangelicals and Revelation-Inspiration

Scripture affirms is true. The inerrancy of Scripture means that Scripture does not affirm anything that is contrary to fact. From its beginning, the church has affirmed this attribute of the Bible. Biblical evidence for it is significant: David affirmed that the words of God are true (2 Sam 7:28); Jesus added that the Word of God is not only true but "truth" itself (John 17:17). The reality that Scripture (which is the Word of God) always communicates the truth—for he does not and cannot lie (Titus 1:2; Heb 6:18)—flows from divine inspiration and divine truthfulness.

The Bible is truthful when it addresses matters that concern salvation through Jesus Christ, promises about eternal life, statements about the nature of human beings, warnings about sinful attitudes and conduct that displeases God, prophecies about the return of Christ and the new heavens and new earth, and so forth. This is also the case when the Bible presents historical facts, lists genealogies, makes statements about the physical universe, and so forth. For example, Scripture is truthful about Jesus' death, burial, and resurrection on the third day. Scripture is equally truthful about Jonah's experience in the belly of the great fish, a story that serves as an analogy of Jesus' death, burial, and resurrection on the third day (Matt 12:40; Jonah 2). Jesus' instructions about marriage between a man and a woman, and a divorce that breaks that marriage, are truthful (Matt 19:3–6); and so are Moses' affirmations about the divine creation of male and female (Gen 1:27) and the institution of marriage (Gen 2:24).

This attribute of complete truthfulness may be affirmed with the following qualifications.[3]

First, the truthfulness of Scripture does not mean that the Bible uses precise, scientific statements when it describes the physical universe. For example, "God made the two great lights—the greater light to rule the day and the lesser light to rule the night" (Gen. 1:16). To be scientifically precise, the sun can be accurately called a "light" but the moon cannot since it only reflects light from the sun. But the use of phenomenological language (referring to something as it appears to human observers) is common, and the Bible uses common, ordinary language. This morning in the place where I wrote this chapter, "sunrise" was at 6:39 a.m. and "sunset" on this day will occur at 9:00 p.m. Technically, this is wrong since the sun neither rises nor sets, but phenomenologically it is correct. Scripture is truthful even when it uses such language.

Second, the truthfulness of Scripture does not mean that the Bible is always grammatically accurate. Biblical writers often used grammatical anomalies. For example, when John received a vision of the seven angels, seven bowls, and seven last plagues (Rev. 21:9), he described "the seven angels who had the seven bowls," adding that the seven angels were "full of the seven last plagues." That is, according to John's grammatical construction, the angels contained the plagues. What he intended to say—and what all readers understand him as saying—was "the seven angels who had the seven bowls full of the seven last plagues." This means that the bowls, not the angels, contained the last plagues. This strange slip may puzzle us grammatically but does not confuse us as to John's intended meaning. Furthermore, truth is a property of sentences, and sentences may communicate adequately and truthfully even when they contain grammatical anomalies. For example, to the question, "Is Mrs. Smith here?" someone may respond, "Her ain't roun'." Though this sentence is a grammatical nightmare, it is nonetheless a true statement since it basically means, "She is not here."

Third, the truthfulness of all Scripture does not mean that the New Testament quotes exactly the Old Testament. Certainly, one way of referring to something that someone else has said or written is to quote it word for word. But there are other ways of referring to it as well: paraphrase may be employed, or a summary may be given, or an allusion may be made. The New Testament authors, when referring to the Old Testament, used these various conventions to do so, and the truthfulness of all of Scripture does not preclude such practice.

Fourth, the truthfulness of all of Scripture does not mean that the New Testament sayings of Jesus contain the exact words of Jesus. If Jesus spoke mostly Aramaic (along with Hebrew as a second language and Greek as a third), then few of the actual words of Jesus are found in the New Testament. Indeed, there are only two phrases of Jesus in Aramaic: *"Talitha cumi"* ("Little girl, I say to you, arise!"; Mark 5:41) and *"Eloi, eloi, lama sabachthani?"* ("My God, my God, why have you forsaken me?"; Mark 15:34; see Matt 27:46). Instead of the exact words of Jesus, the New Testament contains the exact voice of Jesus, meaning that Jesus really spoke the sayings attributed to him by the New Testament authors. Put another way, they were not made up by the disciples and placed in the mouth of Jesus. The Greek of Jesus' sayings is a faithful rendition of the sense of the words that he actually spoke. This does not overturn the truthfulness of all of Scripture.

In the latter part of the twentieth century, Evangelicals were involved in an important debate regarding the truthfulness of all of Scripture. Departing from the historical position of the church on this attribute, some Evangelicals began to affirm the infallibility of Scripture. Stephen T. Davis defined *infallibility* in this way: "The Bible is infallible if and only if it makes no false or misleading statements on any matter of faith and practice."[4] That is, Scripture does not contain any falsehoods in the areas of Christian doctrine such as salvation and holy living. But this leaves open the possibility—indeed, for most if not all of these critics, the actuality—of errors when the Bible addresses matters of history, geography, genealogy, cosmology, and so forth. Specifically, for Davis: "The Bible is infallible, as I define that term, but not inerrant. That is, there are historical and scientific errors in the Bible, but I have found none on matters of faith and practice."[5] In addition, critics of the traditional view who still needed to affirm belief in biblical inerrancy redefined error as "willful deception." Given this definition, they could affirm the complete inerrancy of Scripture because at no point does a biblical author willfully deceive his readers. Clearly, this notion was far removed from the traditional sense of the inerrancy of Scripture.

This challenge was met by the majority of Evangelicals, many of whom championed the Chicago Statement on Biblical Inerrancy (1978). The Chicago Statement affirmed both the *infallibility* and the *inerrancy* of Scripture,[6] with the latter term described in the following way:

> We affirm that Scripture in its entirety is inerrant, being free from all falsehood, fraud, or deceit.
>
> We deny that Biblical infallibility and inerrancy are limited to spiritual, religious or redemptive themes, exclusive of assertions in the fields of history and science. We further deny that scientific hypotheses about earth history may properly be used to overturn the teaching of Scripture on creation and the flood.[7]

The Chicago Statement was followed by what has become the most clear and defensible definition of the inerrancy of Scripture by Paul Feinberg:

> Inerrancy means that when all facts are known, the Scriptures in their original autographs and properly interpreted will be shown to be wholly true in everything they affirm, whether that has to do with doctrine or morality or with the social, physical, or life sciences.[8]

Simply put, the truthfulness of Scripture means that whatever Scripture affirms is true. The inerrancy of Scripture means that Scripture does not affirm anything that is contrary to fact.

The Authority of the Bible

Another corollary of the inspiration of Scripture is its authority. Because it has God for its *author*, Scripture possesses divine *authority*. The authority of Scripture means that all the words in the Bible are God's words; therefore, to believe or obey Scripture is to believe or obey God, and to disbelieve or disobey Scripture is to disbelieve or disobey God.[9]

Evidence of its authority fills the pages of Scripture. The Old Testament prophets proclaimed and wrote with divine authority, prefacing their revelation with "Thus says the Lord!" They spoke the very words of God to the people of Israel. This authority of Old Testament Scripture was affirmed by Jesus and his apostles. For example, to prevent misunderstanding, Jesus explained:

> Do not think that I have come to abolish the Law or the Prophets; I have not come to abolish them but to fulfill them. For truly, I say to you, until heaven and earth pass away, not an iota, not a dot, will pass from the Law until all is accomplished (Matt 5:17–18).

In the Sermon on the Mount, Jesus offered his authoritative interpretation of the Old Testament (Matt. 5:21–48), emphasizing the continuing validity of this part of Scripture. Also, when pressed to justify his use of the expression "Son of God" to refer to himself (John 10:30–36), Jesus appealed to an obscure portion of the Old Testament: "I said, you are gods" (v. 34; Ps 82:6). If the Old Testament permits certain human beings to be called "gods" under certain circumstances, then certainly Jesus can call himself "the Son of God" without being charged with blasphemy (v. 36). Important for our discussion is the attitude Jesus reflected toward this Old Testament passage ("the word of God"): "Scripture cannot be broken" (v. 35). Jesus emphasized the indefectible authority of the Word of God; it can never be broken, set aside, or rendered null and void.

Moreover, Jesus anticipated the authority of the New Testament writings that were to come after his ministry. He promised the Holy Spirit to his apostles so that they would know the truth and remember accurately his teachings (John 14:26; 16:13). With this promise, Jesus authenticated the apostles as the legitimate and authoritative witnesses of his life, teachings, miracles, death, and resurrection. It should come as no surprise, therefore, that as the apostles penned their writings (what would become our New Testament), they were conscious of the authority with which they wrote:

- "When you received the word of God, which you heard from us, you accepted it not as the word of men but as what it really is, the word of God" (1 Thess 2:13).
- "You know what instructions we gave you through the Lord Jesus" (1 Thess 4:2).
- "Stand firm and hold to the traditions that you were taught by us, either by our spoken word or by our letter" (2 Thess 2:15).

Scripture, because it is the Word of God, possesses divine authority. This is true of both the Old Testament and the New Testament. As the one Bible, this and nothing else is the ultimate authority for Christians and for the church.

Thus, any combination of Scripture plus some other authority is a recipe for disaster. The Roman Catholic Church considers its tradition—the communications of Jesus Christ or the Holy Spirit to the apostles that were not written down but transmitted orally from them to their successors, the bishops of the Catholic Church—as a source of divine revelation and thus an integral part of the Word of God. And there is more. Some add reason to Scripture, others join experience to Scripture, while still others add contemporary prophetic revelations to Scripture. Because of the inherent instability of this multisource structure of authority, these additions to Scripture result in detracting from biblical authority. Indeed, these other authorities end up usurping biblical authority and reigning in its place.

As the apostle Paul noted, "Thanks be to God, that you who were once slaves of sin have become obedient from the heart to the standard of teaching to which you were committed" (Rom. 6:17). As people rescued from slavery to sin, Christians willingly submit themselves in obedience and faith to the Word of God. They do not rule over Scripture; rather, Scripture rules over them. As they believe the affirmations and obey the commands of Scripture, they believe and obey God. But tragically, as they disbelieve the promises and disobey the warnings of Scripture, they disbelieve and disobey God.

The Clarity of the Bible

Some will complain that the problem is not submitting to authoritative Scripture but understanding what God is trying to say in his Word. That is, they are convinced that the Bible is a closed book, difficult to read and interpret; thus, they give up trying to understand it. Perhaps others, because of the frenetic pace of life, come home after a weary day at the office or at school, sit down and see their Bible sitting on the coffee table, and even acknowledge to themselves that they should pick it up and read it. In the end, however, they decide to tune in some Bible teacher on the radio or listen to an MP3 file of some pastor's sermon, figuring that they themselves will never be able to get out of the Bible what these professional ministers can deliver for their consumption. Though we know better, the Bible has become the neglected book.

But this should not be since clarity is an attribute of Scripture. "The clarity of Scripture means that the Bible is written in such a way that its teachings are able to be understood by all who will read it seeking God's help and being willing to follow it."[10] The only prerequisite for understanding the Bible is that its readers or hearers "possess the normal acquired ability to understand oral communication and/or written discourse."[11] Understanding Scripture is not dependent on gender (men and women alike can understand it), age (young and old alike can understand it, though adults usually do so more deeply), education (simple people who have never attended school and biblical scholars alike can understand it), language (apparently, the Bible can be translated into every language that exists, so no linguistic barriers stand against its understanding), or cultural background (people from every continent and nation can understand it). However, the level of someone's understanding of Scripture may depend upon and vary with several factors, including spiritual maturity. Generally speaking, more mature Christians understand Scripture more deeply and accurately than do brand-new believers. Such understanding, then, is aided by the Holy Spirit, who illumines Scripture as it is read and studied (1 Cor 2:10–15). Moreover, God himself has ordained that certain people—such as pastors or elders—are to be responsible for helping the church to understand Scripture through the gift and ministry of teaching (1 Tim 3:2; 5:17; 1 Cor 12:28; Eph 4:11).[12]

This is not to say that everything in Scripture is easy to understand; on the contrary, the apostle Peter realistically admitted that the letters of the apostle Paul "contain some things that are hard to understand" (2 Pet. 3:15–16). What Peter did not do is indicate that *all* of Paul's writings are hard to understand; only *some* of them are difficult. And he did not affirm that these difficult portions are *impossible* to understand; they are only *hard* to understand. Moreover, Peter did not prohibit the reading and studying of Scripture because of these difficult parts; rather, he cautioned against those who twisted and distorted these passages and so created heretical teachings from them, which led unsuspecting, gullible people away from Christ. No, a sustained, patient study, undertaken with an expectant attitude, should characterize one's approach to the clear teachings of Scripture.

This is in keeping with biblical metaphors that present Scripture as a "light" or a "lamp" (Ps 119:105; 2 Pet 1:19) that illuminates the pathway of Christians in the midst of the darkness of sin, heresy, temptation, and trials. Such metaphors work only if Scripture is able to be understood. This also accords well with commands and exhortations to read and hear Scripture (1 Tim 4:13; 1 Pet 2:1–3; Col 3:16); such passages would be meaningless if attaining a clear understanding of them is impossible. In addition, the clarity of Scripture makes sense in light of the biblical affirmations of the utility of Scripture. For example, as he appeals to four narratives of Israelite sin and divine judgment (1 Cor 10:1–13, reflecting on Num 14; Exod 32; Num 25; and Num 21), the apostle Paul explained that these events happened to the former people of God and were written down as warning examples (vv. 6, 11) for the instruction of Christians ("on whom the end of the ages has come"; v. 11). In other words, the writers of the Bible assumed its continued intelligibility, for they believed that—even though it was written by and for people who lived with extremely different worldviews than we hold today, light-years removed from our religious circumstance and postmodern culture and social, economic, political, linguistic, ethnic situation—Scripture can be understood by all of God's people at all times.

This means that when Christians open up the Bible to read or study it, their great expectation should be that they will understand it. And it is with this same expectation that they should encourage others to explore Scripture as well.

The Sufficiency of the Bible

When Christians read and study Scripture and grasp its meaning, they can be confident that they are "adequately equipped for every good work" (2 Tim 3:17). The sufficiency of the Bible means that Scripture contained every word that God intended his people to have at each stage of redemptive history, and that it now contains everything Christians need God to tell them about salvation, about trusting him rightly, about obeying him properly, and about pleasing him completely.[13] This means, for example, that for the people of Israel in Moses' time, the Pentateuch (the first five books of the Bible, written by Moses) was the sufficient Word of God. By reading the biblical accounts of Abraham and God's promise to him, the people at that time were given wisdom to understand that God justifies or saves them by his grace through faith alone. Furthermore, it means today that, in the Old and New Testaments combined, Christians have everything they need to please God thoroughly.

In practical terms, this means that Christians can't subtract anything from Scripture or ignore any of its teachings, that would make for an insufficiency of divine instruction. Nor can they add anything to Scripture, like their own personal revelations or legalistic codes of conduct; that would deny the sufficiency of

Scripture. Such prophetic messages and legalistic rules and regulations present major challenges to the sufficiency of Scripture and must therefore be repulsed energetically and completely. Additional "words from the Lord" ("the Lord told me to do such and such") and additional commandments ("you must be a card-carrying, vocal supporter of the Republican Party") and prohibitions ("you must not play video games") do not make their adherents more pleasing to God. Nothing is required by God or forbidden by God that is not commanded or forbidden in Scripture because Scripture is sufficient. Indeed, God will not empower obedience to instructions that he does not give for Christians to follow, and what often ends up happening is the development of pride and arrogance on the part of Christians who heed these extra instructions as they consider themselves superior to Christians who do not engage in these extra measures. In contrast, Christians who uphold the sufficiency of Scripture possess a great confidence that they can be pleasing to God. They realize that when they are faced with a decision about doctrine or practice, if they search out and contemplate all the relevant biblical affirmations, the follow-through from their understanding is pleasing to God. This is the outcome of the sufficiency of Scripture.

The Necessity of the Bible

Because God has willed to give us the revelation of himself and his ways through his written Word, it is necessary for Christians to recognize the Bible as that Word from God.

> The necessity of Scripture means that the Bible is necessary for knowledge of the gospel, for maintaining spiritual life, and for certain knowledge of God's will, but it is not necessary for knowing that God exits or for knowing something about God's character and moral laws.[14]

As we saw earlier, general revelation provides all people at all times and in all places with the knowledge of God's existence, attributes, and moral laws. But general revelation does not provide people with the knowledge of the gospel and instructions in godly living. That comes from Scripture and Scripture alone, just as God willed for it to be. This means that people cannot know about salvation in Jesus Christ unless Christians communicate the gospel, the Word of God, to them. It further means that Christians cannot sustain their walk with Christ and know the will of God so as to please him unless they read Scripture, study Scripture, and hear Scripture taught. They cannot have what God willed to reveal through his written Word without Scripture as that Word from God. As Jesus himself said, "Man shall not live on bread alone, but on every word that proceeds out of the mouth of God" (Matt 4:4 NASB).

On a practical note, the necessity of Scripture means that regularly (each day or more often) Christians are to give attention to reading the Bible, meditating on it, studying it, memorizing it, and applying Scripture through obedience and faith.

The Canonicity of the Bible

Everything that has been affirmed of the attributes of Scripture—its inspiration, truthfulness (inerrancy), authority, clarity, sufficiency, and necessity—has been affirmed of canonical Scripture: the 66 books (39 in the Old Testament and 27 in the New Testament) of the Bible. But why do these particular 66 books compose the canon of Scripture? The word *canon* comes from the Greek word *kanon*, which originally referred to a reed or rod. Later it was used to refer to a measuring rod; figuratively, then, *canon* came to signify a norm or a standard. As developed in church history, *canon* was the term given to the list of all those books that belong in the Bible.

The Hebrew Bible was composed over a long period of time stretching from the writing of the five books of Moses to the last of the prophetic books (Malachi) and the last of the historical books (Ezra, Nehemiah, and Esther). The canon of this Jewish Bible (what Christians call the Old Testament) was set before the time of Christ and consisted of 22 or 24 books (depending on how books were combined or split), organized into three divisions. The first division is **the Law** or the five books of Moses: Genesis, Exodus, Leviticus, Numbers, Deuteronomy. The second is **the Prophets,** which is divided further into the *Former Prophets*: Joshua, Judges, Samuel (1 and 2 Samuel), Kings (1 and 2 Kings); and the *Latter Prophets*: Isaiah, Jeremiah, Ezekiel, and the *Book of the Twelve* (Hosea, Joel, Amos, Obadiah, Jonah, Micah, Nahum, Habakkuk, Zephaniah, Haggai, Zechariah, and Malachi). The third is **the Writings:** Psalms, Job, Proverbs, Ruth, Song of Songs, Ecclesiastes, Lamentations, Esther, Daniel, Ezra (with Nehemiah), and Chronicles (1 and 2 Chronicles). This was the Bible used by Jesus and the apostles. Though arranged differently, the Hebrew Bible and the Protestant Old Testament are identical in terms of the books included in the canon. The order of books in our English Bibles follows the Septuagint, the Greek translation of the Old Testament.

As the early church began to grow and develop, other writings were added to the collection of authoritative Hebrew Scripture: the four Gospels (Matthew, Mark, Luke, John); a historical account of key events in the early church (Acts); twenty-two letters or epistles (Romans to Jude), and an apocalypse, a disclosure of future events (Revelation). Some of these writings point to an expansion of the canon of Scripture. For example, Peter spoke of the letters of the apostle Paul in the context of "the rest of the Scriptures" (2 Pet 3:14–16); and Paul himself connected a saying of Jesus ("the laborer is worthy of his wages") with Deut 25:4, referring to both as "Scripture" (1 Tim 5:18). The books to be included in (what would be called) the New Testament were relatively easy to identify because they fulfilled one and/or two key criteria. The first was *apostolicity,* indicating that the book had an apostle for its author (such as Paul's letters; the Gospel of Matthew; all five of the books of the apostle John), or that an apostle was associated with the writing (such as Mark's Gospel, which was associated with the apostle Peter; and Luke's Gospel and Acts, which were associated with the apostle Paul). The second was *antiquity,* indicating that the book had been long received by the church, which recognized the voice of God speaking to his people through that book. In essence, if the early church had consistently accepted the book as authoritative throughout its history, then that book was held in high esteem and considered equal to the other known authoritative writings. By the middle of the fourth century, the church possessed a canon of Scripture—both Old and New Testaments—that is identical to the one in use among Protestant churches today.

IMPLICATIONS FOR CHRISTIAN EDUCATION

Respect for Revelation

Because the Bible *is* the Word of God, it commands our attention and affirmation. Because the Bible is God's special revelation, Christians, and especially Christian educators, must commit themselves to being a people of the Book. Yet in many instances this devotion to Scripture is lacking in the church. J. Stackhouse stressed the importance of Bible content in Christian education:

> Evangelicals used to be accused of being "biblicistic" and even "bibliolatrous" as they reflexively referred any problem of life to a Bible text. That accusation can rarely be leveled anymore, and it is not necessarily because evangelicals have become more theologically sophisticated. Many instead have become just as ignorant of the Bible as anyone else.
> . . . .
> This is the work of theology, and it is work every Christian must do: learning what God has said and learning how to say it for oneself in one's Christian community. The ignorance of the general public about the fundamentals of the Christian faith is regrettable.

The ignorance of churchgoing Christians about the fundamentals of the Christian faith, however, is scandalous. Christians are somehow expected to think and feel and live in a distinctive way, as followers of Jesus, without being provided the basic vocabulary, grammar, and concepts of the Christian religion.[15]

Christian educators must never allow Scripture to lose its central place in the church's curriculum. The Scriptures must never become neglected or just an ancillary to Christian education. Donald Griggs recommends several ways in which Christian education can guard against minimizing the Bible:

1. Many persons, of all ages, are eager, willing, and ready to commit themselves to a more intentional, disciplined, and fruitful study of the Bible. This means that resources and plans must be provided that call for more commitment, not less.
2. The Bible will be presented whole, not in a piecemeal fashion.
3. The Bible will be the beginning, the end, and the center-point of the preparation and the implementation of teaching.
4. Persons who teach and lead groups that study the Bible, as well as other groups in the church, will be fully equipped for the ministry to which they have been called.
5. Teaching the Bible will incorporate the best of what is known about effective, participatory education.[16]

Perhaps the greatest threat the church faces is not from rival religions, nor from internal differences, nor even from classical liberalism or neoorthodoxy. Perhaps the greatest threat is the neglect of Scripture in instruction.

Teaching beyond Content

To begin this section on implications for Christian education, one more attribute comes into focus: the power of Scripture. As the Bible itself notes, "The word of God is living and active, sharper than any two-edged sword, piercing to the division of soul and of spirit, of joints and of marrow, and discerning the thoughts and intentions of the heart" (Heb 4:12). In addition to the striking, radical ability of Scripture to cut penetratingly both ways, in salvation and judgment (thus, never failing to accomplish the purpose for which God designed it; Isa 55:11), the Word of God's effective power is profitable in many other ways. Indeed, in the same context that he discussed its inspiration, the apostle Paul affirmed four benefits of inspired Scripture (2 Tim. 3:16–17): *teaching*, which is the communication of sound biblical and theological truth; *reproof*, meaning that Scripture exposes sin and convicts of that which is wrong; *correction*, which provides direction about the right way to walk; and *training in righteousness*, the preparation of a mature, Christlike character. As Christians pay attention to the inspired and profitable Word of God, they are adequately equipped or readily prepared for any good work that God requires them to do, such as trusting him in difficult, trying circumstances; finding comfort and peace in the midst of pain and turmoil; obeying him even when the cost of obedience is high; thanking him despite great loss; engaging in ministry in unreceptive contexts, and so forth.

The implication couldn't be clearer: by focusing its attention on and using the Bible as its core curriculum, Christian education profits its participants by teaching, reproving, correcting, and training them in righteousness. Through whatever venue it is offered—Sunday school, VBS, small groups, Bible studies, mentoring—Christian education assists people by helping them please God in everything they do.

Education for Bible Study

Of course, all the previous implications presuppose that Scripture is interpreted rightly and communicated well. A high priority of Christian education is to identify, train, and employ excellent teachers for its many and varied offerings. Certainly, Christians with the gift of teaching should be most highly sought out for these educational ministries. Even though they may possess this needed gift, they still need teaching and training for how to become more effective teachers, and this task is an important element of any Christian educational ministry. Many excellent resources are available to help with this.

Teaching is only half of the story. Each student also needs to be equipped so as to become "a worker who has no need to be ashamed, rightly handling the word of truth" (2 Tim 2:15). Participants at all levels of Christian education should be encouraged to read and study the Bible for themselves. On the basis of the clarity of Scripture, they should be further encouraged to expect to understand what they read and to learn from what they study. Hermeneutics can and should be taught at age-appropriate levels, providing students with the indispensable means to unpack the truth of Scripture for themselves and for others. Helping participants find their way around the Bible as a tool for personal growth and guidance and for leading and counseling others is a necessary component of Christian education.

An important first step in this is for the pastors of the church—specifically, those who preach—to model sound hermeneutical principles. Expository preaching—preaching that moves through entire biblical books from beginning to end and that accurately explains the biblical text—can be a great help in this regard, as it models for the congregational members how they should read and study the Bible. Foregoing certain practices—such as offering complicated explanations, rehearsing lengthy word studies, appealing to Greek and Hebrew words—aids in instructing and encouraging the congregation because it avoids communicating that some kind of esoteric knowledge and training reserved for the elite is necessary to decode the mystery of the Bible. Another important element is to understand and emphasize that there is one interpretation but many varying applications of Scripture. Thus, when people engage in personal Bible study, the question is not, What does this text mean to me? but, What does this text mean? together with, What is an appropriate personal application of this text's meaning? In other words, personal applications must be derived from the accurate interpretation of the text. An important task of Christian education is to equip people to read, study, and apply the Bible.

As they do grasp the meaning of Scripture and apply what is learned to their lives, students must also learn to trust in the authority and sufficiency of Scripture. Again Christian education plays a key role in facilitating this. Trust in the Word of God flows from a deep conviction that all of Scripture is true and truth itself because God, whose Word it is, is wholly trustworthy. Christian educators can facilitate such faith by being constantly and consistently oriented to Scripture in their own personal lives and in their teaching. In terms of fostering a deep respect for biblical authority in the lives of its students, the community of Christian educators must demonstrate that it is itself responsive and submissive to the authority of the Word of God. Practical application of this authority—exhibiting love for one another, moving quickly to reconcile broken relationships, refusing to engage in character-destroying gossip—speaks volumes to those who observe this community and stimulates a similar respect for biblical authority. As for nurturing a high regard for the sufficiency of Scripture, Christian educators must move away from the far too common practice of advocating additional rules and suffocating codes of conduct that have no biblical warrant. Everyone is familiar with the nasty nine, the terrible ten, the dirty dozen—so-called "sins" that violate these legalistic regulations. Though people imagine these to be helpful in avoiding actual sins and living holy lives (Col 2:23), they are no more than personal scruples that may indeed be followed personally, but they cannot be foisted on others as being biblical standards of conduct (Rom 14). Christian educators must first realize for themselves and then emphasize with their students that what these unbiblical restrictions ultimately violate is the sufficiency of Scripture. Then students must be challenged to examine doctrines and practices in light of Scripture so as to ensure that they neither add to nor detract from God's sufficient Word. Repeatedly bringing students back to the question, Is this belief, practice, behavior, or attitude in accordance with Scripture? will help to preserve and apply the sufficiency of Scripture. At times this kind of inquiry may challenge long-cherished ideas, and Christian educators should create and preserve an environment in which such questions and challenges are carried out in an atmosphere of respect and honor rather than quarreling and judging.

Education beyond Scripture

Finally, let's not forget that this chapter is about more than Scripture, for it began with a discussion of general revelation. In terms of implications for Christian education, such revelation demands that educators get out of the classroom! Exposing students to the revelation of God in the created order and through his providential care moves education into the broader context of God's work in the world. Effective study of the glory and nature of God as revealed in this wider context must include (not just reference) creation. In other words, time for observation of God's creation and providential care should be provided, so that clear perception of the evidences of "his eternal power and divine nature" (Rom. 1:20) can take place.

REFLECTION QUESTIONS

1. How would a nonevangelical understanding of Scripture change how and what you teach?
2. In your church what is the place of the Bible in the curriculum? What is taught? Are there portions not taught?
3. Why is instruction in Bible content critical for spiritual growth? What might be the dangers of overemphasizing Bible content? underemphasizing?

4. Why is instruction beyond Bible content critical for spiritual growth?

5. Where in your Christian education ministry are the nature, place, and function of the Bible in Christian education addressed? What would you say if you had to write a statement on the nature, place, and function of the Bible in your Christian education ministry?

---

1   W. Temple, "Revelation," in *Revelation*, ed. J. Baillie and H. Martin (New York: Macmillan, 1937), 83.

2   A. H. Strong, *Systematic Theology* (Valley Forge, PA: Judson, 1985), 211.

3   Adapted from P. D. Feinberg, "The Meaning of Inerrancy," in *Inerrancy*, ed. N. Geisler (Grand Rapids: Zondervan, 1982), 298–302.

4   S. T. Davis, *Debate about the Bible* (Philadelphia: Westminster, 1977), 23.

5   Ibid., 115. Davis did not engender much confidence in his view since he followed up the statement cited above with the following: "Perhaps someday it will be shown that the Bible is not infallible. For now I can only affirm infallibility as the most probable interpretation of the evidence I see" (116).

6   *The Chicago Statement on Biblical Inerrancy*, articles 11 and 12, as cited in W. Grudem, *Systematic Theology: An Introduction to Biblical Doctrine* (Grand Rapids: Zondervan, 1994), 1206.

7   Ibid.

8   P. D. Feinberg, "The Meaning of Inerrancy," in *Inerrancy*, 294.

9   Adapted from Grudem, *Systematic Theology*, 73.

10 Adapted from Grudem, *Systematic Theology*, 108.

11 G. R. Allison, *The Protestant Doctrine of the Perspicuity of Scripture: A Reformulation on the Basis of Biblical Teaching*, unpublished Ph.D. dissertation (Trinity Evangelical Divinity School, Deerfield, IL, 1995), 516.

12 Some of the above was adapted from Allison, *Perspicuity of Scripture*, 516–36.

13 Adapted from Grudem, *Systematic Theology*, 127.

14 Grudem, *Systematic Theology*, 116.

15 J. Stackhouse, *Evangelical Landscapes* (Grand Rapids: Baker, 2004), 71, 193.

16 D. L. Griggs, "The Bible: From Neglected Book to Primary Text," *Religious Education* 85.2 (1990): 246–54.

CHAPTER 5

The Triune God and Christian Education

James Riley Estep Jr.

G*od*. It is no longer sufficient to assume that when someone refers to God, everyone knows which God is in that person's mind. Is God the God of Abraham, Isaac, and Jacob—the God of Judaism? Is he Allah, the God of Islam? Referring to God requires definition and description as to which deity is in view. Additionally, in our contemporary culture, the idea of God has been popularized and even trivialized through politics, sporting events, entertainment, and the media. As a term, *God* is considered politically correct and secularly acceptable as an affirmation of a generic supreme being, ideal, or force. If one were really to consider the generic nature of the term *god*, how many different *gods* are present in one's community? Affirming a belief in God does *not* equate to belief in the God of Christian Scripture or in Jesus Christ as his Son.

While such confusion may reign in our culture, this is not to excuse the faith community from confusion as well. To understand and appreciate the distinction and uniqueness of the Christian faith, one must grasp the Scripture's teachings about God. If education in the church is to be God centered, then it cannot simply focus on whatever *god* might mean in our culture; it must focus on the God revealed in Scripture. Since we are God's creation, and particularly his image bearers, the nature of God informs the Christian life, faith, and community of the church. As K. Gangel and C. Sullivan maintain, the quintessential question on which evangelical education is based is, Whom do we worship?[1]

How does what we as Christian educators believe about God impact how we approach education in the church? This chapter endeavors to present the rationale for a God-centered approach to education by identifying the educational implications of our belief in the Christian God. It will do so by addressing (1) God as Trinity, (2) attributes of the triune God, and (3) essential works of God. A God-centered education should be based on who God is (Trinity), what God is like (attributes), and what he does (works). This chapter is not intended to be a comprehensive treatment of theology proper, the doctrine of God, but rather a presentation of an evangelical portrait of God and its educational implications.

WHO IS GOD? GOD AS TRINITY

The belief in a triune God, the simultaneous and complementary affirmation of the oneness and "three-ness" of God, is perhaps the most distinctive element of Christian teaching about God. While the term *Trinity* does not occur in Scripture (Tertullian used it first in the late second century AD), the doctrine is nonetheless contained in Scripture. The biblical term most frequently associated with the Trinitarian idea is *Godhead* (Acts 17:29; Rom 1:20; Col 2:9). Scripture affirms the essential simultaneous oneness and threeness of God.[2] Three basic affirmations about God are discussed in this section: (1) God is one; (2) God eternally exists as Father, Son, and Holy Spirit; and (3) each of the three persons of the Godhead is fully and equally God.

First, God is one (Deut 6:4; 1 Cor 8:6). The Christian tradition is one of the few monotheistic faiths in the world. Both Judaism and Islam are monotheistic but not Trinitarian; thus, the doctrine of the Trinity separates Christianity from these other monotheistic religions. Being Trinitarian, however, does not make Christianity polytheistic. The simple affirmation that God is one means there is one and only one God, not three. Whatever may be affirmed about the three persons of the Godhead cannot be misconstrued to mean that the Father is one God, the Son is another God, and the Holy Spirit is a third God. The Lord himself does not allow us to think this: "I am the Lord, and there is no other; apart from me there is no God" (Isa 45:5). Erickson explains that "the Trinity must be understood as fundamentally a society. The Godhead is a complex of persons. Love exists within the Godhead as a binding relationship of each of the persons to each of the others. . . . God is love" (1 John 4:8) does not refer to his love toward us but is "a basic characterization of God. . . . The Trinity is three persons so closely bound together that they are actually one."[3]

Second, God eternally exists as Father, Son, and Holy Spirit.[4] This means that the Persons of the Godhead are not interchangeable but rather distinct from one another. The Father is not the Son, and the Son is not the Father. The Father is not the Holy Spirit, and the Spirit is not the Father. The Son is not the Holy Spirit, and the Spirit is not the Son. Thus, the Father, the Son, and the Holy Spirit are different from one another, and they have been so from all eternity. God did not develop into a Trinity but has existed always as the triune God.[5]

Third, each of the three persons of the Godhead is equally and fully God. While each person of the Godhead is distinct, they are equal to one another.[6]

> We must say that the person of the Father possesses the *whole being* of God himself, the Son possesses the *whole being* of God himself, and the Holy Spirit possesses the *whole being* of God himself. . . . [They are individually] *all* of God's being.[7]

Each of the persons of God is of the same essence and attributes and is not inferior or superior to the others in essence or attributes. This means that the same attributes can be applied to the Godhead as a whole as well as to each individual person comprising the Godhead, such as the holiness of the Father (Rev. 15:4), the Son (Acts 3:14), and the Spirit (Acts 1:8). Each person in the Godhead is fully God. Thus, God's oneness and threeness are not contradictory or incongruous.[8]

Relationality of the Trinity

The relationship of the Father, Son, and Holy Spirit has been understood in several ways. The economic model of the Trinity focuses on functionality, how the three persons of the Godhead work together. According to the economic Trinity, the Father has the primary role in *creation*, the Son has the primary activity in *salvation*, and the Holy Spirit has the primary function in *sanctification*. Another approach, the ontological model, focuses on the different relationships they enjoy with one another. According to the ontological Trinity, an eternal characteristic of the Father is *paternity*, an eternal characteristic of the Son is *generation*, and an eternal characteristic of the Holy Spirit is *procession*. These characteristics are revealed in the eternal relationships between the three persons. A third model of the Trinity is the social or communitarian Trinity, which focuses on the Godhead as three persons in community, combining diversity and relationships in unity.

Biblically, the idea of the Godhead precludes certain explanations of their relationship. The Father, Son, and Holy Spirit are not as follows:[9]

- *Three parts of God's being equally divided into the Trinity:* This view denies the oneness of God and instead affirms tritheism.
- *External distinctions added onto God's being:* This makes the Trinity only appear to be three when in reality it is only one person.
- *Three distinct perspectives on God's being:* This would affirm the oneness of God yet make the threeness a human accommodation.

It may help to represent graphically the relationship among the persons of the Trinity. The Trinity can be described as a mystery and fundamentally a spiritual reality. The Godhead is not fully comprehendible to finite human thought. As such, any two-dimensional or physical representation is impossible, not to mention misleading due to the inherent limitations.[10] For example, below are three *erroneous* Trinitarian models that are commonly expressed by Christians.

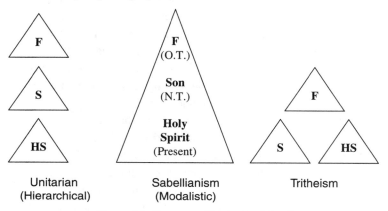

Figure 5.1: Erroneous Trinitarian Ideas[11]

Such models are in violation of both the scriptural portrait of God and the aforementioned affirmations found in Evangelical tradition. For example, the Unitarian model denies the existence of the Trinity, affirming instead that God is one in terms of both nature and person. In most cases the deity of the Son and the Holy Spirit are regarded as created beings. Sabellianism or modalism denies the distinction of the three persons of the Trinity. It affirms the oneness of God but denies that God is three persons simultaneously. In other words, it holds to one representation or manifestation of God at a time: God manifests himself as Father in the Old Testament period, as Son in the New Testament period, and as Holy Spirit in the church age. Tritheism denies the oneness of God and focuses on the threeness, while arguing for the presence of three gods with the same attributes.

We may need to ask if the Trinity can be represented graphically at all and, if so, how. As previously mentioned, every representation of the Triune God falls short of the spiritual, metaphysical reality that is the Trinity. However, endeavoring to affirm the equality, oneness, and threeness of the Trinity, the following graph is presented.[12]

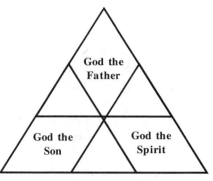

Figure 5.2: Trinitarian Diagram

The figure represents God as a triangle: each person of the Godhead is represented by a triangle, and all three overlap together into one triangle. Hence, the idea of a Triune God is indeed a mystery that cannot be readily represented or fully conceptualized by humanity; however, we can grasp the essential points of his existence from Scripture, as his self-revelation.

WHAT IS GOD LIKE? THE ATTRIBUTES OF THE TRINITARIAN GOD

Another reason for advancing a God-centered approach to education is what God is. The attributes of God are his characteristics or qualities. Generally and commonly speaking, divine attributes can be placed into two general categories. *Nonrelational* attributes, also known as *incommunicable* attributes, are those that emphasize the absolute being and distinctiveness of God. *Relational* attributes, also known as *communicable* attributes, are those that emphasize the relationship he has with creation, including humanity. This section discusses some of the most common of these attributes and also draws educational implications in regard to the dimensions of Christian learning.

Nonrelational Attributes of God

God is spirit. God is nonphysical, spiritual in nature.[13] As such he is not bound by the constraints and limitations of the physical universe in which we live. This is one of the principal distinctions between the God of Scripture and the pagan idols of the Old and New Testaments (Ps 96:4–6; Ezek 20:32; Acts 17:22–28). His spiritual nature, however, is not meant to imply that God is not personal, that he is an impersonal spirit or non-being; rather, he is a personal spirit.

God is independent. God is not contingent on anything or anyone else for his existence;[14] thus, he is independent. The existence of everything else—the universe, the earth, human beings—is dependent on God, but God's being is such that he exists in and of himself.

God is immutable. His essence, character, and will are unchanging; they are constant.[15] As already noted, God eternally exists as triune in nature; he has been, is, and always will be Father, Son, and Holy Spirit. Moreover, the attributes of God have never changed and will never change. And God's will concerning his creation—his plans and purposes for rescuing it—has never and will never fail. While Scripture depicts God as experiencing different emotions and responding to the needs of his creation in a variety of ways, this does not mean that his essence, character, or will are subject to change.

God is eternal. God is temporally without beginning or end and timeless in the sense that the passage of time does not affect him, though he is able to interact with humans in time. He is infinite with respect to time.

God is omnipresent. God is also infinite with respect to space.[16] He is present, in his totality, everywhere simultaneously. He is not restricted by the bounds of his creation. Yet God is present differently in different situations at different times. He is ever-present everywhere.

God is omniscient. God's knowledge is infinite as well. God knows everything without qualification.[17] He does not need to remember things by reaching deep into his memory, and God never comes to learn something new by studying or figuring things out. He just knows everything—past, present, and future—all at once because he is "perfect in knowledge" (Job 37:16) and "his understanding has no limit" (Ps 147:5).

God is omnipotent.[18] God can do whatever he chooses to do. He has unlimited power, as demonstrated in his creation of the universe out of nothing, his decisive liberation of his people from Egypt by means of plagues and miraculous interventions, the incarnation of the Son of God, the resurrection of Christ from the dead, and the transformation of sinful human beings through salvation in Christ. The title for God in the Old Testament that emphasizes his power is *El Shaddai,*[19] which is literally translated "God Almighty." As the sovereign Lord, God reigns over all and is the supreme being. No other authority or power or coalition of them can rival God's.

Relational Attributes of God

God is truthful and faithful. Ultimately, God is the author of all truth, whether it be revealed through his creation (Rom 1:20) or Scripture (John 17:17). Whenever God speaks, he always communicates the truth.[20] This attribute of God indicates that Scripture—the Word of God—is completely true in everything it affirms. Moreover, God is faithful, meaning that he always keeps his promises.[21] He never commits himself to something and then reneges on his word.

God is holy. God's holiness means he is distinct from his creation, exalted above everything else that exists. Furthermore, it points to the sacredness of his presence.[22] He is completely separate from that which is sinful. Yet God appears in glorious holiness and power in the midst of desperately evil situations to rescue human beings from the clutches of sin and temptation, and he enables his people to live holy lives in the midst of this present evil age.

God is righteous. God is a God of perfect standards, righteous judgments, and just acts.[23] He sets the standards according to which his people are to live, demanding perfect conformity to his holy character. His judgments are dispensed indiscriminately; he has no regard to whether those whom he judges are wealthy or poor, strong or weak, wise or gullible. He rewards those who know him but punishes those who disobey him. All his ways are righteous and he acts justly toward everyone.

God is love. God's love means he always gives of himself. Before anything else existed, the Father, Son, and Holy Spirit expressed an eternal, dynamic, and intimate love as persons of the Godhead. Ever since the universe came into existence, God has demonstrated his love in goodness toward his creation, sustaining it by providing everything it needs to flourish (Acts 14:15–18). His love is especially directed toward the people created in his image. Since his image bearers are fallen into sin, God expresses his love in grace, mercy, and compassion to rescue, forgive, and transform them.[24]

WHAT DOES GOD DO? THE ESSENTIAL WORKS OF GOD

We have affirmed the trinitarian nature of God and presented his attributes as revealed in Scripture. But what does God do? What functions does he have with his creation and humanity? Scripture reveals that God plays four essential roles: Creator, Ruler, Redeemer, and End (see Figure 5.3). His works of creating, governing, saving, and guiding toward a goal reflect his nature and exhibit his attributes since it is in these ways that he engages with his creation and humanity as his image bearers.

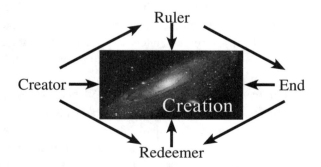

Figure 5.3: The Works of God

God the Creator

Scripture affirms that God chose to create not out of weakness or need but simply by sovereign choice (Ps 115:3; Eph 1:11; Rev 4:11). His creation is both physical and nonphysical, "visible and invisible" (Col 1:16). The tangible universe we can see—together with the realm of angels, demons, and other intangible realities— were both created by him. Creation was accomplished by divine fiat; it was not the mere arrangement of preexisting matter into an orderly universe but a creation *ex nihilo*, "out of nothing." The biblical creation account stands in contradiction to prevailing notions of both monism (that only the spiritual *or* the physical is reality) and metaphysical dualism (that the spiritual and the physical are *equally eternal* realities). By contrast Scripture affirms the reality of *both* the spiritual and the physical as well as their temporal nature and dependency on an eternal Creator.

How does God relate to his creation? God is both immanent and transcendent. *Immanence* means he is near, involved in and with his creation; *transcendence* means he is far removed, qualitatively distinct and separate from his creation. He is present in *and* distinct from his creation. Classical liberalism at the beginning of the twentieth century erred by depicting God as totally immanent, hence removing the necessity for revelation and the possibility of the miraculous.[25] In the mid-twentieth century neoorthodoxy reversed this theological polarity declaring God to be totally transcendent. While this necessitated revelation and allowed for the miraculous, it also meant that God's transcendence limited the intelligibility of his revelation and the authenticity of his miracles.[26] Evangelicals have always rejected these theological poles by affirming that God is *both* immanent and transcendent; hence, revelation is necessary and intelligible, the miraculous is possible, and faith is reasonable.

God the Ruler

We all seek assurance. We need to know that chaos does not reign, promises are binding, and there is order in the universe.

We want to have certainty but seek it in various places. On what is our certainty to be grounded? On what basis can intellectual certainty be reached? For Christians certainty rests on the affirmation of God as the absolute sovereign. The essence of sovereignty is God's absolute lordship or reign. This is not merely the notion of God being King,[27] "for the Lord your God is the God of gods and the Lord of lords, the great, the mighty, and the awesome God" (Deut 10:17; see Dan 2:47). While human leaders may experience a relative sovereignty, God alone possesses divine sovereignty that is *absolute.*

God expresses his sovereignty through a variety of means: decision (such as the selection and call of individuals in accordance with his purpose, Gen. 12:1ff; Rom 13:1ff), causation (Isa 45:7), command (Ps 147:15; Isa 33:22; Acts 5:29; Jas 4:12), permission (Acts 14:16; Rom 1:24,26,28), prevention (Rom 1:13), and judgment (Gen 18:25; Job 33:13; Ps 96:10; Jer 50:44; Heb 12:23; 1 Pet 4:5).[28]

Does God have anything to do with the course of humanity? Is history in effect his-story? In exercising his sovereignty, what is God's mode of operation? Just how involved is God with his creation? Figure 5.4 illustrates the three possible responses to God's involvement along the theological spectrum:

Figure 5.4: Three Views of Divine Involvement

Evangelicals find it impossible to affirm the first view, which produces a worldview similar to deism or a practical atheism at best. Evangelicals do affirm the other two views of divine involvement; with Calvinists leaning more heavily to the third view (divine causation) and Arminians leaning more toward the second view (divine causation and permission).

God has a unique *modus operandi*. These modes of operation are uniquely God's, without human parallel. First, he can create, not simply make but create *ex nihilo*. Second, God can also exercise providence in all its forms to fulfill his will in natural and human history. His providence is evident in two ways: (1) the basic maintenance of the physical universe, that is, the laws of nature; and (2) the intentional intervention in natural processes and history, that is, the subtle manipulation of history and events to fulfill his will. An example of this is God's response to Habakkuk: "Look at the nations and watch —and be utterly amazed. . . . I am raising up the Babylonians" (Hab 1:5–6). Finally, God can also employ miraculous events that may be either disclosed signs and wonders or hidden from observation, spiritual events that are real but unseen.

God the Redeemer

The work of the Triune God is seen clearly in the redemption of humanity. The Father is the sender (John 20:21), the Son is sent as the Savior through sacrifice (John 6:53–58), and the Spirit continues as the sanctifier (2 Thess 2:13). At the same time redemption is a mutual activity.[29] As discussed later in chapter 9, salvation is concerned with more than just conversion; it involves the continual transformation of the lives of believers so that they become totally conformed to the image of Jesus Christ (Rom 8:29–30).

God the End

God is the end of all things, as discussed later in chapter 10. The completion of Christ's work is "when all things are subjected to him," and "then the Son himself will also be subjected to him who put all things in subjection under him, that God may be all in all" (1 Cor 15:28). Accordingly, God's sovereignty should ultimately be considered an eschatological reality wherein his reign will be unchallenged at the end of time. Then the current universe will pass away, and God's redemption of all creation will be completely fulfilled (Rom 8:18–25). What will then exist is a new creation as the glorious temple of God:

> Then I saw a new heaven and a new earth, for the first heaven and the first earth had passed away. . . . And I heard a loud voice from the throne saying, "Now the dwelling of God is with men, and he will live with them. They will be his people, and God himself will be with them and be their God" (Rev 21:1,3).

God is the end. He is our future! And this is our ultimate hope.

TRINITARIAN EDUCATIONAL IMPLICATIONS

Process theologian N. F. S. Ferré endeavored to engage the educational implications of the Trinity by identifying God the Father as Educator, Jesus as Exemplar, and the Holy Spirit as Pedagogue.[30] However, his engagement is rather superficial. Simply placing an educational nuance to each of the persons of the Trinity is a deficient treatment of the possible implications the Trinity poses for the Christian educator. Evangelical theology, however, lends itself to expressing the fullness of the Trinity and its educational implications.

Trinitarian Relationship

The persons of the Trinity are in an eternal relationship with one another, and God has created human beings to be in relationship with himself and one another. We are relational beings. Consequently, human learning requires a *dialogical* element: relationships between one another. Education in the church should enhance the formation of these relationships, not simply for fellowship but to foster a dialogical dimension in learning. More advanced methods of instruction, such as small groups, particularly emphasize this dialogical relationship in an educational setting. This brings to the educational table a level of theological reflection, clarity of thought for clear communication, and intellectual accountability that would be minimized otherwise. In due course this dialogical dimension leads to the formation of community.

Trinitarian Community

Our fundamental concept of community is likewise a reflection of the Trinity since not only do we bear his image individually but also corporately: "In the image of God he created him; male and female he created them" (Gen 1:27). Community implies more than relationship, for it also includes a sense of commonality and a unity in the midst of diversity. Consequently, Christian education is not limited to individual transformation but includes and nourishes community formation as well (see Rom 15:7–14). Such a community shares the unity/diversity paradigm exemplified in the Trinity. Accordingly, Christian educators should encourage and celebrate wide diversity—gender, age, racial, ethnic, socioeconomic—in their educational endeavors. This does not deny the appropriateness of certain segregated educational offerings—age-graded Sunday school, for example—but it does serve as a helpful reminder of the faith community's essential unity and can act as a corrective to the all too frequent penchant toward stratification in the church. Intentional cross-generational mentoring relationships can help overcome church segregation while harvesting the wisdom and experience of senior citizens and investing in teenagers who, in turn, bring an energy and vitality to those who may feel that time for fruitful and fulfilling ministry has passed them by.

Christian education also bears a significant responsibility for the cultivation of God-honoring and God-reflecting cross-gendered relationships. The social Trinity focuses on the reflection of the eternal, dynamic, intimate loving relationships between Father, Son, and Holy Spirit in the temporal, dynamic, intimate loving relationships between men and women made in the divine image (Gen 1:27). The most intensive reflection of this can be found in the marriage relationship between a husband and a wife (Gen 2 focuses on this), but it is not and cannot be limited to this type of relationship only.³¹ Men and women generally, when relating to one another in caring, sacrificing, and loving ways, reflect the self-giving love that has always characterized the Triune God. This should particularly be the case in the church of Jesus Christ, whose members are being renewed in the divine image and have the resources and transformational power to live these cross-gendered relationships in God-glorifying ways.

The church has failed miserably in this matter. Though called to love one another, brothers and sisters in Christ transgress the appropriate boundaries and defraud one another (1 Thess 3:3–8). This should not be so. The initial safe but thoughtless response is often to cut off all cross-gendered relationships, other than marital ones. But the chilling effect this produces prevents Christ followers from obeying the basic commandment to love one another (see Matt 22:39; John 13:34–35; 1 John 3:11; 4:7,11–12,21) and to treat one another as family members (1 Tim 5:1–2 says Christian men are to treat younger women as "sisters, in all purity"). Such imperatives must not be minimized or ignored. Indeed, they demand a certain level of commitment, interaction, and closeness—with full recognition of the inherent dangers in such dynamic, loving relationships. The church does not have the option of setting aside such clear commands to love because of the risks that such love involves. Prudent safeguards are readily available and include Spirit-empowered commitment to sexual purity (physical as well as mental and emotional), deeply honest accountability with others, avoidance of extended contact in isolated meetings, inclusion of one's spouse in such relationships, and so forth. What would it be like if the church became known as the one place in all society where love is pure and relationships between men and women are above reproach and where sexual immorality is so rare that it truly is scandalous? The implication of the doctrine of God—specifically, the social Trinity—gives Christian education the responsibility to make such a vision the reality.

Educational Implications of God's Attributes

For the Christian educator, these following learning principles of education are ultimately rooted in what God is like. The attributes of God provide impetus for educational principles that facilitate Christlikeness in the lives of Christians.

Lifelong Learning. While God is knowable, he is also unknowable due to his infinite nature and our innate finitude. Christians could spend a lifetime studying God and never exhaustively or fully comprehend him. Because of the nature of God, Christians must be lifelong learners, and Christian education must commit itself to providing educational opportunities for believers their entire lives. Christian education must provide graded options for learners of all ages, including adults. No single Christian education program can provide the variety or level of instruction required to facilitate lifelong learning in the church. Sunday school, small groups, Bible study programs, and the church library must be used in concert with one another to provide Christians at every age and level of spiritual maturity with appropriate learning opportunities.

Truth-based Learning. Because of who God is, Christians approach life from a unified view of truth. As was discussed in chapter 4 on God's revelation, God's special revelation of truth is the content of Scripture. Because God is omniscient, truthful, and faithful, Scripture is trustworthy, and we place faith in his Word. However, if God were *not* as described, then his revelation would be questionable, serving as divine opinion or temporarily true, readily dismissed for the voice of another rather than authoritative instruction from the Supreme Being. Equipped with the truthful Word of God, Christian education possesses a firm foundation for truth-based learning.

Transformational Learning. "Be imitators of God, as beloved children" (Eph. 5:1). God's attributes call us to imitation through transformation. Learning that is lifelong and truth based is meant to transform us to become more like God. Learning is meant to change perspectives, values, behaviors—life. While our righteousness could never be equal to his,[32] God nonetheless calls us from a sinful life to a righteous life in him.[33] Christian education planning, curriculum, and execution must always bear in mind that its ultimate goal is life transformation so that its recipients become imitators of God.

Social Justice Learning. God's transformation of us ultimately leads to the transformation of our relationships and society at large. When the gospel of God is propagated through personal evangelism or mission endeavors, transformation of the individual results in a transformation of culture. This requires Christian education, both in terms of its teaching and its learning objectives, to focus beyond individual self-interest so as to foster sensitivity toward culture and others.

Hence, a God-centered education becomes a necessity for the Christian educator in light of the nature and attributes of God. In light of the trinitarian nature of God as portrayed in Scripture, the necessity of a God-centered education becomes obvious to Christian educators.

Educational Implications of God's Works

God the Creator: Education for Identity. If we do not know from where we came, we do not know who we are. We find our identity in our origins. Family heritage, such as last names; familial titles, such as father, brother, grandmother; even family resemblances—all these give us an immediate context for identity. Ultimately, we find our identity in our origins, from where we all came. A *Time* magazine cover story, "How We Became Human," traces the evolutionary trail of the human species to our common ancestry with chimpanzees and apes, complete with a graphic of our "all in the family" tree.[34] In contrast to this scenario, Scripture teaches that our ultimate origins are in a personal Creator God, in whose image we were created (Gen 1:26; John 1:1–3).

The relationship between God and his creation is the macroscopic framework for Christian theology. The implication of creation for humanity is that humans are creatures with meaning, purposefully designed as part of God's creation. Christian education endeavors to engage individuals as we "put on the new self, which is being renewed in knowledge in the image of its Creator" (Col 3:10). Because God is our Creator, we find our identity and meaning in him. Christian education is a ministry that aids individuals in finding their lives in a God who is still involved with his creation.

So what does divine creatorship imply for Christian education? It means that we are creatures of a transcendent and immanent Creator, and so Christian education must address our identity as created beings. Christians approach life with a sense of dependence on, submission to, and thanksgiving for God regarding their existence and provision, as opposed to advocating self-sufficiency, autonomy, and self-adulation (see chapter 8). Christian education is not a means of self-help but the exact opposite. It teaches that we find ourselves in finding our Creator and in placing our lives in his providential care.

God the Ruler: Education for Certainty. A fundamental question for Christian education is by what authority we teach. In contemporary Christian education, appeals are made to a variety of authority sources: church traditions, individual teachers, religious experiences, existential encounters, and Scripture.[35] Evangelicals would not reject any of these but would place a primacy on Scripture as God's special revelation to the church. Without overstating the obvious, the ultimate power and authority in the church is God. Any authority or power that may be present in the church is given by him and extends from him. This places two unique requirements on Christian teachers and educational leaders, which are humility and servitude when exercising authority. Christian teachers approach their task with a servant's attitude, so we are called to a higher standard, ultimately owing our allegiance to God. "And whatever you do, whether in word or deed, do it all in the name of the Lord Jesus, giving thanks to God the Father through him" (Col 3:17).[36] Without God as our Sovereign, Christian educators would lack the certainty and assurance of their teaching and ministry.

God the Redeemer: Education for Transformation. Education must have transformation as its redemptive and salvific element if it is to be Christian. The evangelistic work of the church cannot be separated from the educational ministry of the church since both conversion and nurture through instruction are essential for the transformation of individuals into Christ-like disciples. To make too far a distinction or division between evangelism and education is to create a cavern between them through which individuals could be saved but would never grow beyond the point of spiritual infancy. God as our Redeemer reminds Christian educators that evangelism is not a separate task from education, both must coalesce to fulfill the mission of the church.

God the End: Education for Hope. Education that is Christian cannot simply preserve the past, such as tradition for tradition sake; nor can it merely seek contemporary application, such as succumbing to the call to practical relevance. It must prepare Christians for the future, utilizing the past and present as the trajectories of our hope with its possibilities and opportunities. Hope is by nature future focused: "Now faith is being sure of what we hope for and certain of what we do not see" (Heb 11:1). Scripture teaches that our hope as Christians is that God is not only at the end of our life but at the end of this present universe itself. Christian education is education for eternity, as we assist believers to "set [their] mind on things above, not on earthly things" (Col 3:2).

CONCLUSION

Who is the God we worship? As I noted at the beginning of this chapter, Gangel and Sullivan maintain that the quintessential question upon which evangelical education is based is, Whom do we worship?[37] This chapter has raised and answered that question: God is the Triune Creator, Ruler, Redeemer, and End who is spiritual, self-existing, unchanging, eternal, present everywhere, all-knowing, truthful, faithful, all-powerful, holy, righteous, and loving. In light of this, Christian education must have a God-centered approach to teaching and learning in the church. It focuses on who God is, what he is like, what God does, and how he relates to us. A God-centered education is one that endeavors to glorify him in every aspect of ministry. For Christian educators the rationale and motivation for our educational ministry is ultimately rooted in the God whom we serve and is directly influenced by how we understand him. It distinguishes education in the church from secular education. God is at the center of our unified view of reality, values, and truth—our worldview. As such, Christian education promotes faithfulness to him, individually and corporately as the church. This includes Christian educators themselves, as we too have a personal relationship with the Triune God in the community of the church.

REFLECTION QUESTIONS

1. How is God reflected in your educational ministry? Where does he have obvious voice in your approach to education in the church?
2. If someone were to read any artifacts about your education ministry—such as fliers, handbooks, or training manuals—where would God be referenced? Is he superficial or central in your education ministry?
3. How does your relationship with the Triune God shape what you do as a participant in Christian education?

---

1 K. O. Gangel and C. Sullivan, "Evangelical Theology and Religious Education," in *Theologies of Religious Education*, ed. R. C. Miller (Birmingham, AL: Religious Education Press, 1995), 59.
2 See Matt 28:19; Rom 15:30; 1 Cor 6:11,13–14,19; 12:4–6; 2 Cor 1:20–21; 13:14; Eph 4:14–17; 5:18–20; 1 Pet 1:2–3,11; Rev 1:4–5.
3 M. J. Erickson, *God in Three Persons: A Contemporary Interpretation of the Trinity* (Grand Rapids: Baker, 1995), 221.
4 Gen 1:1–2; Exod 31:4; Judg 15:14; Pss 2:7; 68:18; Isa 6:1–3; 9:6; 11:2; Matt 3:16–17; Acts 5:3–4; 2 Cor 3:17; 1 Pet 1:2; John 1:17; 1 Cor 8:6; Phil 2:11.

5   Deut 3:13–15; 6:4; 20:2–3; 1 Tim 1:17; 2:5–6; 1 Cor 8:4–6; Jas 2:19.

6   Ps 90:2; John 1:2; Heb 9:14; Rev 1:8,17.

7   W. Grudem, *Systematic Theology: An Introduction to Biblical Doctrine* (Grand Rapids: Zondervan, 1994), 252.

8   Matt 28:19; Rom 15:30; 1 Cor 6:11,13–14,19; 12:4–6; 2 Cor 1:20,21; 13:14; Eph 4:14–17; 5:18–20; 1 Pet 1:2–3, 11; Rev 1:4–5.

9   See Grudem, *Systematic Theology,* 252–55.

10   See ibid., 240–41, 252–55.

11   Adapted from H. W. House, *Charts of Christian Theology and Doctrine* (Grand Rapids: Zondervan, 1992), 50.

12   J. Castelein, Course diagram, TH600: Turning Points in Systematic Theology (Lincoln, IL: Lincoln Christian Seminary, 2007).

13   John 1:18; 1 Tim 1:17; 6:15–16.

14   Gen 1:1; 21:33; Ps 90:2; John 1:1; 5:26; 8:58; Rom 11:34–35; Rev 4:11.

15   Exod 3:14; Ps 102:26–28; Mal 3:6; Jas 1:17.

16   1 Kgs 8:27; Job 11:7–10; Pss 90:1–5; 139:7–12; 145:3; Jer 23:23–24; Acts 17:24.

17   1 Sam 16:7; Pss 139:1–4; 147:4–5; Isa 40:21,26–28; Matt 10:29–30; 11:21; Heb 4:13.

18   Job 36:22; Ps 62:11; Matt 19:26; 28:18; Rev 19:6.

19   Gen 17:1; 35:11; 49:25; Exod 6:3; Num 24:4; Job 40:1; Ps 91:1; Ezek 10:5.

20   Titus 1:2; Heb 6:18.

21   Num 23:19; Heb 10:23.

22   Lev 11:44–45; 1 Sam 2:2; Isa 6:1–7; Hab 1:13; Acts 3:14; 1 Pet 1:16; Rev 4:6–11.

23   Ps 119:137; Acts 10:34–35; Rom 2:11.

24   Neh 9:17; Pss 86:15; 103:8; 111:4; 116:5; 145:8; Isa 54:10; Joel 2:13; Luke 15:20; Eph 3:4–5; Titus 3:5; Jas 2:13; 1 Pet 1:3; 1 John 4:7–8.

25   See J. R. Estep Jr., "Liberal Theology," in *Evangelical Dictionary of Christian Education,* ed. M. Anthony (Grand Rapids: Baker, 2001), 429–30.

26   See Estep, "Neo-Orthodoxy," in *Evangelical Dictionary,* 503–4.

27   1 Chr 16:31; Pss 22:28; 93:1–2; 96:10; 97:1; 99:1; 103:19; Isa 52:7.

28   One major divide in Evangelicalism is how God exercises his sovereignty, especially in regard to human will, which involves the debate between Calvinism and Arminianism (discussed in chapter 9).

29   Eph 2:13–22; John 14:13–15; 17:5,26.

30   N. F. S. Ferré, *A Theology for Christian Education* (Philadelphia: Westminster, 1967), 99–150.

31   This must be the case because (1) the account of humanity's creation in the image of God as male and female precedes the account of the first husband and wife; and (2) men and women who do not marry (in the case of Christians, for the reason that they have the gift of celibacy for complete dedication to the cause of Jesus Christ; 1 Cor. 7:25–35) are

still created to reflect the eternal, dynamic, intimate loving relationships between the Father, Son, and Holy Spirit—the God who created them in his image—as single persons.

32   Ps 143:2; Isa 64:6; Zech 3:1–7.

33   Rom 6:13; Gal 2:21; Eph 6:14; 2 Tim 3:16.

34   M. D. Lemonick and A. Dorfman, "What Makes Us Different?" *Time* (October 9, 2006), 44–53.

35   See R. B. Zuck, "The Problem of Authority in Christian Education," *Bibliotheca Sacra* 119.473 (1962): 54–63.

36   J. R. Estep Jr., "A Theology of Administration," in *Management Essentials for Christian Ministries*, ed. M. J. Anthony and J. R. Estep Jr. (Nashville, TN: B&H, 2005), 39–41.

37   Gangel and Sullivan, "Evangelical Theology and Religious Education," 59.

CHAPTER 6

Christology and
Christian Education
Michael J. Anthony

CHRISTOLOGY: THE PERSON AND
WORK OF JESUS CHRIST

The category of theology known as Christology concerns itself with the many facets of the person and work of the Son of God. It encompasses a time prior to his incarnation as Jesus of Nazareth, looking back into eternity past to ascertain his preexistent state. It also examines the nature of his unique birth, incarnate existence, earthly ministry among his people, and substitutionary death on the cross. Finally, Christology concerns itself with his ongoing ministry in our lives after his resurrection and ascension.

His preexistent state, earthly life, and postresurrection continuation have been the subjects of church councils throughout the history of the Church. Controversy regarding the person and work of the Son of God started almost from the first mention of the coming of the Messiah, and it has not stopped since. Some theologians draw a distinction between Christology, the *person* of Christ, and soteriology, the *work* of Christ, but this chapter draws no such boundary.

This chapter will provide a firm foundation for the person and work of Christ in addition to discussing some unique educational implications of Christology for Christian educators in the twenty-first century.

THEOLOGICAL FOUNDATIONS

Being able to articulate one's understanding of the deity, humanity, earthly ministry, and work of Christ is essential to one's spiritual maturity. Furthermore, having a firm grasp of Christology when a member of a contemporary cult knocks at one's door is a sure defense against aberrant theology.

The Deity of Christ

Understanding the deity of Christ is of the utmost importance for believers today.

> The deity of Christ sits at the pinnacle of controversy and belief concerning the Christian faith and has real value to the believer concerning knowledge of God, new life, personal relationship with God, and the ability to worship Christ for who he is.[1]

This doctrine has been hotly debated since the formation of the early church. Factions held to a belief that the Son of God was not eternal, and therefore he could not be God. Ebionism believed that "the Christ"—the power and presence of God—came upon the man Jesus at his baptism and remained with him until shortly before his crucifixion, at which time it departed. Thus, the man Jesus experienced the power of God but was not himself the God-man. Arianism, a belief that the Son of God was a created being, albeit a unique one, had implications for the deity of Christ. Arianism reasoned that since God cannot share his essence with anyone or anything else, the Son of God must be a created being. Furthermore, if Christ was not eternally present before creation, then he cannot be God but is simply a unique aspect of creation itself. This latter doctrinal controversy is still prevalent today, and the denial of the deity of Jesus Christ serves as a foundational distinctive of several sects such as Jehovah's Witnesses and the Mormons.

The Preexistence of Christ

Strictly speaking, discussing the deity of Christ involves the period of time when he lived on earth. Many theologians also include the eternal aspect of his life prior to his incarnation. That is, since the Son of God was involved in the acts of creation, he obviously existed prior to his birth in Bethlehem. This topic is important because if the Son of God came into existence at some point in time, then he did not exist in eternity past and could not have been involved in creation as Scripture claims (John 1:3; 3:31; 6:62; Col 1:16; Heb 1:2). Furthermore, if he did not exist prior to creation, then the Son was not God since eternality is a divine attribute. In addition, without the preexistence of Christ, there can be no Trinity.[2] Therefore, the doctrinal distinctive of the Son's preexistence is no trivial matter.

Jesus claimed to be preexistent to his incarnation. In John 8:52–59, Jesus stated that before something in the past occurred ("before Abraham was"), he already existed ("I am"). The religious leaders who heard this emphatic and solemn affirmation immediately understood that Jesus was claiming to be the eternally existing God, for the title "I am" was the exclusive name of God. The only possible response from the religious leaders to such a bold claim was capital punishment, so "they took up stones to kill him."[3]

As the preexistent Son of God, he eternally existed with the Father and the Holy Spirit (John 1:2), enjoying their mutual love (John 5:20; 17:24,26), relishing in their unity (John 17:11,21–22), and sharing in their divine glory (John 17:5,24). When the universe came into existence, the Son was engaged as the agent of creation (John 1:3,10; Col 1:15–16).

The Incarnation of Christ

Nearly two thousand years ago, the preexistent Son of God became incarnate as the God-man, Jesus Christ. Though the word *incarnation* itself does not appear in Scripture, its components ("in" and "flesh") certainly do. The apostle John wrote that the Word became flesh (John 1:14) and later referenced the Son's coming in the flesh (1 John 4:2; 2 John 7). The human flesh that the Son of God took on was human nature in its entirety— not only a body but a human mind, emotions, will, motivations, and needs as well. At that point he became human.[4]

The incarnation came about in a miraculous way: the virgin birth. The prophet Isaiah foretold this (Isa 7:14) and both Matthew (1:18–25) and Luke (1:26–38) attest to it. Mary was betrothed to Joseph, but the two did not have sexual intercourse before she became pregnant with the incarnate Son of God through the power of the Holy Spirit. Through this miracle Mary conceived and gave birth to the God-man, Jesus Christ.

The incarnation means that Jesus was a real and fully human being, as can be documented from the record of the four Gospels. In all of the following examples, Jesus can be seen to be fully human.

- He became hungry and needed to eat food to nourish his body. After fasting forty days and nights in the wilderness, Jesus became hungry (Matt 4:2).
- He became weary and thirsty. A weary Jesus gave instructions to the woman of Samaria to give him some water from the well (John 4:6–7).
- Jesus became sleepy and needed to catch up on his rest. On one occasion Jesus was so exhausted that he slept peacefully during a violent windstorm that threatened to sink the boat in which he and his disciples were traveling (Matt 8:23–27).
- Jesus periodically retreated from his exhausting ministry to the crowds so he could be alone. After he miraculously fed the five thousand, Jesus dispersed the crowds and "went up on the mountain by himself to pray; and when it was evening, He was there alone" (Matt 14:22–23 NAS).

- Besides engaging in personal prayer to the Father (Luke 6:12), Jesus also attended worship at his local synagogue (Luke 4:16).
- During his ministry, Jesus developed and enjoyed close friendships with his disciples—Peter, James, John (Matt 17:1–9; Mark 14:32–42) and the rest of the twelve (Matt 10:2–4)—and others, such as the women who supported his ministry (Luke 8:1–2), and Lazarus, Mary, and Martha (John 11:5).
- Beyond this deep love that bound him to his friends, Jesus was often moved with compassion for people he did not even know—the leper he cleansed (Mark 1:40–42), the blind men he healed (Matt 20:29–34), the dead he raised to life (Luke 7:11–15), and tax collectors and sinners he forgave (Matt 11:19).[5]

The incarnation also means that Jesus Christ was fully divine, possessing all of the attributes of God. These would include eternality (John 8:58; 17:5), omnipresence (John 1:48), omniscience (Matt 16:21; Luke 6:8; 11:17; John 4:29), and omnipotence (Mark 5:11–15; John 11:38–44). Moreover, in his life he engaged in activities that could only be attributed to God. He forgave sins (Mark 2:1–12), gave spiritual life (John 5:21), raised the dead (John 11:43),[6] and was given the divine responsibility to exercise judgment (John 5:22,27).

Both the humanity and deity of Christ are essential to soteriology, the doctrine of salvation. The problem of human sin is not something that can be solved by human beings themselves. God is infinitely superior to his human creatures, and if human beings are going to be reunited to their Creator, they will have to depend on God to take the initiative. The moral gap that was caused by man's sinful nature, the guilt that accrues from disobedience and faithlessness, and the severed relationship with God that occurred in the garden leave human beings at a loss for resolution. Reconciliation must take place on God's terms and in his timing. Any reconstitution of the fellowship that was once enjoyed must be at the invitation and initiation of God himself. The gap is too vast for any means other than God himself to overcome.[7]

This chasm was bridged by Christ. In eternity past the Godhead decided that the Son would reconcile humanity to its Creator, coming as "a lamb without blemish or spot" to offer his "precious blood" on the cross (1 Pet 1:19). God would have to take the initiative by becoming man and serve as the divine rescuer of mankind. Deity would have to be united with humanity and joined as one (Heb 2:14–18). The incarnation of the Son of God made that possible.

> If, however, Jesus were not really one of us, humanity has not been united with deity and we cannot be saved. For the validity of the work accomplished in Christ's death, or at least its application to us as human beings, depends upon the reality of his humanity, just as its efficacy depends upon the genuineness of his deity.[8]

The incarnation of the Son was God's remedy for a fallen world. The penalty of sin is death (Rom. 3:23), and because God cannot die (because he is eternal) and man could not satisfy God's requirement (because of his sin), it was necessary for God to become man on our behalf. Furthermore, as God who became a real and fully human being, Christ can serve as a model and guide for our own living.

The Work of Christ

Regarding the work that Christ came to fulfill, one need look no farther than Jesus' own words. He said he came to seek and to save those who were lost (Luke 19:10). He came to proclaim the good news to the poor, to give liberty to those who were held captive, to give sight to the blind, and to proclaim the acceptable year of the Lord (Luke 4:18–19; see Isa 61:1). He also came not to be served but to serve by giving his life as a ransom for many (Matt 20:28). Much of what he accomplished during his earthly visit among us can be explained in terms of one of these categories.

Christ came to restore mankind to a relationship with the eternal God. This relationship was broken in the garden by man and could only be restored at God's initiation. Living outside this fellowship with God, human beings had developed a distorted concept of what God was like. Being God himself, Jesus was able to correct that misconception, both testifying of and displaying his Father's grace and mercy for those who came to him with a humble heart (John 14:8–9; Heb 1:3).

Throughout the earthly ministry of Christ, he had a divine appointment with the cross; until that day transpired, however, he was busy doing the work of his heavenly Father (Luke 2:49). There were people who needed healing, religious leaders who needed to be corrected, a nation in desperate need of hope, and disciples who needed training for their upcoming ministry. Jesus' calendar was filled with divine appointments and supernatural engagements.

The ultimate step toward reconciling the world to his heavenly Father was Christ's death on the cross. Having taken on real and full human nature (Phil 2:6–7), Jesus was able to experience the pain and suffering of a sacrificial death. Moreover, because he lived as a human being in the midst of heartache and suffering, Christ was well fitted to make the ultimate sacrifice (Heb 5:7–9). He was well acquainted with fatigue, hunger, thirst, and weariness. He understood the force of betrayal as only one who has been betrayed can know. He experienced the disappointment, discouragement, and isolation associated with being human.[9] As a real and fully human being, Jesus Christ was fully prepared to suffer on the cross and satisfy his Father's criteria for reconciling mankind to himself.

But the death of Christ was not the end of his existence. In fulfillment of Scripture, Jesus rose from the grave on the third day through the miraculous power of God. This event confirmed that the Father was satisfied with the death of his Son for the salvation of humanity (Rom 4:25). Moreover, to demonstrate the reality of his resurrection, Christ appeared to his disciples and many others for a period of forty days (1 Cor 15:3–9; Acts 1:1–3). After this he ascended into heaven, leaving this world as the embodied God-man until he returns in the same physical manner (Acts 1:9–11).

Today Christ sits at the right hand of his Father (Mark 14:62; Rom 8:34; Heb 1:3,13) to act as our intercessor (Rom 8:34; Heb 7:25), as our advocate (1 John 2:1), and as head of his body, the Church (Eph 1:22–23). He is ever watchful over our activities and seeks to empower us through the Holy Spirit and guide us where he so wills. He has promised to be with us (Matt 28:20) and to come again in glory for the establishment of his kingdom (Acts 3:20–21).

The study of Christology provides us with a rich understanding of God's love and grace and enables us to see how God throughout human history has planned for the reconciliation of mankind to himself. Jesus' birth, earthly ministry, atoning death, and resurrection were the fulfillment of the Father's plan (Isa 53; Luke 24:44–47; 1 Pet 1:18–19). That plan does not end at the cross, for today Christ brings us hope that our future is secure and provides us with guidance for our lives today. So much can be drawn from his short years of earthly ministry, and examining some of those experiences in the following sections teaches a great deal about how we can continue his ministry through Christian education.

EDUCATIONAL IMPLICATIONS OF JESUS THE MASTER TEACHER

Throughout the Gospel accounts the title that is used most often (48 times) to describe Jesus is "teacher." Although the title was indicative of his ministry emphasis, sometimes it is hard for us to envision him in this role because our concept of teacher is vastly different from what was evident in his day. Our concept of a teacher is one who stands in front of a classroom in a rigid academic setting lecturing and demanding the mastery of facts. However, this is not the image we glean of Jesus as we read through the Gospel accounts. Jesus neither taught in a formal academic setting nor advocated one. When we encounter Jesus teaching, he may be walking along the side of a lake, sitting on the side of a mountain, or stopping under the shade of a tree long enough to tell a story or explain an Old Testament passage. Certainly, he did teach formally in synagogues and in the temple courtyard, but the vast majority of what we see and hear from him comes from informal instructional locations.[10] Jesus serves as a unique example to the Christian educator, as Warren Benson explains:

> The Savior was the quintessential teacher. Being God in human flesh He had no weakness as a pedagogue. He modeled the truth in an ultimate sense. Christ never lost touch with those He was teaching despite the loftiness of His content or the holiness of his character. He knew how to adapt to their level of understanding and use the familiar to explain the profound.[11]

Jesus was remarkable because of his character and his message. He communicated with a deep personal conviction yet a balanced compassion. He was forceful when necessary yet gentle with those who needed more time to grasp the concepts he was teaching. He was forthright with the religious leaders but patient with his own disciples. The character and methods of Jesus warrant detailed examination, for in both we find the secret to what made this individual the Master Teacher that he is known for nearly two thousand years later.

The Character of Jesus the Teacher

Jesus came to reveal the character and nature of his heavenly Father. Throughout the course of human history, man had corrupted the image of God and transformed it into one mired by his own distortions. Pagan idols propagated an image of God as

aloof, self-centered, sensual, and abusive. Thus, God was someone to be feared and appeased through offerings designed to
pacify and keep him at bay. People no longer worshipped God
out of a sense of awe and wonder but for fear and trepidation
instead. Being God himself, Jesus knew better and came, in part,
to set the record straight. He came to reveal his heavenly Father
as one filled with compassion, long-suffering, tenderhearted-
ness, and attentiveness to the petitions of the humble. Many of
his stories and parables focused on these themes. However, he
also expressed the reality of God's judgment, wrath, vengeance,
condemnation, righteous jealousy, and severity—all calling for
repentance.

Jesus initiated this corrective process of revelatory instruction and entered his teaching ministry with persuasive passion
and personal zeal. But it isn't just the content of his message
that is so captivating and engaging. Rather, the combination of
his lifestyle, inherent authority, and unique methodology cap-
tures his hearers' attention. The Jewish leaders were threatened
by his popular influence, while the Roman government was
confused by his persuasive power. But how could a man devoid
of academic pedigree, political savvy, or economic status wield
such influence? The answer is found in what makes him such a
unique figure in human history. Unlike others of his day Jesus
Christ possessed and taught with moral authority, led an uncom-
promising lifestyle consistent with his teaching, demonstrated
an authentic simplicity for all to see, and directed his teaching
at an unlikely audience.

Jesus taught with authority. One of the unique elements
of Jesus' instructions was the authority that accompanied his
teachings. Since Jesus had never attended one of the acclaimed
rabbinic schools in Palestine, it was understandable that those
who heard him teach responded with wonder and amazement.
Obviously, he did not receive his authority from an educational
degree. Those who knew he had grown up as a tradesman in
Nazareth wondered, "Is not this the carpenter, the son of Mary,

and brother of James and Joses and Judas and Simon? Are not his sisters here with us? And they took offense at him" (Mark 6:3). Others asked, "Where then did this man get all these things?" (Matt 13:56). Clearly they were shocked to hear such profound teachings coming from someone who never had formal theological training.

People would gather from miles around to hear Jesus' stories and profound insights. He provided clear application of biblical truth and gave people hope that God really did care about the details of their lives. Jesus communicated to his listeners that the Creator of the universe cared about them and invited them into a personal relationship with him. Jesus taught people that God was approachable and actually wanted to give them eternal life. This was shocking news to them, and it set Jesus' teachings apart from the instructions given by the religious leaders of the day.

The result was that "when Jesus had finished these words, the multitudes were amazed at his teaching; for he was teaching them as one having authority, and not as their scribes" (Matt 7:28–29 NASB). Jesus' authority was God-given, tied to the uniqueness of his teachings, and flowed from a character that could not be accused of injustice or self-centeredness. Jesus gave freely and sought the welfare of others above his own. A lifestyle like that gave his message authority and power.

Jesus' lifestyle was consistent with his teaching. Jesus teachings flowed out of who he was, not from his lesson plan for the day. In essence Jesus was the lesson plan. If he wanted his disciples to learn a lesson on humble servanthood, he simply took off his outer garment and washed his disciples' feet (John 13:1–17). When he wanted them to learn how to trust God for protection, he took them out on the lake in a storm and calmed the violent seas (Matt 8:23–27). Jesus taught his disciples to love their enemies (Matt 5:43–48), and some of his last words from the cross were about forgiveness for his persecutors (Luke 23:34).

Jesus' personal integrity was not lost on his detractors. The Pharisees and Herodians said, "Teacher . . . we know you are a man of integrity and that you teach the way of God in accordance with the truth. You aren't swayed by men, because you pay no attention to who they are" (Matt 22:16). This was profound testimony of Jesus' consistent lifestyle when even his enemies confessed his personal integrity. Indeed, Jesus challenged the religious leaders to find fault in him: "Can any of you prove me guilty of sin?" (John 8:46). Pilate examined Jesus and reluctantly admitted he found no fault in him (Luke 23:4), and the centurion who observed his crucifixion declared, "Surely, this was a righteous man" (Luke 23:47). Jesus' lifestyle of integrity went a long way toward reinforcing his message.

Jesus lived a life of authentic simplicity. There was nothing ostentatious about Jesus' character as Master Teacher. He was authentic and unpretentious. He associated with the poor and downcast and was comfortable visiting with those the world had cast aside. Much to the shock and consternation of the religious leaders of his day, Jesus went to weddings, attended banquets, and enjoyed fellowship with sinners. For example, he invited himself to dinner at the home of Zacchaeus, a hated tax collector (Luke 19:1–10), and chose another tax collector, Matthew, to become one of his trusted disciples (Matt 9:9–12). He met in the open with a Samaritan woman who had anything but a spotless reputation in her community (John 4:1–45). Jesus was a frequent participant at parties attended by the despised people of his society, and he said of himself: "The Son of Man came eating and drinking, and they say, 'Look, a glutton [one who eats far too much] and a drunkard, a friend of tax collectors and sinners!'" (Matt 11:19). Jesus touched and cleansed revoltingly decrepit lepers (Matt 8:1–3) and talked to and liberated the maddeningly uncontrollable demon possessed (Matt 15:22–28). When most religious leaders would have been too busy to waste time on children, Jesus welcomed them into his presence and admonished his followers to become like children if they hoped to one day enter the kingdom of God (Matt 18:3; 19:14).

Jesus came to tell those who were lost how they could find their way home. Having been accused of associating with the destitute, Jesus responded, "It is not the healthy who need a doctor, but the sick. I have not come to call the righteous, but sinners" (Mark 2:17). This explains why Jesus, who lived a life of authentic simplicity, expressed disappointment, anger, and indignation at religious and political leaders who would not lift a finger to help people in need. Only one who was not a hypocrite, as they were, could expose such blatant and tragic hypocrisy without fear of being charged with duplicity.

Jesus was genuine, authentically simple, and unpretentious. He made no effort to pretend to be anything other than who he claimed to be. In his humility he was appealing; in his simplicity he was engaging; and in his honesty he won over multitudes to his message. He was a powerful force but not because of his might or demeanor. His authentic and simple lifestyle lived out in the open for all to see became a most powerful weapon.

Jesus directed his teachings at an unlikely audience. To this unlikely audience of tax collectors, prostitutes, poor, sick, and other marginalized people, Jesus directed his teachings. Specifically, "His teaching flowed out of the needs of the people he taught. It flowed out of problem situations they presented. It flowed out of the real crises of life."[12] One example of this is Jesus' encounter with the Samaritan woman at the well (John 4:1–45). At this time, contact between a man and a woman (v. 27), let alone a Jewish man and a Samaritan woman, was taboo, "for Jews have no dealings with Samaritans" (v. 9). As unlikely as this was, Jesus addressed her and her particular situation. Multiple marriages and a dysfunctional pattern of behavior reinforced the real focus of Jesus' teachings, as he led her to realize that her deepest need was not for physical water but for "water welling up to eternal life" (v. 14).

Jesus knew the hearts of the people he addressed (Matt 12:25; Mark 2:8; Luke 5:22) so he directed his teachings to their most pertinent needs. An example of this was Jesus' conversation with the rich young man who sought to know what he needed to do to have eternal life (Matt 19:16–22). After ascertaining from the man that he was blameless in the keeping of the command- ments, Jesus exposed what the man still lacked, saying to him, "If you would be perfect, go, sell what you possess and give to the poor, and you will have treasure in heaven; and come, follow me" (v. 21). Knowing that this young man was wealthy and attached to material goods, Jesus offered a challenge that cut directly to the man's greedy heart. Indeed, "when the young man heard this he went away sorrowful, for he had great posses- sions" (v. 22). Because Jesus had this unique ability to discern the hearts of those in his audience, he was able to direct his teaching with pinpoint accuracy to their greatest needs. And he did so with the most unlikely cast of characters.

The Variety of Jesus' Teaching Methods

Much can be said about the varied teaching methods employed by Jesus, who was a master craftsman in the art of teaching. A summary of his varied methods reveals this craftsmanship.

Jesus frequently asked questions. Jesus was extraordinary in his use of this dynamic teaching method of asking questions. His questions exposed his hearers' misconceptions, revealed his listeners' incorrect theological presuppositions, and forced his learners to divulge their motives. Sometimes Jesus asked ques- tions to elicit answers, but most of the time they were crafted to create cognitive disequilibrium—that is, to cause Jesus' hearers to question themselves and to ponder and think before offering a response. Indeed, when reviewing the evidence in the Gos- pels, we find that Jesus asked questions for many reasons, such as the following:

1. *To make one think*: "If one of you has a son or an ox that falls into a well on the Sabbath day, will you not immediately pull him out?" (Luke 14:5).
2. *To secure information for himself:* "What is your name?" (Luke 8:30).
3. *To express an emotion:* "You brood of vipers, how can you who are evil say anything good?" (Matt 12:34).
4. *To introduce a story:* "What is the kingdom of God like? What shall I compare it to?" (Luke 13:18).
5. *To follow up a story:* "Who then is the faithful and wise manager, who the master puts in charge of his servants to give them their food allowance at the proper time?" (Luke 12:42).
6. *To rebuke criticism:* "Have you never read what David did when he and his companions were hungry and in need?" (Mark 2:25).
7. *To awaken conscience:* "You blind fools! Which is greater: the gold, or the temple that makes the gold sacred?" (Matt 23:17).
8. *To elicit faith:* "But what about you? Who do you say I am?" (Mark 8:29).
9. *To clarify the situation:* "What did Moses command you?" (Mark 10:3).
10. *To create a dilemma:* "If then David calls him 'Lord,' how can he be his son?" Matt 22:45).[13]

Jesus' frequent use of the question method of instruction served these many purposes:

> Jesus asked clear, direct, purposeful questions that made his teaching stimulating, spirited, and soul-searching. His queries aroused interest, provoked thought, requested information, elicited response, clarified issues, applied truth, and silenced critics.[14]

Jesus taught using parables. In addition to questions, Jesus employed various methods of teaching. The most noted of these are his parables: "The parables of Jesus are unique and famous throughout the world. They are very short stories which convey truth in vivid pictures with which most of his listeners were familiar."[15] Parables teach important spiritual truths (with which people are unfamiliar) by means of analogy with something concrete (with which people are familiar). Many of Jesus' analogies used either metaphors (speaking of someone who communicates the gospel as a "sower") or similes ("the kingdom of God is like"). Certain elements of the parables, but not all of them, are symbolic, representing someone or something else.[16] Some of Jesus' most notable parables include the good Samaritan (Luke 10:30–37), the talents (Matt 25:14–30), the prodigal son (Luke 15:11–32), and the separation of the sheep and the goats (Matt 25:31–46).

On most occasions the disciples needed Jesus to explain his parables in order for them to understand his meaning. When they posed the question, "Why do You speak to the people in parables?" (Matt 13:10), Jesus offered two reasons for this teaching method. The first reason had to do with the favored position of the disciples in Jesus' kingdom mission: "To you it has been granted to know the mysteries of the kingdom of heaven, but to them [the crowds] it has not been granted" (Matt 13:11). This reason underscores why Jesus often explained his parables to his disciples: He wanted to ensure that they understood his meaning and grasped important truths about the kingdom he was building and which they would be leading. The second reason focused on God's sovereign choice that the crowds around Jesus would not be permitted to comprehend his teaching: "Therefore I speak to them in parables; because while seeing they do not see, and while hearing they do not hear, nor do they understand" (Matt 13:13). As difficult as this might be for us to grasp, the fact remains that God did not will for the crowds watching and listening to Jesus to "see" and "hear" (that is, "understand") him. So Jesus taught the crowds in parables, partially hiding the truth he was communicating. This was both by divine design—God would not grant understanding to the crowds following Jesus—and due to the dullness of those same followers—they had failed to carry out their human responsibility to pay attention to and learn from Jesus.[17]

Jesus took advantage of teachable moments. Jesus' teaching often took place as he walked along a dusty trail or sat in a boat crossing a lake, that is, in what would have surely been seen as routine moments. On one occasion, when Jesus and his disciples were eating at the home of a Pharisee, he omitted the ritual premeal washing, then used it as an opportunity to teach on the priority of inner cleansing (Luke 11:37–41). At another meal hosted by a Pharisee, Jesus noticed that the guests were pushing and jostling to secure a seat near the host or guest of honor and interrupted the moment to teach on the importance of humility (Luke 14:7–11). It seems that Jesus used what came along as fodder for his curriculum: "For Jesus, every event or encounter was an important learning situation in which God was speaking. Being alert to these opportunities would disclose an unusual and deeper meaning behind what might be ordinary occurrences of each day."[18] Whether he was watching people put their offerings in the temple treasury (Mark 12:41–44) or healing a blind beggar (John 9:1–3), Jesus used teachable moments to reveal truth and disclose divine instruction.

> Days were filled with teachable moments for his disciples. Jesus went to where the people were. He hung out with the commoners in their natural environments, spending time with them. He talked with them about their daily experiences. He was very accessible to people as a wandering charismatic teacher. Simply by being with people in the midst of their daily activities, in the streets, in their homes, sharing meals, around the docks, in the fields, and so forth, Jesus taught.[19]

Jesus' miracles provided a unique type of teachable moment. Generally speaking, he preferred not to draw attention to his miraculous powers and often commanded those who were the recipients of his miraculous healings not to tell anyone about it (e.g., Mark 1:40–45). He knew that the miracle itself could overshadow the importance of his message, and ultimately it was the message that he came to bring. But Jesus did perform miracles on occasion and used them as a springboard for his teaching. One example is the case of the paralyzed man who was lowered through the roof of a house by his friends (Matt 9:2–7). Jesus was most concerned that his learners would understand that he had the power to forgive sins. The fact was, however, that speaking the words to the man that his sins were forgiven was easy (and unverifiable), certainly far easier than actually healing the bedridden man. In order to prove he had the authority to forgive sins, Jesus performed the miracle, restoring the paralytic to full health. This object lesson—this teachable moment—drove home Jesus' teaching on the forgiveness of sins. Indeed, throughout his ministry, Jesus' miracles punctuated his message and made people stop and think about what he was teaching.

Jesus used Scripture as his curriculum. One of the more remarkable things about Jesus' teaching is how much of it comes from Scripture—what we now call the Old Testament—and his heavenly Father. He often began his teaching with the phrase, "You have heard that it was said to those of old" (Matt 5:27,31,38,43), or with the question, "Have you not read?" (Matt 12:3,5; 19:4; 22:31). This was Jesus' way of making sure that his learners knew the source of his material, which in turn emphasized the authority with which he addressed them. When he clarified the Old Testament and its application to current living, it was always in fulfillment of Scripture (Matt 5:17–19). Jesus appealed to such Old Testament stories as Jonah's three days in the belly of the great fish (Matt 12:40) and Moses' bronze serpent in the wilderness (John 3:14–15) to indicate and drive home a particular aspect of his saving work.

Beyond references to Scripture, Jesus was also generous in attributing his teachings to his heavenly Father (John 17:16–18; 8:28; 12:49–50; 14:24). Having been sent by the Father, Jesus' mission was to communicate the Father's message to those who would hear it. There was no doubting the source of Jesus' teaching or the focus of his instruction.

Jesus taught confrontationally. Because of his authority and focused mission, Jesus never strayed off course or capitulated to those who sought to sidetrack him. This was true, even when it put Jesus in conflict with the people of his day. For example, as a devout Jew, he sought to abide by the laws that were presented in Scripture. However, when conflicting interests developed between keeping the law—especially when it was distorted by additional man-made regulations—and helping a person in need, aiding that person always won (Mark 3:1–6). Jesus knew the difference between the commands of his Father, together with the true intent regarding the Sabbath, and the rules and regulations of the religious establishment. So, when he healed a man's hand in the synagogue on the Sabbath, it is no surprise that Jesus was rebuked by the religious leaders. Rather than apologizing and backing down to avoid a confrontation with them, however, Jesus turned the moment into an opportunity for instructional correction by confronting the leaders and revealing the true nature of the Sabbath. Indeed, he punctuated another such episode of healing on the Sabbath by teaching, "My Father is always at his work to this very day, and I, too, am working" (John 5:17).[20] Time and again, Jesus refused to back down from a confrontation which he then turned into a teaching opportunity.

APPLICATION AND REFLECTIONS
FOR THE CHRISTIAN EDUCATOR

Jesus the Master Teacher teaches us through a prayer to his Father: "This is eternal life: That they may know you, the only true God, and Jesus Christ whom you have sent" (John 17:3). One of the ultimate goals of Christian education is to make Christ, his person and work, known so that all who are involved may in turn know God and his Son Jesus Christ. Through many and various venues, both short-term and on-going—such as

Sunday school, vacation Bible school, small groups, long-term Bible discovery groups, women's breakfast, men's sports get-togethers—the highest priority is communicating Christ to those who have not yet come to know him and to those who have already embraced him and must continue to know him more deeply.

As Christian educators engage in their endeavors of all types, the character of Jesus serves as a role model for them to follow. Their lifestyle, like that of their Master Teacher, must be consistent with their teaching. They dare not communicate (either explicitly or implicitly) the cliché, "Do as I say, not as I do." Actions speak as loud as words, and any teaching, mentoring, discipling, modeling, or other educational actions that are not backed up by consistent Christian living will at best fall on deaf ears or, at worst, cause others to fall badly. This means the lifestyle of Christian educators must be above reproach (1 Tim 3:2); they must be people of integrity and known as such. This regards not only their outward behavior but their motives as well. As the Master Teacher lived authentically, so too must Christian educators be typified by genuineness without even a hint of hypocrisy.

As for the people to be addressed by Christian education, one critical lesson to learn from Jesus focuses on the unlikely audience that engaged with him: he attracted all types of people to himself without judgment or prejudice. Furthermore, he made it a point to reach out to all kinds of people, overcoming ethnic barriers (he taught Jews, Samaritans, and Greeks), gender barriers (he taught women as well as men), generational barriers (he taught both young and old), socioeconomic barriers (he taught rich and poor), and political barriers (he taught Romans and Jews). Christian educational endeavors must learn from this and, wherever it is possible to do so, overcome the barriers that infect current society. There simply is no room for bigotry, prejudice, favoritism, partiality, superiority, boasting, and arrogance, for all people are created in the image of God and are equal at the cross of Jesus Christ.

As for the methods to be employed by Christian education, Jesus as the Master Teacher again provides some important principles. Scripture must be the center of the curriculum. As divinely revealed, truthful, authoritative, sufficient, necessary, and clear teaching, Scripture deserves this priority. But Jesus demonstrated that this does not limit Christian educators to only one method of communicating the Bible. His method of asking questions—the so-called "Socratic method"—continues to work remarkably well in the hands of competent teachers. There are times when a question should be answered with another question in order to challenge people to engage in critical thinking.

Well-crafted and well-timed questions provoke thought, help listeners draw conclusions, awaken the conscience, elicit faith, clarify issues, and create dilemmas; that is, they make people think for themselves rather than relying on their teacher for answers, and they facilitate spiritual maturity.

> The ability to ask thoughtful questions is an art that can lead to profound learning experiences. Asking questions forces students to think, to analyze in such a way that they reach conclusions for themselves rather than having them spoon fed. Articulating an answer requires a further learning process of sifting through thoughts, prioritizing, organizing, and synthesizing them into a coherent answer.[21]

When educators are asked a question and are tempted to give an answer, they should catch themselves first and ask themselves, "Is there a way to redirect this question through asking another question that will help the student discover truth?"

Beyond this questioning method, many other excellent teaching approaches are available for educators. Personal stories and anecdotes, discussion of headlines from news reports, excerpts from books and movies, humor, illustrations from participants themselves, small-group discussions that are well guided and well directed, and many other methods present themselves for use in Christian educational settings. All the while, educators are being sensitive to and looking for teachable moments, which they then seize to drive home crucial truths, even when the lessons to be learned deviate from the plan of the day. In both the mundane and miraculous aspects of life, these teachable moments may be discerned and utilized for teaching. In this Christian educators should not shy away from confrontation. When needed, teaching confrontationally with the appropriate respect, humility, and demeanor called for by the situation may result in a significant breakthrough.

Finally, it has been said that Scripture teaches that two things will last for eternity: God's Word (Isa 40:8) and people. The task of Christian education is to put the two together. The curriculum is God's Word, which is taught so as to be applicable to the needs of people. Wise educators take time to study their students, seeking to know and understand their life experiences. In this way they have a more focused target in mind when they take God's Word and apply it to their needs. Following Jesus, the Master Teacher, Christian educators have the most excellent model to help them in their task.

REFLECTION QUESTIONS

1. How would you say your affirmation of Jesus as the Christ impacts your teaching as a Christian educator?
2. Can you identify at least three ways Jesus' model of teaching and discipleship influences or challenges you as a Christian educator?
3. What are some innate limitations of comparing our teaching ministry to that of Jesus'? In what areas should they *not* be compared? Why?
4. How is Jesus Christ reflected in your education ministry? As one person once asked, "Where is Jesus in what we do?"

1   M. J. Erickson, *Christian Theology* (Grand Rapids: Baker, 1998), 699.

2   C. C. Ryrie, *Basic Theology* (Wheaton, IL: Victor, 1986), 237–38.

3   Wayne Grudem, *Systematic Theology: An Introduction to Biblical Doctrine* (Grand Rapids: Zondervan, 1994), 545–46.

4   Ryrie, *Basic Theology,* 241.

5   G. R. Allison, *Jesusology: Understand What You Believe about Jesus and Why* (Nashville: B&H, 2005).

6   His followers also raised the dead but did so in his name.

7   Erickson, *Christian Theology,* 722.

8   Ibid., 723.

9   Ibid., 790.

10 "Although Jesus frequently taught in the formal setting of a synagogue, most of his time was spent as a traveling teacher whose students followed him wherever he went. Jesus had a peripatetic school: he taught in the open air on the mount of beatitudes (Matt 5:1–2); on the seashore (Mark 4:1); in the temple area (Mark 11:17)." See J. A. Grassi, *Jesus as Teacher: A New Testament Guide to Learning "the Way"* (Washington, DC: St. Mary's College Press, 1982), 26.

11 W. Benson, "Christ the Master Teacher," in *Christian Education: Foundations for the Future,* ed. R. E. Clark, L. Johnson, and A. K. Sloat (Chicago: Moody, 1991), 89–90.

12 R. Yount, "Jesus, the Master Teacher," in *The Teaching Ministry of the Church,* ed. Daryl Eldridge (Nashville, TN: B&H, 1995), 35.

13 L. R. Reeser, *Jesus' Use of the Question in His Teaching Ministry,* unpublished thesis (La Mirada, CA: Talbot School of Theology, 1968), 35–36.

14 R. B. Zuck, *Teaching as Jesus Taught* (Grand Rapids: Baker, 1995), 236.

15 D. E. Clark, *Jesus Christ: His Life and Teachings* (Elgin, IL: David C. Cook, 1977), 121.

16 A helpful though somewhat technical definition of a parable is the following: "It expresses or implies the logic of analogy in the language of either simile or metaphor elaborated into a form of allegory that is selectively, but not pervasively, symbolic." See J. W. Sider, *Interpreting the Parables* (Grand Rapids: Zondervan, 1995), 259.

17 Adapted from G. R. Allison, *Jesusology: Understand What You Believe about Jesus and Why* (Nashville, TN: B&H, 2005), 51–54.

18 Grassi, *Jesus as Teacher,* 62.

19 V. L. Blackwood, "Teaching of Jesus Christ," in *The Evangelical Dictionary of Christian Education,* ed. M. J. Anthony (Grand Rapids: Baker, 2001), 686.

20 "The rabbis held that even though the Scriptures said that God 'rested on the Sabbath,' his creative work really continued each day. Jesus appealed to this teaching for justification of his healing work on the Sabbath. He was really doing no more than imitating the Father." Grassi, *Jesus as Teacher,* 37.

21 D. Falls, "Socratic Method," in *The Evangelical Dictionary of Christian Education,* 650.

CHAPTER 7

Pneumatology and Christian Education

Michael J. Anthony

PNEUMATOLOGY:
THE DOCTRINE OF THE HOLY SPIRIT

*I*n Genesis 1, following the account of the creation of the inanimate world and the animate creatures, the narrative reaches its pinnacle with an extraordinary divine deliberation. Prior to his creation of human beings, God says, "Let *us* make man in *our* image, according to *our* likeness" (Gen 1:26). These plural pronouns (*us, our*) indicate that God is not a solitary being. From Genesis 1, we understand that the Godhead includes both the Father, who spoke the universe and all it contains into existence (Gen 1:3–25), as well as "the Spirit of God, who was hovering over the face of the deep" (Gen 1:2).[1] Thus, in the opening section of Scripture, we are introduced to the Holy Spirit and his participation in the creation of the world. The dimension of theology that seeks to understand the person and work of the Holy Spirit is referred to as pneumatology.[2]

Some have referred to the past 100 years as the century of the Holy Spirit. The Holy Spirit has always been active with great power in the church age—from its beginning on the day of Pentecost to the rapid and decisive spread of Christianity throughout the Roman Empire and from the recovery of biblically grounded theology and practice in the Reformation to the waves of revival that shook colonial America during the Great Awakening that propelled missionaries to spread the gospel throughout the world. But the twentieth century was a unique era in certain ways as greater attention was directed to the Holy Spirit and as a new emphasis was placed on him and his powerful ministries that brought salvation to new frontiers and empowered Christians for godly living and fruitful ministry. This was in no small part due to the Pentecostal movement that began in Azusa Street in Los Angeles and spread from there to every region of the world by unleashing a phenomenal movement of God's Spirit.[3] New churches and denominations—the Assemblies of God, the Church of God, the Church of God in Christ—came into existence, characterized by the baptism of the Spirit after conversion, speaking in tongues, and evangelistic fervor. Sixty years later this Pentecostal theology and ministry had spread to mainline denominations—Anglican/Episcopal, Methodist, Presbyterian, Baptist, Catholic—bringing the charismatic renewal. A third wave of Pentecostalism influenced some aspects of Evangelicalism through John Wimber and the Vineyard Fellowship at the end of the twentieth century. Indeed, the Pentecostal/charismatic phenomenon continues today to account significantly for the rapid spread of Christianity throughout Central and South America, Africa, Asia, and much of the rest of the world. At the forefront of this movement is the Holy Spirit.

But who is the Holy Spirit, and in what activities is he engaged? The Christian tradition has generally understood the work of the Holy Spirit—who is himself fully God, the third Person of the Trinity—to fall within three broad categories: revelation, salvation, and holy living. Accordingly, this chapter will explore both the person and work of the Holy Spirit and then discuss the educational implications for the lives of believers (individually) and the church (corporately) today.

The Names of the Holy Spirit

Scripture includes more than twenty different names for the Holy Spirit. Like a mosaic each name provides a piece that, together with others, forms a portrait of this Person of the God-head. His most common names are "the Spirit" and "the Holy Spirit." The term "Spirit" is closely associated with "breath," as seen in Job 33:4: "The Spirit of God has made me; the breath of the Almighty gives me life." This is reflected also in Christ's interaction with his disciples: "He breathed on them and said, 'Receive the Holy Spirit'" (John 20:22). Another important name is the Greek term *paraklētos*, often rendered "Paraclete," but it can also be translated "Comforter," "Helper," "Counselor," or "Advocate." Other phrases describing the Holy Spirit are "the Spirit of God," "the Spirit of Christ," and "the Spirit of Truth."[4]

The Personality and Deity of the Holy Spirit

The Holy Spirit is a divine *Person*, not some type of imper-sonal force or energy. As a Person, he possesses an intellect (he understands the deepest mysteries of the Godhead; 1 Cor 2:10–11), he exhibits emotions (he can be grieved or saddened; Eph 4:30), and he exercises his will (he sovereignly distributes spiritual gifts to Christians; 1 Cor 12:11). Moreover, he engages in personal activities, like speaking (Acts 8:29), praying (Rom 8:26–27), teaching (John 14:26), and bearing witness (Rom 8:16). Because of their personal names, we may find it easier to consider the Father and the Son as divine Persons, but it would be heresy or blasphemy to say that the Holy Spirit is just an impersonal force or power rather than a divine Person in his own right.

Along with the Father and the Son, the Holy Spirit is a *divine* Person, the third Person of the Trinity. One of the clearest pas-sages of Scripture that helps us affirm the deity of the Holy Spirit is the story of Ananias and Sapphira in Acts 5. Like many of the new disciples at the start of the Christian movement, this husband and wife team sold a parcel of land belonging to them and presented part of the proceeds from the sale to the apostles for distribution to the members of the church in Jerusalem. As generous as this was, it was also problematic because Ananias and Sapphira made it seem as though they were giving all of the proceeds from the sale of the land rather than only a portion. This deceit would not remain secret, however, as Peter became aware of it: "Then Peter said, 'Ananias, why has Satan filled your heart to lie to the Holy Spirit....You have not lied to men but to God." The parallel statements "lied to the Holy Spirit" and "lied to God" clearly indicate that the Holy Spirit is God.

Moreover, the Holy Spirit is characterized by divine attributes and engages in divine activities. Some of the Spirit's attributes are the following: omnipresence (David acknowledged that anywhere and everywhere he goes, the Holy Spirit is present; Ps 139:7–10), omniscience (the Holy Spirit knows everything, "even the deep things of God"; 1 Cor 2:10); omnipotence (nothing is impossible for the Holy Spirit; Luke 1:35–37), and eternality (Heb 9:14). Concerning his activities, the Holy Spirit engages in works that can only be done by God himself. Chief among these is the act of creation itself (Gen 1:2; Job 33:4). The Holy Spirit is also active in causing people to be born again at the start of their Christian lives (John 3:5–6; Titus 3:5), and he will bring salvation to its magnificent climax when he accomplishes the resurrection of all believers through the glorification of their physical bodies (Rom 8:11). Moreover, the Holy Spirit was responsible for the inspiration of Scripture, as Peter affirmed: "For prophecy never had its origin in the will of man, but men spoke from God as they were carried along by the Holy Spirit" (2 Pet 1:21). These divine attributes and divine activities affirm the deity of the Holy Spirit. He is a *divine Person*.

The Holy Spirit in Relation to the Father and the Son

Christians affirm the doctrine of the Trinity, the eternal existence of *three divine Persons*—the Father, the Son, and the Holy Spirit. This raises the question of the relationship between these three Persons. Historically, the church has acknowledged that the Holy Spirit is *homoousios*—of the same essence or nature— as the Father and the Son. This means that the attributes that are possessed by the Father and Son alike—such as independence, unchangeableness, eternality, omnipresence, omniscience, omnipotence, wisdom, love, holiness, righteousness, jealousy, truthfulness, faithfulness, sovereignty, mercy, grace, and wrath—are the same attributes that the Holy Spirit possesses. The Holy Spirit is God, fully divine and equal in essence and nature in every way to the Father and the Son.

Historically, the church has also affirmed that the Holy Spirit proceeds from both the Father and the Son. They did not create him, and he is himself God, but he eternally proceeds as the Spirit from them both. This explains why both the Father and Son sent the Spirit at Pentecost on his mission, a point that Jesus himself emphasized in his teaching on the Holy Spirit (John 14:26; 15:26; 16:7). In accordance with one of the early creeds, the church affirms that the Holy Spirit "proceeds from both the Father and the Son."[5] Thus, while the Father, Son, and Holy Spirit are equal in terms of their deity, they are three distinct Persons of the Trinity.

The Work of the Holy Spirit in the Old Testament

The Old Testament is replete with examples of how the Holy Spirit was actively engaged in the events of both world and human history. God's Spirit played a critical role in the creation of the world (Gen 1:2; Job 33:4) and continues actively to preserve and sustain all that was created (Ps 104:27–30). Moreover, his gifts to human beings—understanding and reason (Job 32:8), wisdom and discernment (Gen 41:38–39), and skillfulness in craftsmanship (Exod 28:3; 31:3–5; 35:30–35)—are particularly noteworthy.

The Old Testament concentrates on the Spirit's activities in regard to his work among key figures in Israel. This does not mean that the Holy Spirit was inactive in the lives of other people to save and sanctify them, but the Old Testament focuses on his work among the leaders of the people of God. Three groups—prophets, judges, and kings—were the particular recipients of the Spirit's powerful activity.

The Holy Spirit spoke by the mouths of the prophets. Specifically prophecies declared the mind and will of God as revealed by the Spirit through the prophets. The prophet Ezekiel stated: "The Spirit of the LORD fell upon me, and He said to me, 'Say, Thus says the LORD'" (Ezek 11:5 NAS). The prophet Micah explained: "As for me, I am filled with power, with the Spirit of the LORD, and with justice and might, to declare to Jacob his transgression and to Israel his sin" (Mic 3:8). The New Testament comments on this role of the Spirit, saying that "no prophecy ever came by the will of man; instead, moved by the Holy Spirit, men spoke from God" (2 Pet 1:21).

The Holy Spirit stirred up judges and empowered them to deliver Israel from its oppressors. Seemingly like clockwork, the people of God would rebel against him, and for judgment God would give his people into the hands of their enemies, and they would languish in oppression for an extended period of time. In desperation the people would cry out to God to save them, and he would raise up a judge—such as Othniel (Judg 3:9–11), Gideon (Judg 6–8), Jephthah (Judg 11–12), and Samson (Judg 13–16)—who by the power of the Spirit would deliver them and grant them peace from their oppressors.

Other special empowerments were directed to the national leaders of Israel as the Holy Spirit came upon kings and equipped them to rule the people of God. David enjoyed this enablement from his earliest anointing by Samuel: "The Spirit of the Lord came mightily upon David from that day forward" (1 Sam 16:13). But the Holy Spirit could—and did, in the case of Saul—withdraw his empowering presence in the case of grievous and persistent sin (1 Sam 16:14). Knowing that the Spirit had left his predecessor Saul, David pleaded with God not to remove the Holy Spirit from him (Ps 51:10–12) during times of failure so he could continue to fulfill God's purposes throughout his life.

One other important theme regarding the Holy Spirit echoes through the prophetic portion of the Old Testament. Prophets such as Jeremiah (31:31–34), Ezekiel (36:25–27), and Joel (2:28–32) looked forward to a new, fresh, and unprecedented outpouring of the Holy Spirit at some point in the future. At that time God would write his law on people's hearts, sprinkle them clean from sin, give them a new heart, put his Spirit within them so they would obey him; and he would do so on all people: the people of Israel as well as the Gentiles, both men and women, young and old alike, and all classes of people. In this way the Old Testament anticipated the new covenant ministry of the Holy Spirit.

The Holy Spirit in the Gospels

John the Baptist picked up on this Old Testament anticipation and heightened this expectation by associating this fresh new work of the Holy Spirit with the coming of the Messiah. As John explained: "I baptize you with water. But One is coming who is more powerful than I. I am not worthy to untie the strap of his sandals. He will baptize you with the Holy Spirit and fire" (Luke 3:16). Of course, John referred to the coming of the Son of God incarnate as Jesus the Messiah. The incarnation itself was the product of the miraculous work of the Holy Spirit (Luke 1:35; Matt 1:18,20). At the start of Jesus' messianic ministry, the Holy Spirit descended on him as he was being baptized (Luke 3:21–22) and then propelled him into the wilderness to be tempted by Satan (Luke 4:1–13). Jesus conducted his ministry through the Holy Spirit—teaching, discipling, confronting, exorcising demons, and walking with God—by means of the Spirit's resources and power (Matt. 12:22–29; Luke 4:14–21).

Jesus himself continued and heightened the Old Testament anticipation of a new, fresh, and unprecedented outpouring of the Holy Spirit to come. Looking to the future, Jesus promised that "streams of living water" would one day flow from his disciples: "He said this about the Spirit, who those who believed in him were going to receive, for the Spirit had not yet been received, because Jesus had not yet been glorified" (John 7:37–39; see 14:17). After his death and resurrection, yet still before his glorification would be complete with the ascension, Jesus commanded his disciples "not to leave Jerusalem, but to wait for the Father's promise. 'This,' he said, 'is what you heard from Me; for John baptized with water, but you will be baptized with the Holy Spirit not many days from now'" (Acts 1:4–5 HCSB). The expectation of the fulfillment of the long-awaited promise of a new, unprecedented outpouring of the Holy Spirit—prophesied in the Old Testament, reinforced by John the Baptist—must have been palpable! The fulfillment was just around the corner.

In more detail Jesus foretold this coming Holy Spirit: He would be "another Paraclete" ("Counselor," "Helper"), "the Spirit of truth" given not to unbelievers of this world but to the followers of Jesus Christ "forever" (John 14:16–17). The Spirit would teach these disciples "all things" and remind them of everything Jesus had communicated to them (John 14:26); thus, because the Holy Spirit would "testify" about Jesus Christ, his disciples would also "testify" about Jesus Christ (John 15:26–27).[6] Furthermore, the Spirit would "guide" the disciples "into all the truth," not speaking on his own initiative but communicating all that he learns—including "what is to come"—from the Father and the Son. By this the Holy Spirit would glorify Jesus Christ (John 16:13–15). Fittingly, even before the coming of the Holy Spirit after the ascension, Jesus "breathed on [his disciples] and said, 'Receive the Holy Spirit'" (John 20:22). This vivid, tangible, and symbolic action was a harbinger of the Spirit's coming at Pentecost not many days afterwards. Before that could take place, however, the disciples established themselves in Jerusalem, just as Jesus had commanded them, and awaited the fulfillment of the promise concerning the Holy Spirit (Luke 24:49; Acts 1:4–5).

The Holy Spirit on the Day of Pentecost

Jesus' disciples were a diverse group: the original twelve; a larger group of seventy; some key women supporters of Jesus' ministry, including his mother Mary (Luke 8:1–3); and by the day of Pentecost, which was after Jesus' resurrection, another group of 120 (Acts 1:14–15) that likely included Jesus' half brothers. Although they did not grasp the full significance of the promise of the Holy Spirit during the 10 days of waiting and expectation in Jerusalem, they experienced firsthand the baptism and filling of the Spirit once he arrived on the day of Pentecost. This is one of the most significant events in the history of the world because Pentecost: (1) was the fulfillment of the anticipated and unprecedented outpouring of the Holy Spirit; (2) marked the inauguration of the new covenant; (3) gave birth to the church; and (4) was accompanied by miraculous signs— "a sound like that of a violent rushing wind," "tongues like flames of fire," and the verbal rehearsal of the "magnificent acts of God" (Acts 2:2–4,11). Speaking in tongues refers to the disciples' ability to speak languages that they had never studied or previously spoken. This miraculous day of Pentecost launched God's Spirit on his new covenant mission.

This innovative mission has several features that differentiate it from the Holy Spirit's former, old covenant ministry. Chief among these differences is his permanent indwelling of believers. Unlike the temporary manifestations of the Holy Spirit, who came upon and empowered the people of Israel but whose presence could be withdrawn, the Holy Spirit now indwells Christians and remains in them forever. Another difference is that this filling of the Holy Spirit is for all people—Jews and Gentiles, rich and poor, powerful and weak, old and young, men and women—who are Christ followers, rather than primarily for a select group of leaders in Israel. According to Peter's first sermon on the day of Pentecost, the presence of the Holy Spirit in God's people is characteristic of the new covenant ministry as his mission has come to the forefront of God's plan of redemption through the church.[7]

The Ministries of the Holy Spirit Today

The new covenant work of the Holy Spirit consists of numerous ministries, which could be described as encompassing the whole range of experiences in salvation for Christ's followers. Indeed, even before people embrace Jesus Christ for salvation, the Holy Spirit is powerfully at work to convict them of personal sin, self-righteousness, and worldly judgment (John 16:8–11). As this conviction sets in, the Holy Spirit brings about regeneration, or the giving of new spiritual life in the place of spiritual death (Titus 3:5–6). People are "born again" and remade into a "new creation" (John 3:3–5; 2 Cor 5:17). Moreover, these new Christians are sealed with the Holy Spirit (Eph 1:13–14), marked out as belonging to God with the Spirit as the firstfruits of their salvation (Rom 8:23), and given the Spirit as a pledge or down payment (2 Cor 1:22; 5:5), which is the guarantee that they will one day experience the fullness of God's presence and blessing when Christ returns. Subjectively, the Holy Spirit bears witness to believers in Christ that they truly belong to God forever (Rom. 8:16). As if this were not enough, Jesus Christ baptizes new believers in the Holy Spirit, thereby incorporating them into the body of Christ (1 Cor 12:13). These are the various ministries of the Holy Spirit at the beginning of salvation.

This powerful working of the Spirit continues throughout the lives of Christians as they are progressively transformed by him into greater and greater conformity to the image of Jesus Christ (2 Cor 3:18). Indeed, the Holy Spirit is particularly responsible for sanctification, the ongoing process by which Christians break more and more with sin and become more and more like Christ (1 Pet 1:2). The Holy Spirit provides everything that is needed to overcome the power of sin, and by the fruit he bears Christians exhibit the character of Jesus Christ more and more in their lives (Gal 5:16–23). The key is for Christians to be guided by the Spirit (Rom 8:4–8) or filled with the Spirit (Eph 5:18)—that is, controlled by and submissive to his leading.

In terms of specific activities of the Spirit, he engages in prayer for Christians (Rom 8:26–27). When believers are weakened and confused so they do not know what to pray, whether from failure to grasp God's will in particular situations or from being overwhelmed by life, they can be confident that the Holy Spirit intercedes for them in those times of struggle. And they can know with certainty that the prayers of the Holy Spirit, though expressed in a way that Christians cannot understand or offered in some unspoken manner, will be answered by God because the Spirit always prays in accordance with the Father's will and is thus always heard. Even the prayers that Christians do express find their access to God through the Spirit (Eph 2:18).

Another important activity of the Spirit is his illumination of the Word of God. When Christians read and study the Bible, they should always do so requesting and relying upon the Holy Spirit both for help in understanding what they read and in applying what they understand. As one Christian prayed each and every day, he and a group of pastors would gather for Bible study:

> Almighty, eternal and merciful God, whose Word is
> a lamp unto our feet and a light unto our path, open
> and illuminate our minds, that we may purely and per-
> fectly understand your Word and that our lives may be
> conformed to what we have rightly understood, that
> in nothing we may be displeasing to your majesty,
> through Jesus Christ our Lord. Amen.[8]

As for ministries of the Holy Spirit directed at the building up and strengthening of churches, one of his key activities is his distribution of spiritual gifts (1 Cor 12:11). The Spirit himself sovereignly decides on the gifts that each believer should receive, which include teaching, leading, faith, mercy, serving, and many more. The overriding purpose for these gifts is to bring blessing to the church; their exercise is for "the common good" (1 Cor

11:7). This common good is also promoted by the Holy Spirit, who is the Creator and Sustainer of unity in the community of faith. Churches do not have to attempt to create unity among their members; that is already provided by the Spirit (Eph 4:3). What must instead happen is that churches are to work hard to maintain that unity, which seems to be fragile and undergo breakdowns because of the sinfulness of church members (Eph 4:30; 1 Thess 5:19). Mindful that they are natural enemies who have been brought together, not naturally but by the grace of God through Jesus Christ,[9] church members must rely on the Holy Spirit to be able to express genuine love to one another (Rom 15:30; Col 1:8) in an atmosphere of righteousness, peace, and joy fostered by the Spirit (Rom 14:17). Moreover, church leaders have been installed by the appointment of the Holy Spirit (Acts 20:28; 13:2–3). By these means the Holy Spirit works powerfully to build up and strengthen churches.

Finally, the work of the Holy Spirit—begun with the conviction of sin and regeneration and continuing through sanctification in general and many specific ministries like prayer and commissioning church leaders—will one day find its culmination in the reality of glorification. Just as God raised his crucified Son Jesus Christ from the dead, so will the Spirit of God who lives in believers raise up their mortal bodies when Christ returns (Rom 8:11). This powerful work of resurrection will bring about the completion of the salvation that was begun in the lives of Christians, a glorification that is itself guaranteed and wrought by the Holy Spirit. It is little wonder, then, that Zechariah encourages us with these words: "'Not by might, nor by power, but by my Spirit,' says the Lord" (Zech. 4:6).

THE HOLY SPIRIT AND EDUCATION

Throughout the pages of the New Testament, God reveals the unique instructional role that the Holy Spirit plays in the life of the church. Among other things we discover that the Spirit is intimately involved in four ways: serving as a *teacher* of spiritual truth, as a *guide* in matters that pertain to the spirit, as a *declarer* of God's intentions, and as a *revealer* of God's truth. Each aspect is critical to the spiritual formation of the individual believer as well as the corporate body of Christ. Therefore, each will be explored in detail in order to gain a fuller understanding of the Spirit's role in the instructional process.

The Holy Spirit as Teacher

One of the focal aspects of the Spirit's work is to serve as a teacher, as stated in John 14:26: "But the Counselor, the Holy Spirit, whom the Father will send in my name, will *teach* you all things and will remind you of everything that I have said to you." The Greek adjective *didaktos*, which is related to the verb for "teach" in John 14:26, occurs twice in 1 Cor 2:13: "This is what we speak, not in words *taught* us by human wisdom but in words *taught* by the Spirit, expressing spiritual truths in spiritual words."

Together these verses affirm a spiritual truth that one of the primary purposes of the Spirit's coming is to serve as a teacher of spiritual truth. Indeed, were it not for the Holy Spirit teaching us the truths of God, we would be grossly inadequate. The verb *didasko* carries the meaning of instructing, delivering a discourse, explaining truth. The verb's indirect object "you" and its direct object "all things" point out the relevant, active nature of imparting truth from one person (the teacher) to another (the student).[10] The Holy Spirit's teaching is directed toward instilling biblical truth in such a manner that it develops and nurtures the believer.

A word here needs to be said about the value of the teachable moment. The opportunity to teach God's Word usually comes during prearranged opportunities of instruction such as a class, home Bible study, or seminar. However, there are also times when God has a different agenda for our day, and he brings us into an encounter with someone for the express purpose of revealing his Word to them. This may be during a coffee chat with a neighbor, meeting with a colleague at work during a break in the routine of the day, or perhaps with someone on school campus between classes. We call these encounters "teachable moments" because hindsight confirms that divine opportunities compelled us to share his Word with someone in need of guidance and direction. A biblical example of this is when Jesus encountered two strangers on a seemingly mundane walk along the road to the village of Emmaus (Luke 24:13–35). These are special meetings arranged by the Spirit for the express purpose of teaching God's Word.

The Holy Spirit as Guide

The apostle Paul wrote to the believers at Rome that "as many as are led by the Spirit of God, these are sons of God" (Rom 8:14). This passage reveals to us the guiding nature of the Holy Spirit in the life of the believer. Those who received the harshest of criticism from Jesus during his earthly ministry were those who preferred to use the law as a rod of correction rather than to look beyond the letter of the law and consider its intent. He condemned the rulers of the temple for being more concerned with the legality of healing on the Sabbath than with celebrating a miraculous work of God during a worship service (Mark 3:1–4). Those who live by strict adherence to the law have no need of the Spirit to guide their behavior. But life is rarely so simple. Sometimes life is more complex than that, so the ministry of the Holy Spirit as a guide is necessary.

The Spirit applies the Scriptures to our needs, but guidance goes beyond that to areas of critical thinking. This was greatly lacking in the religious leaders of Jesus' day. They knew the Word of God (especially the law) but lacked the critical thinking necessary to look beyond the law to the heart of God. In matters pertaining to keeping the Sabbath, the fulfillment of Old Testament prophecies, and the requirement of grace, the scribes and Pharisees lacked a deeper understanding of God's Word that the Spirit is able to provide for us. Sometimes solving complex moral and ethical decisions requires the application of seemingly conflicting verses, and this is where the Holy Spirit guides us and directs us to the correct interpretation and application of the Scriptures.

During times of life when sin complicates our walk or blurs our vision, we need the Holy Spirit to show us the way of escape and to guide us back into righteous living. Sometimes we need the benefit of a spiritual counselor to help us navigate the path, and the Holy Spirit (and other human spiritual leaders as well) are a necessary part of the redemptive equation. This is one of the blessed ministries in the life of the believer for which we as teachers are deeply grateful.

The Holy Spirit Declares

Jesus spoke to his disciples about the coming of the Holy Spirit, which likely left some of them wondering what the Spirit would do in Jesus' absence. Perhaps anticipating this question, Jesus revealed to them that part of the Holy Spirit's ministry would be to announce (John 16:13–15). The Greek verb *anangello* is used three times to clarify his work. We read:

> When the Spirit of truth comes, he will guide you into all truth. He will not speak on his own but will tell you what he has heard. He will tell [*anangello*] you about the future. He will bring me glory by telling [*anangello*] you whatever he receives from me. All that belongs to the Father is mine; this is why I said, "The Spirit will tell [*anangello*] you whatever he receives from me" (NLT).

Thus, one of the Holy Spirit's roles is to declare or announce something on behalf of God the Father or Jesus.[11]

The Holy Spirit Reveals

Luke records an amazing story about an encounter that Jesus' parents had as they entered the temple to dedicate their new son to God. Upon entering the temple courtyard, they met a devout and righteous man by the name of Simeon. Scripture tells us that he had been waiting a long time for God to show him the promised Messiah. "And it had been revealed to him by the Holy Spirit that he would not see death before he had seen the Lord's Christ" (Luke 2:26). Although we do not know how the Spirit revealed this to Simeon, the Spirit's message to Simeon was clear, so he approached the parents and blessed the young Jesus. Here we see the Spirit speaking to the heart of man in ways that people cannot. God's Spirit finds unique ways to confirm his message as he communicates with the innermost spirit in a man or woman. In an educational context this work of the Spirit to reveal his truth can be profound and impacting.

As teachers we need to be reminded of our dependency on the Holy Spirit to speak to students in their hearts where lasting life transformation takes place. If you have taught for any length of time, you know that you cannot reason someone into changing habits and long-established patterns of behavior. Only God can do that, and he chooses to do so by transforming the person from the inside out—often through the use of his still small voice deep inside the soul of the believer. Sometimes it takes more than a convincing argument from an impassioned teacher. Changing habits of the heart requires heart surgery, not brain surgery, and that is what the Holy Spirit brings to the learning encounter.

> The author of the divine address helps the hearer to understand the address itself. The Spirit assists hearers to "understand what God has freely given us" (1 Cor 2:12). Unless the Spirit is active to penetrate our self-deceptions, how could we, trapped in a history of sin, recognize this address? The Spirit works preveniently to make the mind receptive, to enable openness to divine address, and to prepare the believer to be unafraid of receiving the truth.[12]

Character development comes through transformation. Rarely does it in occur in the classroom with others watching. Most of the time it takes place on the walk back to the dorm or the commute home during rush hour when believers have time to think and reflect on the things God is speaking to them about. "God knows the secrets of the heart" (Ps 44:21), and it is to him that the Spirit reveals our thoughts and motives. Perhaps we are in denial and unable to recognize truth when we see it, but the Spirit of God is able to remove our blinders and reveal truth to us in ways that others cannot. God convicts us of sins in our lives (John 16:8) that perhaps years of hard-heartedness has prevented us from seeing. But the Spirit of God reveals our sins and leads us to a path of righteous living.

When Paul wrote to the believers in the church at Corinth, he spoke forcefully about the ministry of the Spirit of God as a revealer, as in 1 Cor 2:6–10 (italics added).

> Yet we do speak wisdom among those who are mature; a wisdom, however, not of this age nor of the rulers of this age, who are passing away; but we speak God's wisdom in a mystery, the hidden wisdom which God predestined before the ages to our glory; the wisdom which none of the rulers of this age has understood; for if they had understood it they would not have crucified the Lord of glory; but just as it is written, "Things which the eye has not seen and ear has not heard, and which have not entered into the heart of man, all that God has prepared for those who love him." For to us *God revealed them through the Spirit*; for the Spirit searches all things, even the depths of God.

Here Paul acknowledged the work of the Holy Spirit in revealing to him spiritual insights that the world could not possibly know or understand apart from the Spirit. This same Spirit is able to reveal spiritual insights and wisdom to us as well as we wait on him and remain open to his ministry in our lives.

THE HOLY SPIRIT AND SPIRITUAL GIFTS

Clearly one of the dominant roles of the Holy Spirit in the church today is his impartation of at least one gift to every believer at the point of spiritual conversion: "Each one should use whatever spiritual gift he has received to serve others, faithfully administering God's grace in its various forms" (1 Pet 4:10). Speaking to the believers in the church at Corinth, Paul declared, "Now to each one the manifestation of the Spirit is given for the common good" (1 Cor 12:7). He went on to provide a partial list of these gifts with the intent that whoever possesses a gift will employ it for the benefit of other believers in the church.

If one compares the four major lists of spiritual gifts (Rom 12:6–8; 1 Cor 12:4–11; 1 Cor 12:28–28; Eph 4:11–16) with other passages that cite an individual gift (celibacy, martyrdom, craftsmanship), it is possible to construct a list of nearly thirty spiritual gifts. The length of the list largely depends on definition (such as those who want to equate the first-century apostle with the modern missionary) and whether one considers the sign gifts (tongues, interpretation of tongues, miracles, healings, and exorcisms) active today. Others debate whether some behaviors are considered gifts or simply character traits that all believers should possess, such as the fruit of the Spirit (Gal 5: 22–23).

Upon examination of the biblical evidence on spiritual gifts, we come to several conclusions:

1. No one person possesses all of the spiritual gifts. They are designed to be spread out among all the believers in a local church (1 Cor 12:14–21).
2. No particular gift is more essential to the body of Christ. Each is important and plays a vital role. Although the gift of prophecy is the only gift cited in all four New Testament passages, that does not necessarily mean it is the most important, especially in light of Rom 12:4–8 and 1 Cor 12:22–26.

3. The purpose of spiritual gifts is to benefit all believers in
   the local church, so as each gift is exercised, the members
   of the church mature in their faith and service to others
   (Eph 4:11–16).
4. The Holy Spirit decides who receives which particular
   gift, and he gives them according to his sovereign plan
   (1 Cor 12:11).
5. Natural talents are given by God to benefit the individual
   in natural life (such as earning a living as a musician or
   artist), whereas a spiritual gift is given for the express purpose of building up the body of Christ (Eph 4:11–16).

The gifts of the Holy Spirit for the church today are significant
in that they provide a point of contact between us and the eternal
God of the universe. When we are operating under the control
of the Spirit, using the gift that he has provided, it is a glorious
opportunity for us to experience deep personal fulfillment and
meaning. We are not investing in ourselves through some selfish
act but using our God-given abilities for the express purpose of
helping others. It is a blessed experience indeed to be so led and
controlled by the Spirit to accomplish his purposes.

THE HOLY SPIRIT AND PERSONAL
APPLICATIONS AND REFLECTIONS

When we take the time to reflect on the ministry of the Holy
Spirit and its application for believers, we must feel a certain
sense of awe to realize that an eternal and all-powerful God has
chosen to limit himself to work through his human creation.
Without people speaking on behalf of God, no one would come
to know Christ. Without someone teaching God's Word, no one
would grow in their spiritual maturity. God needs his church to
carry out his purposes for mankind. It is a strange concept, but
it brings us to a state of humility.

God's sovereign plan before the very foundations of the earth
were laid included the coming of the Holy Spirit for the purpose

of carrying out the continuing work of Jesus Christ. After Jesus'
ascension, the Holy Spirit was dispatched to carry on in Jesus'
absence. It is for this reason that a more accurate title for the
book of Acts is "The Acts of the Holy Spirit" rather than "The
Acts of the Apostles." Throughout the pages of the Old Testament, there is an emphasis on the Person and work of God the
Father in his dealings with mankind. Throughout the pages of
the four Gospels, we develop an understanding of Jesus Christ,
his character, and his relationship to man. But throughout the
remainder of the New Testament, we have a record of the Holy
Spirit's ministry in the lives of individual believers and the
church as a whole.

The Holy Spirit calls us to repentance, indwells us at the
point of spiritual rebirth, fills us as we yield control of our lives
to him, works a lifelong process of sanctification in our lives,
and seals us until the day of our passing into eternity. It is a
close and bonding relationship that we enjoy with this third
member of the Godhead.

The Holy Spirit brings about our redemption in partnership
with the Father and the Son. The Spirit gives the new believer
a gift which, once it has been identified and developed, is
employed as a means of bringing about spiritual renewal to others and spiritual maturity to the body of Christ. Each of us is
essential to the life of a healthy church. We each play a role and
contribute in some significant way.

The Holy Spirit and the Teacher-Learner Process

In relation to the teacher-learner process that we discussed
earlier in the book, the Holy Spirit plays a critical role in each
step of the process. His presence is critical to the learning process and plays an important role throughout it.

The Holy Spirit revels in a vessel that is open to being used.
Teachers that begin the lesson preparation in prayer, confessing sin and acknowledging their dependency on the Holy Spirit
for guidance, begin with the right attitude. Teachers who serve

under the leadership of the Holy Spirit experience more robust lessons and spiritual fruit from their teaching.

The Holy Spirit desires to partner with teachers in the development of each element in the lesson. The Holy Spirit wants to influence all aspects of the learning encounter—the prayerful consideration of the lesson aim, the construction of the lesson plan, the choice of the methods and materials, and the consideration of the learning environment. Teachers who are yielded to the Holy Spirit and quietly wait on his influence and support know the benefit of partnering with God while teaching.

Remember that one of the primary reasons the Holy Spirit was dispatched by the Father is to lead and guide mankind into biblical truth. Thus, he desires to give you wisdom in leading people who lack such understanding into a fuller knowledge of it. God wants to use you and seeks ways to make your teaching effective. There is nothing more powerful than a teacher yielded to the control of the Holy Spirit in front of a class of students with an open Bible. It makes Satan tremble and rattles the gates of hell. If you stand in the power granted by God's Spirit, you will realize that you teach with the backing of all God's resources to communicate biblical truth for his glory.

Many passages in the New Testament indicate that Jesus knew the thoughts of those he encountered. Some came to challenge and confront him while others came in humility with great need. Jesus took this attitude into consideration when he selected his content and methods. For example, no group of people received greater condemnation than the scribes and Pharisees, yet when Nicodemus, a leader among the Pharisees, came to him at night with a teachable spirit, Jesus neither condemned nor rebuked him. Attitude made the difference.

Not all students come into the content of learning with the same attitude. Some students come because their parents demanded their participation while others can't wait to get in the door. They sit next to each other while staring at the teacher. One has an open mind to learn while the other is a closed book.

The reality is that most teachers may not be able to tell the difference as they sit in front of them. However, the Holy Spirit knows as he judges the motives and intentions of their hearts. The Holy Spirit is able to take what is said by the teacher and make it applicable to one student in a specific way yet say something completely different to another—because they each come from different starting points.

The Holy Spirit is the real communicator of truth, not human teachers. We are simply the vessel that God uses as a mouthpiece to communicate his lesson. What happens after the word leaves the lips of the teachers is up to the Holy Spirit as he takes it and uses it to penetrate the heart of the student. We have limited control over this part of the learning process, but it is better this way since it leaves the process in God's hands.

Children have different needs from their older adolescent siblings. Likewise adults are different depending on the particular life stage they are experiencing at the time. New parents have different concerns from empty nesters. It is not realistic to expect that one lesson will have the same meaning to everyone assembled in the audience. In these situations the Holy Spirit is able to take the content and relate it to the particular needs of those assembled. This does not negate the importance of giving the lesson aim some concerted forethought, but it does acknowledge the connection the Holy Spirit plays between the teacher and the learner.

The Holy Spirit and Curriculum

Some may be of the opinion that because of modern publishing companies, curriculum writers, and mass-marketed media materials we no longer have as much dependency on the Holy Spirit for teaching methods. Many think that all we really need to do is teach the curriculum provided by the church and let the Holy Spirit work with the result.

The problem with this line of reasoning is that it neglects one of the essential steps in the process of learning. The curriculum is the backbone of the learning process in that it supplies the content of the message. Without attention to the substance of what is being offered through the curriculum, there is little control over the outcome of learning.

Some have swung the pendulum a little too far and proclaimed that "only the Bible" will be taught. And while that is a noble aim, it is a bit misguided since some parts of the Bible are not appropriate for young children due to the limitations of understanding. For example, reading a Bible story about the demon-possessed child (Luke 9:37–43) or the hemorrhaging woman (Mark 5:24–34) may not be age appropriate for young children. Some lessons may be better left until they are of an age where such stories, and their background explanations, can be communicated with clearer focus.

The Holy Spirit is employed in this step of the learning process by finding appropriate stories from the Bible according to the age appropriateness of the student and by helping the teacher craft the lesson in such a way that makes it understandable and applicable to the child's world. Simply reading a Bible story without guidance in its relevant application is insufficient for most Sunday School lessons today. The Holy Spirit provides wisdom for teachers by helping them design the lesson around the Bible story and by making it more relevant for the context of their particular lives.

L. LeBar argued that the Holy Spirit is related to the curriculum in three ways: he guides writers and editors as they develop lessons; he guides church leaders in the selection of the materials; and he guides teachers in both the use of the lesson and its adaptation to the specific needs of the students assembled.[13]

The Holy Spirit and Education

The Holy Spirit knows the hearts and lives of students far better than teachers do. When a teacher begins lesson development in prayer, asking God for guidance in the selection of the appropriate lesson aim, he opens himself up to a more reliable focus of the lesson. Now the Holy Spirit is free to direct the teacher to select particular Bible passages with the appropriate methods and specific applications that help the lesson hit its intended target. Only the Holy Spirit can know the mind of the learner, so allowing him the freedom to select the outcome of the lesson makes for a far more meaningful lesson.

Jesus was a master communicator by anyone's definition. He held large crowds captive with his storytelling techniques. Audiences were mesmerized by his revelation of truth and the manner in which he communicated it. His ability to blend biblical truth with relevant application and creative instructional methods was nothing short of miraculous at times. He was able to take a small lesson and bring out a large meaning. Even in an audience of hostile religious leaders, Jesus held his ground and taught in the face of opposition.

Jesus was able to command such attention because he was a master craftsman of instructional methodology. At times he used a simple object lesson (such as a fish or a coin; Luke 11:11–13; Matt 18:1–6; 22:15–22) while at other times he used an individual (a small child or a crippled man) as a springboard to a lesson of eternal truth. Methods were used as a means to an end—never the end in themselves. Otherwise the lesson was lost in the moment of amazement.

We use a variety of methods in our instruction today because, like seasoning in a meal, we prefer variety. It brings out what's special and allows particular elements of the lesson to stand out beyond others. As teachers, our weakest method is the one we use the most. That's why we need variety but not just for variety's sake. Too much variety and our instructional objective is lost in the constant shuffle.

Some creative methods might include using media (movie clips, music segments), storytelling, drama, small groups, debates, agree/disagree, role play, neighbor nudge, expert panels, guest speakers, creative writing assignments, quizzes, problem-solving exercises, brainstorming activities, field trips, and projects. The Holy Spirit can assist the teacher in the appropriate selection of instructional methodology given the lesson aim, the students present, and the environment available.

The Holy Spirit is creative and assists the teacher in the selection of methods which need to be used to enhance the lesson and provoke critical thinking. Perhaps starting the lesson with a brief video clip can captivate the audience at the beginning of the lesson, or maybe breaking the whole class into small groups would allow the content to be explored more fully with specific application in mind. Whatever method you use, it should enhance the lesson and clarify the biblical truth being taught.

Jesus taught in many different environments: along the pathway while watching a farmer casting seed, at the seashore while fishermen mended their nets, on a mountainside, and in vicious storms. Jesus taught in so many places that it is obvious the environment was secondary to the truth he taught. The Holy Spirit can use just about any environment where a willing teacher and a teachable student meet together to discuss biblical truth.

CONCLUSION

The Holy Spirit is a vital element in the dynamic process of teaching biblical truth. Human teachers are merely vessels of opportunity for God to speak and communicate his lesson. In spite of our own weakness and human frailty, God has chosen in his sovereignty to use teachers to communicate his Word. Total submission of our wills to his ensures a more profitable learning outcome for our students. This dependence on the Holy Spirit is one of the hallmarks of distinction between secular education and Christian education. There can be no Christian education apart from the power and influence of the Holy Spirit.

Our goal in Christian education is the spiritual maturity of our disciples: "to present every man complete in Christ" (Col 1:28). The outcome of our lesson is usually not short-term behavior change—though at times that may be appropriate given the conditions of the students present. The outcome should be long-term life transformation. The teaching-learning process is a lifelong learning dynamic that can get messy at times. Ministry is a contact sport not intended for spectators, and as such it involves a long-term perspective. Remember, the Holy Spirit was given to the church for the purpose of assisting in life transformation. As we yield to the Spirit's control, we find ourselves partnering with God to help fulfill the Great Commission of "baptizing them . . . and *teaching* them to obey everything" Christ commanded us to do (Matt 28:19).

REFLECTION QUESTIONS

1. How would you describe the Holy Spirit's role in Christian education?
2. Where in your own life have you sensed the Holy Spirit's presence in your teaching?
3. How does the Holy Spirit influence and interact with the teacher? the learner? the teaching-learning process?
4. What might teachers do to enhance or improve the presence of the Holy Spirit in their lives and teaching?

---

1   The Spirit's hovering indicates his activity in protecting the "formless and void" creation and preparing it for the subsequent creative activity of God. Furthermore, we learn from later Scripture (John 1:1–3; Col 1:16; Heb 1:2) that the Son of God was also included in this creative activity. See chapter 6 for further discussion.

2   The word *pneumatology* comes from two Greek words: *pneuma*, meaning "Spirit," and *logos*, meaning "word" and implying "study of." Thus, *pneumatology* is "the study of the (Holy) Spirit."

3   For a recent account of this movement, see C. M. Robeck Jr., *The Azusa Street Mission and Revival: The Birth of the Global Pentecostal Movement* (Nashville: Thomas Nelson, 2006).

4   For a more detailed examination of the names of the Holy Spirit, see R. A. Torrey, *The Person and Work of the Holy Spirit* (Grand Rapids: Zondervan, 1974), 35–65.

5   In affirming the procession of the Holy Spirit from both the Father and the Son, we follow the historic position of the Western (that is, Roman Catholic and Protestant) church and its *Filioque* ("and the Son") addition to the Nicene-Constantinopolitan Creed.

6   With this promise and provision, Jesus validated his disciples as the legitimate witnesses to his person and work. This is a key element in

establishing the inspiration and authority of the New Testament as the canonical Word of God.

7   W. Grudem, *Systematic Theology: An Introduction to Biblical Doctrine* (Grand Rapids: Zondervan, 1994), 1018.

8   H. Zwingli, as cited by G. W. Locher, *Zwingli's Thought: New Perspectives* (Leiden: E. J. Brill, 1981), 28.

9   D. A. Carson, *Love in Hard Places* (Wheaton: Crossway, 2002), 61.

10   Roy B. Zuck, *Spirit-Filled Teaching* (Nashville: Nelson, 1998), 22.

11   Ibid., 28.

12   T. C. Oden, *Life in the Spirit* (San Francisco: Harper Collins, 1992), 73.

13   L. LeBar, *Education That Is Christian*, rev. ed. (Old Tappan, NJ: Fleming H. Revell, 1981), 227.

CHAPTER 8

Humanity, Sin, and
Christian Education

Gregg R. Allison

Any sustained thought about humans cannot help but conclude that we are amazingly complex beings. On the one hand, we possess significant physical, intellectual, creative, social, and relational abilities. The explosive speed of a 100-meter sprinter, Einstein's brilliant formula $E=mc^2$, the artistic genius of Michelangelo's fresco *The Last Judgment* in the Sistine Chapel, the simple yet profound casting of votes in democratic elections, Anne Sullivan's befriending and teaching of Helen Keller to help her overcome physical barriers—all of these excellent achievements underscore the fact that human beings are full of wonder. On the other hand, we are capable of horrific abuses of our many abilities so as to wreak havoc among ourselves. Brute strength turned against women and children to rape and molest, scientific and technological discoveries (mis)employed to produce weapons of mass destruction, Robert Mapplethorpe's artistic acumen (mis)used in exhibitions of degrading photographs, the Holocaust and other genocidal atrocities, rampant divorce—all of these tragic failures emphasize the fact that human beings are full of woe. Both dignity and depravity typify the human race, human institutions, human aspirations and achievements, human communities, and human beings individually.

Two Christian doctrines address this wonderful and woeful reality: the doctrine of humanity, or theological anthropology, and the doctrine of sin. In terms of the overall story of Scripture, these two doctrines correspond to its first two major themes: creation and fall (the other two are redemption and consummation). That is, God created the heavens and the earth in general and human beings in particular. Specifically, he created humans in his image, and the first man and the first woman were created in a state of integrity, enjoying face-to-face conversation with their Creator, the bounty of a fertile environment, and transparency as husband and wife in their relationship with one another. But they did not remain in this state of integrity; they fell headlong into sin. With this tragedy came the destruction of their relationship with God and alienation from him leading to death, the cursing of the earth and its subjection to futility, and the disruption of their marital relationship with the introduction of competition for control and harsh domination in response. Sin entered the human race and spread so as to wreak havoc with everything human beings touch; thus, it is "not the way it's supposed to be."[1]

This chapter focuses on the doctrines of humanity and sin, emphasizing both the dignity that is true of human beings as creatures made in the image of God and the depravity that is true of human beings as sinful, fallen creatures. Furthermore, and most importantly for our purposes, these two realities will be examined for their implications for Christian education. Indeed, what it means to be human and fallen is one of the most influential factors in developing an approach to education that is decisively Christian.

HUMANITY, DIGNITY, AND THE IMAGE OF GOD

The creation of humanity in the image of God is recorded in Gen 1:26–31. In the preceding narrative the heavens and the earth are created—including light and its separation from darkness; the expanse and the separation of the waters above from the waters below; the dry land and vegetation; the sun and

moon, with the separation of day and night; the creatures of the
sea and the birds of the sky; and cattle, creeping things, beasts
of the field, and other creatures on the earth—in anticipation
of and preparation for the apex of God's creative work: human
beings. This culminating act begins with divine deliberation,
as the triune God—Father, Son, and Holy Spirit—purposes to
create human beings in his image (v. 26). This plan is then actu-
alized as the first two human beings are created in the divine
image, one male and one female (v. 27). God's blessing follows
and with it the mandate to his first two human beings to "be
fruitful and multiply and fill the earth and subdue it and exercise
dominion" over everything else that had already been created (v.
28). The evaluative judgment—"And God saw that everything
he had made, and behold, it was very good" (v. 31)—is regis-
tered because the entire creation, with humanity as its crowning
effort, corresponds exactly and completely to the divine design
and purpose for it.

The first chapter of Genesis provides the "Goodyear blimp"
perspective on creation, and the second chapter gives the "tele-
photo lens" view on the formation of the first man and the first
woman. "God formed the man from the dust of the ground"
(Gen 2:7), and then he energized the physical being of the man
with a life force ("the breath of life") so that "the man became a
living being."[2] In what amounts to a shocking statement, God's
evaluative judgment of the isolated man so created is, "It is not
good for the man to be alone" (2:18). After promising to provide
a being that would be the corresponding fit and helper for the
man, God paraded the animals before the man for him to name
(2:19). This was not an unsuccessful attempt on the part of God
to find some creature that would be suitable for the man, but it
served to arouse in the man the realization that he had no corresponding mate (2:20). As promised, God provided the man with
his missing counterpart, which God did without the involvement or cooperation of the man whom God put to sleep (2:21).
Having fashioned the woman from the rib and skin of the man,

God presented her to him (2:22). The "man" (Hb. *ish*) named her "woman" (Hb. *ishshah*) as he joyfully acknowledged that she exactly corresponded to him (2:23). (Notice that the word for *man* is imbedded in the word for *woman* in both English and Hebrew.) Though this narrative does not speak about the institution of marriage *per se*, Moses interrupted the story with an editorial comment giving a general principle about marriage (2:24). The narrative concludes with a comment about the physical pleasure that the man and the woman derive from sexual intercourse in their marital relationship (2:25).

These two grand narratives of the origin of human beings created in the image of God are rich in terms of implications for the doctrine of humanity. First, human beings are created as dependent beings. The fact of the first man's creation out of the dust of the ground establishes that we are earthly, not divine or heavenly, beings. This means that our existence is contingent, not necessary. It could be the case that we do not exist. Our existence in this world is contingent on God's purpose and our parents producing us; remove either factor, and we do not now exist. As far as I can see, only two possible responses can be given to this created contingency: either rebel against it and attempt to live autonomously and independently of God; or accept it and live in humble submission to and dependence on God.

Second, human beings are created as holistic people. Though we may distinguish between our material aspect (body) and our immaterial aspect (soul or spirit), the two cannot be separated— at least not in this life. Tragically, the church has been overly influenced in this regard by Platonic philosophy, which affirms that immaterial reality is inherently good while material reality is inherently evil. This philosophy infiltrated the church and results in some Christians considering the body and its physical appetites to be a hindrance to spiritual maturity and the root of human sinfulness. This viewpoint further results in the church's emphasis on spiritual matters—Christians "save souls" and exercise "spiritual disciplines"—to the great neglect of physical needs. But the human body is included in God's redemptive work. Indeed, "the Lord is for the body" (1 Cor 6:13) in that his complete work of salvation includes bodily resurrection. Moreover, "the body is for the Lord" (1 Cor 6:13) means that Christians are to "glorify God in their body" (1 Cor 6:20) by yielding it to God for his purposes (Rom 6:12–14), worshipping him (Rom 12:1–2), avoiding sexual immorality (1 Cor 6:18; 1 Thess 4:3–8), and being holistically sanctified (1 Thess 5:23). Furthermore, being holy in body means that Christians should engage in physical discipline (1 Tim 4:8; 1 Cor 9:24–27). Because human beings are created holistically, ministry to people in their entirety—intellect, emotions, will, body, motivations, purposes, relationships—is incumbent upon the church.

Third, human beings are "fearfully and wonderfully made" (Ps 139:13–16). Though we have focused on the creation of the first man and the first woman, God's creative work did not stop with our original parents; it is expressed through his personal and intimate designing of each and every individual human being since the original creation. The proper response as we contemplate ourselves—a body-soul unity—is to be full of wonder and worship our Creator God. This means that we should never attempt to minimize the abilities and accomplishments of human beings in some desperate and misguided attempt to protect the honor and glory of God. Whatever any individual human being is and does that is good, and whatever the collective human race is and does that is good—all of these are the result of creation in the divine image and the common grace of God to his human creatures. And all of this is worthy of applause and thanksgiving—to both creature and Creator.

Fourth, every human being is created as one of two genders, male or female. God created human beings in his image as male and female. The first human being created was male; the second, female. God did not originate the human race as an androgynous creature that later differentiated into men and women, as Greek mythology taught. Neither did God change humans into

males and females as an afterthought. A person's gender, therefore, is a fundamental characteristic of life. It is not a secondary
characteristic, like blond or black hair, blue or green eyes. This
means that we enjoy a relationship with God as either male or
female, we relate to others either as a male or a female, and we
know and relate to ourselves as either a male or a female. Thus,
our existence is determined by our gender. Try as I might with
all the encouragement of my wife, I can never see and experience life from her (female) perspective. But, as with all matters
regarding our existence, one's maleness or femaleness is not a
mistake; it is divinely designed as part of God's plan for each
individual person (Ps 139:13–16).

I have so far skirted around an important question: What
is the image of God? What does it mean for human beings to
be created in the divine image? Throughout the church's history, numerous answers to this inquiry have been supplied:
the image of God is human rationality, or human freedom and
moral responsibility, or humanity's spiritual capacity for a relationship with God, or humanity's exercise of dominion. For
discussion's sake these various options can be categorized as
four main proposals: (1) The image of God is *substantival*. It
is something that a human being *is*, some attribute or characteristic. If the image distinguishes human beings from all other
created beings, then identification of the image involves comparing human beings with these other creatures so as to discern
what makes them different. Leading contenders for this human
differential include reason and free will. (2) The image of God
is *functional*. It is something that a human being *does*, some
activity or role. The activity is often understood as dominion
because of the close proximity between creation in the divine
image and the divine intention and mandate for human beings
to exercise dominion over the rest of the created order. (3) The
image of God is *relational*. It consists of the human being's
relationship with God and with other human beings. It is in the
plurality of gender—male and female—and in the relationship

between men and women that human beings reflect the plurality
of persons—Father, Son, and Holy Spirit—and their trinitarian
relationship with one another. As the Triune God exists as persons in relationship, so the image of God consists in the relationships between men and women and, ultimately, between human
beings and God himself. (4) The image of God is *teleological*. It
consists in human destiny, the *goal* or purpose for which human
beings are created. Jesus Christ is the perfect image of God to
whose image Christ followers will one day be fully conformed
(Rom 8:29–30). This transformation into the divine image is
an ongoing process through the Holy Spirit (2 Cor 3:18) and
the renewal of human nature (Col 3:9–10; Eph 4:22–24), so the
image is both a future blessing and reality—the goal of God's
good work in Christ followers.

The problem is that all of these ideas tend to reduce the
image of God to one particular part or aspect of our humanness;
thus, they miss a key point: we human beings are not made in a
piecemeal way and put together, like the many pieces of a jig-
saw puzzle, to become what we are. Rather, in our humanness,
we are constructed holistically with a wholeness and complete-
ness that does not allow us to be divided into this part and that
part. We as human beings in our entirety—not a part of us, not
one particular ability or function or relation—are created in the
image of God. So Adam, the holistic first human being, was the
image of God. Similarly, as the holistic second human being,
Eve was the image of God. Moreover, you are the image of
God. I am the image of God.

More specifically, *God created us in his image so that we,
like a mirror, would reflect him in the world in which we live.*
This reality provides us with the answer to most important
questions about life that could ever be asked: "Why do I exist?"
"Does human existence have meaning?" "What is the purpose
for my life?" We exist to reflect God in the world in which we
live. Human existence has meaning because we are created with
dignity and significance as the image bearers of God. Our pur-

pose is to imitate him. As we do, we give others a glimpse of
what God himself is like. This is most clearly and convincingly
accomplished as we live relationally, building a community of
men and women characterized by dynamic, loving relationships, and as we further the interests of God and his kingdom in
the world in which we live.[3]

If this is what it means to be created in the image of God, can
anything more be said about the constitution of human nature?
In the past, discussion has focused on two positions: trichotomy
and dichotomy.[4] According to the first, human nature is composed of three elements: the material body, the immaterial soul
(generally thought to consist of intellect, emotions, and will),
and the immaterial spirit (generally thought of as the capacity
for a spiritual relationship with God). According to the second
position, human nature is composed of two elements: the material body and the immaterial soul or spirit, the latter two terms
being interchangeable.

Both positions, philosophically speaking, are dualist in nature
and are opposed to monism. Both trichotomy and dichotomy pro-
pose a material aspect and (at least one) immaterial aspect for the
constitution of human nature. All monistic views reduce human
nature to one aspect—either (in the vast majority of cases) to the
material aspect or (much more rarely) to the immaterial aspect.
Monism denies that human nature is complex and composed
of multiple elements, insisting instead that it is indivisible and
simple. In the latest manifestation of materialistic monism, the
physicalist position claims that human consciousness, thought,
memory, decision making, self-awareness, moral conviction,
learning, motivation, intention, purposing, action, even religious
conviction can be explained in terms of neurological processes
operating in the brain and central nervous system in addition to
the chemical reactions initiated and sustained by such processes.[5]
This view is often (and correctly) associated with the loss of
human meaning, purpose, freedom, and responsibility. Of course,
a further implication of the physicalist position is that once one's

physical organism ceases its functioning, one does not (and cannot) exist as a person. Death is the end of human existence.

This position flies in the face of both Scripture and Christian theology. Jesus himself insisted that human beings consist of both body and soul (Matt 10:28). According to Scripture, human existence continues after death, either in the comforting and joyful presence of Jesus Christ ("the spirits of the righteous made perfect"; Heb 12:23) or in the misery of torment and punishment (Luke 16:19–31). Christian theology has always affirmed the intermediate state, the period of existence between a person's death and bodily resurrection at the return of Jesus Christ. This existence is a disembodied one: the believer's soul lives in Christ's presence without the body which has been sloughed off and laid in a grave. The apostle Paul describes this as being "naked," "unclothed," and "away from the body" (2 Cor 5:3–4,8; see Phil 1:22–24). He looks almost with horror at this possibility for himself,[6] indicating that the intermediate state is an abnormal condition. This means that our normal condition is to be embodied people and, except for the intermediate state, we will always exist as embodied people. Specifically, our current earthly existence is an embodied one (now with perishable, dishonorable, weak, dying bodies), and our future existence with the Lord in the new heavens and new earth will be an embodied one (then with imperishable, glorious, strong, Spirit-dominated, resurrected, glorified bodies; see 1 Cor 15:42–49). Even though we will be in the presence of Jesus Christ in heaven during the intermediate state, because our existence will be a disembodied one, it is not our ultimate hope. We will long for the completion of our salvation at the second coming of Christ, when we will once again possess physical existence in our resurrection bodies.

In summary, both Scripture and the Christian doctrine of the intermediate state demand some type of dualism and categorically rule out monism or physicalism.[7] The constitution of human nature is both material and immaterial.

HUMANITY, DEPRAVITY, AND
THE FALL INTO SIN

Human beings were created at the apex of creation week as the image bearers of God, and they are fearfully and wonderfully made, but regretfully this is only part of the Christian story. These same human beings are also frightfully and tragically fallen creatures, having tumbled into the depths of depravity so as to be guilty before God and tainted, corrupted, spoiled, sin-stained image bearers.

The origin of this reality is recorded in Genesis 3. Present in the original creation was a singularly magnificent creature, the serpent. Choosing "from among the animals that which he saw would be most suitable for him . . . Satan perverted to his own deceitful purposes the gift that had been divinely imparted to the serpent."[8] Thus, through the agency of the serpent, Satan crafted an atmosphere of deceit and trickery, laying a trap for the first woman to fall into. Part of the deception was to raise doubt about whether God had actually said what the woman thought he said concerning the prohibition against eating—was it "of any tree in the garden?" By this question Satan cast suspicion on God, bringing doubt on the veracity of his word while perverting it at the same time (Gen 3:2). The woman corrected the serpent's twisted rendition of the prohibition, underscoring that God threatened disobedience with certain death (3:3). The serpent counterattacked, asserting the complete opposite— "You will not surely die!" (3:4)—which amounted to calling God a liar. The serpent heightened the temptation by assuring the woman that eating the prohibited fruit would enable her to become just like God, which would be a good thing. It was so good, in fact, that it should lead the woman to question the goodness of God in withholding such a treasure from her (3:5).

With her gaze firmly fixed on the forbidden tree, she saw it as good for food and beautiful to look at but also as desirous as a supply of wisdom for divine-like knowledge of good and evil (3:6; see 2:9). The satanically induced and stimulated atmosphere of trickery was intense at this point, and the woman caved in to the deception. She took of the fruit of the prohibited tree and ate it in willful disobedience to the command of God. She elevated herself and her desire as the authority above God and his will. As the apostle Paul would later comment, "The woman was deceived and became a transgressor" (1 Tim 2:14). In a frightful perversion of the created order, "she also gave some to her husband who was with her, and he ate" (Gen 3:7; see v. 17). Though the woman had been terribly deceived by Satan, the man was not fooled (1 Tim 2:14); he knowingly and deliberately chose to disobey the command. Together, the man and the woman experienced the promise of the prohibited tree: "The eyes of both were opened." But they got far more than they bargained for: "They knew that they were naked," yet such knowledge was too much for them to handle properly. Their knowledge was now accompanied by a sense of shame, so they engaged in a futile attempt to cover their nakedness (3:7).

Other consequences followed hard on their disobedience: hiding from the presence of God (3:8), self-indictment in the matter of guilt (3:9–11), and shifting of responsibility from self to another (3:12–13). So God pronounced his furious judgment: humiliation and abasement of the serpent and the ultimate defeat of Satan (3:14–15); painfulness in childbearing and attempted usurpation of rightful male authority by the wife, and harsh domination of the wife by her husband (3:16); a curse on the earth in terms of unfruitfulness, a sentence to hard labor, and physical death for all human beings (3:17–19).

In a startling commentary on the Genesis 3 account of the fall and the last mentioned consequence, Paul described the deadly contagion that spreads from that sin to all human beings (Rom 5:12–19): "Just as sin came into the world through one man, and death through sin, and so death spread to all men because all sinned" (v. 12). Clearly Paul placed the blame on the first man and his first sin for the sin-death connection that prevails among all human beings. Some type of solidarity exists between Adam and his sin-death reality and human beings and their sin-death reality. The last phrase, "because all sinned," is crucial for understanding this. To avoid misunderstanding, Paul specified that he was not referring to the actual sins of people being the cause of their death. As an illustration, he turned to the period between Adam and Moses, who was responsible for the giving of the law (vv. 13–14). During this period, even though people were sinning, their sin was not counted against them; this was so because there was no law for them to transgress. They did not sin—indeed, they could not sin—as Adam had sinned, who transgressed the divine law and sinned by eating the fruit. So if these particular people were not held accountable and were not found guilty before God because of their personal sin (their personal transgressions of the divine law), why did all of them die? Why was the penalty for sin still assessed though no accountability for sin was in effect?

Paul responded by offering a loose parallel between Adam and Christ (vv. 15–19). On the one hand, death and judgment came through the one sin/transgression/disobedience of the one man Adam, leading to condemnation for all people; they are made sinners by his act. On the other hand, the free gift of God's grace came through the one act of righteousness/obedience of the one man Jesus Christ, leading to justification and eternal life for all people who receive that gracious gift; they are made righteous. Thus Paul established this connection:

- The reason that all people die is "because all sinned" (v. 12).
- The reason that all people die is the one sin of the one man Adam (vv. 15–19).

The solidarity between Adam and the human race is such that his sin-death connection is imputed to all human beings. Because of his sin, together with the concomitant penalty of death, all human beings are guilty of Adam's sin, made sinners, die physically, and are judged and condemned by God.

Historically, this is referred to as *original sin*. From birth all human beings are reckoned guilty before God and are corrupted by sin. The first aspect of original sin—*original guilt*—has reference to the legal status of human beings in relationship to God and his law: we are guilty and thus liable to suffer punishment. The second aspect of original sin—*original corruption*—has reference to sin's effect on human beings: we have a sinful nature. This corruption is so extensive that it infects every element of human nature—intellect, emotions, will, body, motivations, purposes, conscience—resulting in total (or pervasive) depravity. Moreover, this corruption is so intensive that it renders human beings totally unable to do anything that will ultimately please God and totally incapable of changing themselves so as to take steps toward a relationship with God. Calvinists affirm both original guilt and original corruption being traced back to Adam's transgression while Arminians affirm that original corruption was from Adam but claim that the guilt of sin is received when individuals themselves sin.[9]

Furthermore, because of the corrupting influence of the sinful nature, eventually all human beings commit actual acts of sin. Sin is not only an evil action, however. Nor can the idea of sin be limited to evil thoughts. As just noted, sin may also refer to human nature. Accordingly, sin can be defined as any lack of conformity—in act, thought, word, feeling, intention, and nature—to the character and moral law of God.[10] Such sin is described biblically as missing the mark, transgressing a law, disobedience, rebellion, unfaithfulness, abomination, lawlessness, hard-heartedness, idolatry, injustice, doing wrong, stiff-necked stubbornness, perversion, wickedness, deviation from the way, and so on. Common and helpful approaches to classifying actual sins include distinguishing between sins of presumption (defiant sins, or sins with a high hand) and sins of ignorance (see Num 15:27–31; Lev 5:17–18); sins of commission and sins of omission; sins that can be forgiven and the unpardonable sin (Matt 12:30–32); sins for which prayer should be offered and the sin leading to death (1 John 5:16–17); and less serious sins and more serious/cardinal/capital sins, which may include the seven "deadly" sins of pride, envy, lust, gluttony, anger, sloth, and greed.[11]

Tying together discussions of both humanity's dignity and depravity, we may trace the image of God and the disastrous effects of sin on God's image bearers through the grand story line of Scripture.[12] With the prefall state we may speak of the *original* image of God. Adam and Eve were holistically created by God and were image bearers of God in a state of integrity. This was not a perfect state because though it was possible for the first man and first woman as people of integrity not to sin, it was also possible for them to sin. The latter possibility is what actually happened (as recounted above); thus, the postfall state initiated the *perverted* image of God. Since that time all human beings are born with original sin, involving both guilt and corruption. As fallen image bearers, all human beings are enslaved to sin—unable not to sin. This frightful parody of the original image is defaced, deformed, perverted, yet not annihilated completely. And unless God intervenes in this desperate situation, sinful human beings are destined for physical death, divine judgment, wrathful condemnation, and eternal separation from God.

Through God's work of salvation in the history of his people Israel and especially through his Son, this hellish nightmare is overcome; the *redeemed* or *renewed* image of God becomes the new identity. God intervenes in the life of fallen, sinful human beings with his multifaceted work of salvation. Included in this mighty work is justification, by which the guilty verdict assessed to all human beings is overturned. God declares the one who has faith in Jesus Christ "not guilty!" but righteous instead. Moreover, the Holy Spirit causes the new birth; and with a regenerated, new nature and the work of the Spirit of God and the Word of God in sanctification, the broken image of God is progressively restored. Though never completed during this earthly life, this renewal touches and influences all areas of human nature. Finally, when Jesus Christ returns, we look forward to the *perfected* image of God. Then, Christ followers will be fully conformed to the image of Christ. Every aspect of their nature—intellect, emotions, will, body, motivations, purposes, conscience—will be fully restored to (or, better, beyond) the original divine design. As image bearers now redeemed and perfected by the grace of God, they will flourish beyond what was possible for Adam and Eve. Not only will they be able not to sin; they will not be able to sin. And they will live eternally with God in the new heavens and new earth, which will bear a striking resemblance to the garden of Eden, from which they were once expelled as a result of sin. Thus, the divine image bearers will come full circle with the curse of sin reversed and the image of God shining brightly, strongly, and unwaveringly forever.

IMPLICATIONS OF THE DOCTRINES OF HUMANITY AND SIN FOR CHRISTIAN EDUCATION

Education for Human Finitude

The first implication of the doctrines of humanity and sin for Christian education is that human beings are created as finite beings. This explains the need for education in general, for if human beings were infinite like God, they would have no need to learn anything. Being finite, however, human beings are limited in what they know and pursue education to further their knowledge. This also explains the particular need for Christian education for Christ followers. Salvation through Christ does not result in a sudden increase in knowledge, much less infinite knowledge; rather, Christ followers dedicate themselves to the pursuit of the knowledge of God and his will through the study of Scripture. Indeed, renewal of the mind, which is enjoined on all Christians (Rom 12:1–2; Eph 4:22–24), comes through this pursuit, and progressive renewal in the image of God comes by means of knowledge (Col 3:9–10). Part of this pursuit and transformation is aided by Christian education. Education that is worthy of the qualifier *Christian* must seek to inculcate sound biblical and theological truth in its students. Moreover, as a corporate reality, the church seeks "a spirit of wisdom and of revelation in the knowledge of God" (Eph 1:17). So it is appropriate that Jesus Christ continues to give the church pastor-teachers (Eph 4:11), elders who are able to teach (1 Tim 3:2; Titus 1:9), and other teachers (1 Cor 12:28) so that the church may "attain to the unity of the faith and of the knowledge of the Son of God, to mature manhood, to the measure of the stature of the fullness of Christ" (Eph 4:13). In this corporate sense, then, "Christian education" takes place through sermons, Sunday school lessons, small-group teaching, counseling, personal mentoring, and any other venue in which the communication of Scripture takes place.

Holistic Education for Holistic Beings

Second, human beings are created as holistic beings, and this creaturely reality has important implications for education. We are not mere "heads" to unlatch, open up, and pour content into; imparting knowledge is not enough. The apostle Paul explained that "knowledge of the truth" through education never stands alone; it must always be "in accordance with godliness" (Titus 1:1). Such godliness involves the appropriation, development, and expression of sanctified thoughts, emotions, decisions, actions, motivations, and purposes. Yet this is not moralism, legalism, or behaviorism, for all of these reductionistic strategies fall short of producing authentic Christian godliness. Rather, Christlikeness is appropriated, developed, and expressed as divine image bearers are transformed through the power of the Word of God, the filling of the Spirit, life together in community, dying to the sinful nature, the imitation of Christ, thankfulness, rejoicing in suffering, fleeing from temptation, obedience and faithfulness, and a foundational orientation to a Christian worldview. Christian educators seek to initiate and stimulate such genuine godliness through means that go beyond the communication of knowledge alone; these include modeling Christlikeness, developing personal relationships with students, "walking the walk" themselves, exhibiting an appropriate transparency about life's ebb and flow, and so forth.

Education in Human Relationship

Third, from a holistic dualism perspective, human beings are created holistically as complex beings; that is, human nature is composed of both material and immaterial aspects. This does not contradict the above affirmation of the holistic nature of human beings; rather, it nuances it and functions to stave off any unwanted moves toward a Platonic dualism with its strong emphasis on the dichotomy between material and immaterial aspects of human nature. Though human beings cannot be compartmentalized into intellectual, emotional, volitional, and physical components (as is commonly done), and though the holistic nature of human creatureliness calls for educating people in their entirety, the complex composition of human beings still demands attention to both material and immaterial realities. For example, human embodiment must be treated seriously in the educational process. This may be as simple as providing more physical space in classrooms for younger children—and a Disney-like Sunday school wing of the church may make for an even better educational environment for them! As long as it promotes creativity, legitimate self-expression, and a sense of ownership rather than adolescent self-indulgence, educating high school students in rooms or buildings that they have painted, furnished, and in other ways "decorated" may contribute to the process. Even for adults, certain spatial situations—such as a physical environment that is aesthetically pleasing and arranged so as to facilitate adult-level and adult-style learning—may enhance their learning experiences; in many cases, a lecture hall is the least suitable for this.

Human relationships must also be treated seriously in the educational process. For young children this may entail teaching them how to share, take turns, and respect one another and their adult teachers. Among middle school and high school students, attention should be paid to the exciting yet angst-producing discovery of the opposite gender. In a secular educational context, instruction in this regard takes on a very different form from that in churches. In one sense Christian education should supplement the instruction in male-female relationships, dating, and romance as supplied by Christian parents. Yet among students who do not have this home environment, Christian education may need to supply most or all of the instruction as a counterpoint to what they receive from other sources. As for adults, working to overcome the "dog eat dog" competitive syndrome so typical of secular worldviews is incumbent on Christian education. Ongoing, long-term relationships of mentoring, accountability, modeling, and ministering together should be encouraged and facilitated by Christian educators.

Education for Awe of God

Fourth, human beings are fearfully and wonderfully created, and Christian education that factors in this reality approaches its task with a deep sense of wonder and gratitude. Christian educators count it a privilege and an honor to be "God's fellow workers" (1 Cor 3:9) in helping to shape people with remarkable physical, intellectual, creative, social, and relational abilities so as to further their transformation into the image of Christ. Encouraging Christ followers to reorient the use of their God-given gifts from selfish ends to God-honoring ones—promoting the cause of Christ and furthering the kingdom of God—is the high calling of Christian education.

Education for God's Purpose

Fifth, human beings are created purposefully as the divine image bearers: *God created us in his image so that we, like a*

mirror, would reflect him in the world in which we live. This
has important implications for Christian education in terms of
both its strategy or approach and its teleological orientation
(thus, both its means and ends). In one sense Christian education
begins with the end in mind; its opening question is "For what
is education designed?" Its goal is the total transformation of
divine image bearers so they are fully conformed to the image of
Christ (Rom 8:29). With this end firmly established, the means
are then constructed and a plan for transforming lives is devised.
Clearly, this strategy must be in keeping with the Word of God
and undergirded by the Spirit of God. Christian educators should
not imagine that inclusion of approaches that are not biblically
sanctioned (explicitly or implicitly) and Spirit empowered will
be "fruitful"—at least in terms of fruitfulness that is genuine
and lasting (John 15:16). Christian educators can be helped in
this by the wisdom of God, both as it is extended to them in the
work and as it serves as an example for them. God's wisdom
means that he always chooses the best goals and the best means
to accomplish those goals. Wisdom is far more than mere effi-
ciency, however. The wise God values the highest good in terms
of what will bring him the greatest glory and what is of greatest
benefit to his image-bearers. So in his infinite wisdom, God con-
structs his purpose in keeping with his highest values for his own
glory and our greatest good, and the steps he chooses to accomplish his plan are certain to be the very best ways.[13] As applied
to Christian education, this wisdom pattern affirms that matters
of highest value—the glory of God, total transformation into the
image of Christ—constitute its goals, and carefully selected and
developed strategies or approaches constitute its means.

This may sound easy, but those who work in Christian education know that such is not the case. The main reason for the
difficulties that come with the task is the second doctrine treated
in this chapter: human depravity because of sin. Not only does
human finitude dictate the need for education; human sinfulness demands it and tragically taints it as well. Possession of the

knowledge of good and evil did not work out as the first man and first woman envisioned it would, and the human race has been confused by it ever since those first fateful eye-opening bites. Christian education thus wrestles with a host of difficulties due to human fallenness.

Spiritual warfare is one such difficulty. This may manifest itself in Christian educators having to overcome entrenched sinful situations, false teachings that Paul called "teachings of demons" (1 Tim 4:1), and persistently sinning people whose conflicts are often battles "against the rulers, against the authorities, against the cosmic powers over this present darkness, against the spiritual forces of evil in the heavenly places" (Eph 6:12). Resistance to transformation, both personal and corporate, is a second difficulty that flows from human sinfulness and presents substantial problems for Christian education. Individuals fail to take advantage of educational opportunities in their churches; even when they do, they refuse to engage actively in preparation for class and/or participation in it. Similarly, churches themselves become comfortable with the status quo in their programming, worship, ministry, and the like. Sunday school classes that have existed for years or even decades become sacred cows that, even years past their vital contribution to the church, stubbornly refuse to change rooms, curriculum, organization, purpose, or goals. A third difficulty created and nourished by human corruption is lack of engagement in Christian educational ministries as teachers, facilitators, mentors, and leaders. How often does the scenario repeat itself, that one week before VBS or the start of the new Sunday school year, the church is still desperately searching for volunteer Bible story readers and fifth-grade teachers? C. Plantinga creatively called this the sin of "going limp":

> Making a career of Nothing—wandering through malls, killing time, making small talk, watching television programs until we know their characters better than our own children—robs the community of our

gifts and energies and shapes life into a yawn at the God and savior of the world. The person who will not bestir herself, the person who hands herself over to Nothing, in effect says to God: you have made nothing of interest and redeemed no one of consequence, including me.[14]

Even darker, more sinister, problems are created for Christian education by sin. An increasingly common practice in churches is requiring parents to register their children when they are dropped off for Sunday school; the parents are then given an identification badge that associates them with their own kids. This security measure hopes to prevent some stranger from entering into the educational area, claiming some innocent victim as her own, and kidnapping a child. Church safety procedures dictate that, instead of one person, two responsible people must accompany a child into the bathroom. This security step hopes to prevent a physically abusive person from being alone with and molesting a child. Someone on the youth staff is designated to be responsible for shadowing the juvenile delinquent—out on parole and excited about attending the youth group to know more about the Jesus he met while in prison—everywhere he goes. This safety measure hopes to minimize as much as possible any potential incident involving this youth and the other members of this community of grace and forgiveness. Likewise, prudence demands that a former pedophile, amazingly and thoroughly saved by the cross of Christ, is not assigned to be on a team engaging in ministry with children.[15]

The pervasive depravity with which human beings are beset also has implications for Christian education. Specifically, the transformation targeted as its goal must reach into each and every area of its human recipients' lives—with the knowledge that corruption and (as a corollary) resistance to transformation will be found at every juncture. Sin in the mind must be overcome; but so must sin in the emotions, sin in the will, sin in the body, and sin elsewhere.[16] When people transition from an educational opportunity into "real life" with only good intentions to change—and who does not have such good intentions?—the task is unfinished. Christian education must help to develop a character of discipline that moves beyond good intentions after Sunday school and Bible classes to actual life change. Portable truth is required, even demanded. And this truth is not just about what constitutes right belief (*orthodoxy*); it includes concrete practice (*orthopraxy*) as well as proper feelings (*orthopatheia*). Indeed, Christian education cannot rest content with success in one or a few areas of life transformation. As Newman underscored, "Integrity on one side of our character is no voucher for integrity on the other side."[17] Appealing to a familiar metaphor for sin, Plantinga noted that "sin is a plague that spreads by contagion or even by quasi-genetic reproduction. . . . People rarely commit single sins."[18] Victory over sin—any sin, even in only one area of entrenched corruption—is to be applauded; but the ultimate goal of Christian education is the making of full-fledged disciples of Christ, whose entire existence has been radically transformed into full conformity with the image of Christ.

Education within Human Development

Sixth, God created us as developmental beings. While we are wholly human from conception, we are not wholly formed adults for many years. We grow up! We grow and mature through a process of human development. However, the Scriptures are not a developmental psychology text. They simply reflect the observable growth of individuals and report on them phenomenologically. "And the boy Samuel continued to grow in stature and in favor with the Lord and with men" (1 Sam 2:26). Similarly, "And the child [Jesus] grew and became strong; he was filled with wisdom, and the grace of God was upon him. . . . And Jesus grew in wisdom and stature, and in favor with God and men" (Luke 2:40,52). Such passages at least offer observations on the growth process in human beings, including the physical, cognitive, social, and spiritual dimensions. Similarly, these changes occur from childhood to adulthood: "When I was a child, I talked like a child, I thought like a child, I reasoned like a child. When I became a man, I put childish ways behind me" (1 Cor 13:11).

Social scientists such as Jean Piaget, Lev Vygotsky, Erik Erickson, Lawrence Kohlberg, and James Fowler have formed developmental theories based on their observations of humans; each provided insights into the developmental processes. As Christian educators we affirm that part of God's image in humanity is this developmental pattern that moves us from infancy to childhood toward adulthood. We must recognize and respect the difference between how a five-year-old learns and how a 15-year-old learns, and teach responsibly—not simply for effectiveness in the classroom but out of respect for each divine-image bearer. Christian educators must also acknowledge that development has it limits. Human development cannot overcome sin, nor can mere cognitive development or any other developmental process in humanity restore a right relationship with God through Christ. Christian educators must become familiar with such theories to aid them in effective instruction, but they must not allow these theories to supplant the value of humans as more than the sum of their developmental parts since they are made in the image of God.

Lifelong Learning for Spiritual Formation

Finally, Christian education understands from the doctrine of sin and depravity that it faces a formidable, cunning, and persistent foe. The educational enterprise, therefore, is never complete in this lifetime. Moreover, it may never rest or let down its guard; no halfhearted or stunted effort is allowed. Furthermore, because sin is so entrenched in human lives, human relationships, human institutions, and even human churches, Christian education must offer all available means consistent with the Word of God for help in overcoming sin. A partial or selective effort, one that knowingly refuses to endorse or provide a

legitimate means of whole-life transformation, cannot be coun-
tenanced. Only a full-orbed and full-power attack against sin
will do. Thankfully, this monumental task is not left to human
ingenuity, planning, and resources (as important as these are).
Christian education echoes and agrees with "the word of the
Lord to Zerubbabel: Not by might, nor by power, but by my
Spirit, says the Lord of hosts" (Zech 4:6).

REFLECTION QUESTIONS

1. How does your education ministry foster the formation of relationships in the church? If it does not, what
   changes need to be made so that it will?

2. How well does your church's education ministry
   promote the idea of humanity's uniqueness and special
   place in creation?

3. Given the discussion on human depravity, what might
   education be like if one were to affirm human goodness
   or innocence?

4. Where in your congregation's programs do you prepare
   Christians to do spiritual warfare? How?

---

1   From the book title: C. Plantinga Jr., *Not the Way It's Supposed to Be: A
    Breviary of Sin* (Grand Rapids: Eerdmans, 1995).

2   Though Christian interpreters of Scripture have traditionally understood
    "the breath of life" to refer to the spirit (Hb. *ruah*) or some immaterial
    aspect of human beings, while others understand the last phrase "and the
    man became a living soul" (Hb. *nephesh*) to refer to the soul as another
    element of the immaterial aspect, neither is my position. First, "the breath
    of life" is a property that is shared by all living creatures (Gen 1:30),
    and it is that energizing principle that is given at birth and withdrawn at
    death (Gen 7:22; Eccl 12:7). Second, the last phrase says that "the man
    became a living being" and does not indicate that a soul was added to his
    immaterial aspect. If a complaint is registered that this demeans man's
    existence by relegating him to the same level as all other living creatures,
    it should be noted that the text specifies that God himself breathed this
    breath of life into the man's nostrils, something that is not said of any of
    the other creatures. This personal impartation of the energizing principle
    to the man distinguishes and elevates him above all other creatures.

3   Some of the above has been adapted from G. Allison, *Getting Deep: Understand What You Believe about God and Why* (Nashville: B&H, 2001), 38–43.

4   The root word is the Greek *temno* ("to cut") with either *tricha* (three-fold) or *dicha* (twofold); thus the term literally means "cut threefold" or "cut twofold." The former position is supported by appeal to 1 Thess 5:23; Heb 4:12; and 1 Cor 15:44. The latter position is supported by appeal to Gen 2:7; Eccl 12:7; Matt 10:28; 1 Cor 5:3,5; and the inter-changeability of the terms "soul" and "spirit" in Luke 1:46–47; John 12:27; and 13:21.

5   This position is fueled by the discoveries of neuroscience, which has added new data from functional MRIs and PET scans to the consideration of how human beings function. Thus, neurophysiology has moved into the realm of metaphysics, reducing human nature to the physical organism only.

6   In 2 Cor 5:2,4, Paul wrote of groaning, "Longing to put on our heavenly dwelling. . . . being burdened—not that we would be unclothed."

7   It is with great consternation and deep concern that we watch some so-called Evangelicals jettison the historic doctrine of the intermediate state in favor of some type of monism, whether it is N. Murphy and her nonreductive physicalism, K. Corcoran and his constitution view, J. Green, or others. W. Hasker's emergentism or emergent personalism stands against this trend, as does J. Cooper in his splendid biblical and philosophical treatment of this issue in *Body, Soul, and Life Everlasting: Biblical Anthropology and the Monism-Dualism Debate* (Grand Rapids: Eerdmans, 1989).

8   J. Calvin, *Commentary on the Book of Genesis* (Grand Rapids: Baker, 1989), 140. The identity of the one behind the serpent's deceptive activity is not revealed in the Genesis narrative, but later revelation establishes that it is "the devil and Satan, the deceiver of the whole world" (Rev 12:9; 20:2). This Satan was "a murderer" and "has been sinning from the beginning" (John 8:44; 1 John 3:8), that is, from the beginning of the biblical accounts of the creation of human beings and their existence on earth. A good case can be made that Isa 14:12–17 alludes to the fall of Satan. Though the text is directed as a taunt against the king of Babylon (14:3–11), the heightened language of vv. 12–17 seems to point beyond this fallen historical figure to another fallen being. If this is so, then the fall of Satan is attributed to his pride and rebellion; he was not satis-fied with his finite, limited, creaturely role, so he overreached the bounds assigned to him (see Jude 6) in a futile attempt to ascend to heaven and make himself like God. Apparently, this Satanic rebellion involved one third of the angelic realm (Rev 12:4). The punishment of Satan and his minions was banishment from heaven; indeed, they were cast down to earth as part of the retributive judgment of God against them (Rev 12:9). They are bound in some limited manner until the day God will mete out his ultimate judgment on them (Jude 6; 2 Pet 2:4) when they will be "thrown into the lake of fire and sulfur" and "will be tormented day and night forever and ever" (Rev 20:10).

9   Pelagius would have rejected both original guilt and original corruption, affirming human innocence and perfectability.

10 This should remind us that the moral law of God is not some external standard outside of God to which he himself is beholden. It should also serve to dispel the notion that the moral law is arbitrary; that is, that because of the absolute freedom of the divine will, God could just as easily have properly required murder, adultery, stealing, and lying as he did in prohibiting those activities. Rather, the moral law of God is an expression of his holy, righteous, and just character. Thus, as the life-supplying, covenant-keeping, need-providing, and truth-telling God, he prohibits the above-mentioned activities because they violate his own character, and he enjoins protection of life, faithfulness in marriage, hard work to earn a living, and speaking the truth because these activities reflect his very nature.

11 The Roman Catholic distinction between mortal and venial sins derives from some of the above considerations but is then extended too far and in an unbiblical direction. For example, the sacrament of penance or reconciliation is prescribed as the necessary solution for mortal sin, and temporal suffering in purgatory accrues from venial sins that leave their stain on one's soul, necessitating both purgation and the rendering of satisfaction before that soul may enter heaven.

12 Thanks to A. Hoekema's book, *Created in God's Image* (Grand Rapids: Eerdmans, 1986), for the springboard of this discussion.

13 Some of the above has been adapted from G. Allison, *Getting Deep: Understand What You Believe about God and Why*, 49–51.

14 Plantinga, *Not the Way It's Supposed to Be*, 188.

15 I have always made a point to bet on grace; it *can* ultimately win and conquer all. At the same time, however, I insist (like Jesus) that we be "wise as serpents and innocent as doves" (Matt 10:16).

16 The compartmental nature of this discussion is literary only. I am not implying that human nature in its holistic reality is so compartmentalized.

17 J. H. Newman, "Secret Faults," in *Sermons and Discourses, 1825–39*, ed. C. F. Harrold (New York: Longmans, Green, 1949), 5; cited in Plantinga, *Not the Way It's Supposed to Be*, 47.

18 Plantinga, *Not the Way It's Supposed to Be*, 53–54.

CHAPTER 9

Salvation and
Christian Education

Gregg R. Allison

T he drama of salvation is an all-encompassing phenomenon. It involves God's gracious and powerful work
to rescue his created yet fallen people from sin and its
penalty through the person and work of Jesus Christ, and the
human response to this divine initiative. The first dramatic act
occurred in eternity past, before any human person—or anything
else, for that matter—was created. Although already enacted in
part, the last dramatic act for the completion of salvation awaits
future divine intervention, including the return of Jesus Christ
and the remaking of all of creation for a new eternity future. In
between these opening and closing acts, the drama of salvation
includes a summons to forsake one's old reality and embrace
a new one through the *calling of God*; a replacement of deadness with new spiritual life through *regeneration by the Holy
Spirit*; a human response to the gospel that entails turning from
sin and exercising faith in Jesus Christ in *conversion*; a divine
declaration that one is no longer guilty before God but righteous
instead by means of *justification*; a new family identity with
brothers and sisters in Christ through *adoption*; an identification
with his death and resurrection by *union with Christ* and place-
ment into his body, the church, through *baptism with the Holy
Spirit*; a forward progress in forsaking sin and becoming more
and more like Christ by means of *sanctification*; and an ultimate
conformity to the fullness of Christ's image through *glorifica-*

tion. Most importantly for our purposes, each and every act in this drama of salvation has implications for Christian education—its goals, content, methods, programming, environment, and much more.

DRAMA OF SALVATION
ACT 1: THE ETERNAL CHOICE OF GOD[1]

Though it is difficult for us even to imagine, we know something about what reality was like before this universe and everything in it was created. Only God—the eternal Father, Son, and Holy Spirit—existed. In this reality before creation—often called *eternity past*—love was shared and enjoyed between the three, their radiant glory was splendid, their sense of pleasure with one another was perfect. And purpose existed in the Godhead. Part of that purpose eternally shared between the Father, the Son, and the Holy Spirit was to create a universe consisting of the heavens and the earth and all that they contain. Part of that purpose was the creation of human beings in the image of God. Part of that purpose was the sending of the Son to earth to give his life for the salvation of fallen human beings, as Peter explained:

> You were not redeemed with perishable things like silver or gold from your futile way of life inherited from your forefathers, but with precious blood, as of a lamb unblemished and spotless, the blood of Christ. For He was foreknown before the foundation of the world (1 Pet 1:18–20 NAS).

Before the world was created, God had purposed as part of his eternal plan that Jesus Christ would be the perfect sacrificial lamb whose blood would be shed in order to rescue his human creatures from their sinfulness. What God eternally purposed concerning his Son was brought about in the space-time reality of the created world when Jesus died on the cross for sinful human beings.

One other aspect of that eternal project of God deserves our attention. Part of God's plan includes his own choice of some human beings to experience his love and forgiveness through Jesus Christ. Paul explained:

> Blessed be the God and Father of our Lord Jesus Christ, who has blessed us with every spiritual blessing in the heavenly places in Christ, just as He chose us in Him before the foundation of the world, that we would be holy and blameless before Him. In love He predestined us to adoption as sons through Jesus Christ to Himself, according to the kind intention of His will, to the praise of the glory of His grace, which he freely bestowed on us in the Beloved (Eph 1:3–6 NAS).

Before the world was created, as part of his eternal plan, God chose or predestined people in Jesus Christ to belong to him as his adopted sons and daughters. This is often referred to as *election*. Election was certainly not based on anything these chosen people would ever be or would ever do; his choice was not conditioned on beauty or attractiveness, intelligence or wisdom, outstanding efforts or good works. Speaking of God's gracious choice, the Bible states that "if it is by grace, it is no longer on the basis of works, otherwise grace is no longer grace" (Rom 11:6 NAS).[2] Indeed, human sin had separated all people from God and rendered them unlovable in themselves. Rather, God's election was free, gracious, and completely unconditional; it was based only on his sovereign will and good pleasure. God chose people in Christ because he freely desired to do so, because it pleased him to do so—period. But this wasn't a capricious choice. God's choice was not a fickle, random selection; rather, it was his eternal choice of fallen people to pursue them, find them, draw them, and intimately and personally love them forever.

This should not surprise us because, according to Scripture, all that comes to pass is the outworking of the comprehensive, sovereign plan of God:

> In him we have obtained an inheritance, having been predestined according to the purpose of him who

works all things according to the counsel of his will,
so that we who were the first to hope in Christ might
be to the praise of his glory (Eph 1:11–12 ESV).

So God's choice of some people to experience salvation through Jesus Christ is just one aspect of his overall purpose regarding everything that comes to pass. Clearly then, those who are chosen can offer only one response to this undeserved act of God's love: dedicate their lives entirely to Christ and give all honor and praise to their glorious God and his magnificent grace. Nothing else would be worthy of God's eternal purpose in choosing them to be his children forever. Election is the gracious choice of God that took place in eternity past, and it constitutes the first act in the drama of salvation.

DRAMA OF SALVATION
ACT 2: BEGINNINGS IN TIME

The second act in the drama of salvation takes place in time when the work of Jesus Christ on behalf of sinful human beings is applied to the lives of specific individuals. As Paul explained:

We should always give thanks to God for you, brethren beloved by the Lord, because God has chosen you from the beginning for salvation through sanctification by the Spirit and faith in the truth. It was for this He called you through our gospel, that you may gain the glory of our Lord Jesus Christ (2 Thess. 2:13–14 NAS).

In thanking God, Paul repeated what we have already seen about election: God has eternally chosen some people to enjoy the experience of salvation. This experience comes about through two important actions in the lives of the ones he chose. One is the work of the Holy Spirit and call of God who summons people to himself. This is God's own activity to bring about salvation in the lives of sinful people. The other is belief in the truth, faith, that involves a deliberate and willful acceptance of God's invitation to salvation when the good news about Jesus Christ is heard and understood. This is the human response to God's initiative in providing and offering salvation to sinful people. Both activities are crucial: God must work to bring salvation, and people must respond to the divine work to appropriate salvation. These two activities bear some fleshing out.

By *the call of God* is meant "an act of God the Father, speaking through the human proclamation of the gospel, in which he summons people to himself in such a way that they respond in saving faith."[3] Specifically, God calls people "out of darkness into His marvelous light" (1 Pet 2:9 HCSB), which includes "fellowship with His Son, Jesus Christ our Lord" (1 Cor 1:9 HCSB) and demands that his summoned people "walk worthy of God, who calls [them] into His own kingdom and glory" (1 Thess 2:12 HCSB). That this divine calling is part of the drama of salvation can be seen in Paul's placing it in the midst of his description of God's mighty acts on behalf of his children. Paul noted five specific (though not exhaustive) acts in the drama of salvation: God's foreknowledge of those who will become Christians, his predestination of those people to become fully conformed to the image of his Son, *calling*, justification, and glorification (Rom 8:29–30). Furthermore, God's call always comes through the gospel (2 Thess 2:14) and so is intimately linked with the communication of the good news. This divine calling is part of the act of salvation at the beginning of God's powerful work to rescue sinful people.

For this powerful work of divine salvation to take root in the hearts of people, human sinfulness must be overcome; otherwise, how could people that Paul described with the following words from Eph 2:1–3 (HCSB) ever change from deadness to life?

> And you were dead in your trespasses and sins in which you previously walked according to this worldly age, according to the ruler of the atmospheric domain, the spirit now working in the disobedient. We too all pre-

viously lived among them in our fleshly desires, carrying out the inclinations of our flesh and thoughts, and
by nature we were children under wrath, as the others
were also.

This horrifying description of human sinfulness and deadness
paints the backdrop against which we can understand Jesus'
affirmation to Nicodemus in John 3:5–8 (NAS):

Truly, truly, I say to you, unless one is born of water
and the Spirit he cannot enter into the kingdom of God.
That which is born of flesh is flesh, and that which is
born of the Spirit is spirit. Do not marvel that I said to
you, "You must be born again." The wind blows where
it wishes and you hear the sound of it, but do not know
where it comes from and where it is going; so is everyone who is born of the Spirit.

According to Jesus, one thing is essential for overcoming
human sinfulness so as to enter into the life of the kingdom
in which God as king reigns and rules: *the new birth.* This is a
spiritual birth—a new life that comes from above, from God,
through the cleansing forgiveness of sin and the indwelling
presence of the Holy Spirit.[4]

All who experience the new birth enter into a new reality, a
new life in the Spirit of God. As Jesus himself indicated, this is
quite mysterious. We cannot see and control the wind, but we
detect its presence and power by hearing its sound and observ-
ing the bended trees and the leaves that are whipped here and
there by it. In the same way we cannot grasp and control the
Holy Spirit. But we can observe the presence and power of the
Spirit through the new birth as experienced by the followers of
Jesus. All who are born again live a new reality. The old reality,
dominated by concerns of sinful human nature and life in this
world, is cancelled. What once loomed large in stress-producing
importance—wealth, security, popularity, comfort, independence, power, career success, human recognition—begins to

fade away. In its place God and his priorities—purity, integrity, faithfulness, love, dependence, forgiveness, patience, worship, thankfulness, service—begin to reign increasingly supreme.

This new birth is also called *regeneration*. This word emphasizes the reality of spiritual death out of which people are delivered by the new birth. This takes place, as we have seen, by the Holy Spirit. Indeed, God plays the sole role in our regeneration; we can contribute nothing at all to being born again, as John explained: "But to all who did receive Him, He gave them the right to be children of God, to those who believe in His name, who were born, not of blood, or of the will of the flesh, or of the will of man, but of God" (John 1:12–13 HCSB). The new birth is solely by divine intervention. Moreover, regeneration comes about by the Word of God:

> You have been born again—not of perishable seed but of imperishable—through the living and enduring word of God. For,
>
> > All flesh is like grass,
> > and all its glory like a flower of the grass.
> > The grass withers, and the flower drops off,
> > but the word of the Lord endures forever.
>
> And this is the word that was preached as the gospel to you (1 Pet 1:23–25 HCSB).

When people hear the gospel of Jesus Christ communicated, God uses his Word to bring about the new birth in their lives. Again, the Bible affirms: "In the exercise of His will He brought us forth by the word of truth" (Jas 1:18 NAS). This means that regeneration (or the new birth) is not a decision or action on our part but is the work of God the Holy Spirit through his Word. It removes us from spiritual death and imparts to us new spiritual life. Regeneration is part of the act of salvation at the beginning of God's powerful work to rescue sinful people.

This mighty divine work must be followed by a human response, commonly called *conversion*.[5] Conversion consists of two activities: repentance from sin and faith in Jesus Christ. The first activity of repentance, or turning from sin, is a key part of the gospel message. As he launched his earthly ministry, Jesus challenged people: "Repent, for the kingdom of heaven is at hand" (Matt 4:17, NAS). As Jesus commissioned his disciples to communicate the gospel throughout the entire world, he said: "Thus it is written, that the Christ would suffer and rise again from the dead the third day. and that repentance for forgiveness of sins would be proclaimed in His name to all the nations, beginning from Jerusalem" (Luke 24:46–47 NAS). Moreover, in the first Christian sermon ever delivered, Peter urged his listeners: "Repent, and each of you be baptized in the name of Jesus Christ for the forgiveness of your sins" (Acts 2:37–39 NAS). Furthermore, as Paul spoke with the philosophers of Athens, he challenged them with these words:

> having overlooked the times of ignorance, God is now declaring to men that all people everywhere should repent, because He has fixed a day in which He will judge the world in righteousness through a Man whom He has appointed, having furnished proof to all men by raising Him from the dead (Acts 17:30–31 NAS).

Repentance, or turning from sin, is an essential element of conversion, a human response to God's work of salvation when the good news of Jesus Christ is heard.

Repentance includes three elements. The first element is an intellectual understanding that sin is wrong and deeply grieves and offends God. This involves a change of perspective, for unbelievers accept and even excuse their sinful behavior, but at conversion a person realizes the awfulness and harmfulness of sin. The second element is an emotional sorrow for sin. This involves a change of feeling, for unbelievers enjoy their sinful passions, but at conversion a person senses regret and remorse for his sinfulness. The third element is a willful decision to renounce sin and to forsake it. This involves a change of purpose, for unbelievers choose to live in sin, but at conversion a person intentionally commits to abandon his sinful living. All three aspects—intellectual, emotional, willful—are involved in repentance from sin.

The second activity of conversion is faith, or turning to Jesus Christ. This is also referred to as trust because in conversion people cease relying upon themselves and their own efforts to please God and trust in Christ and Christ alone to bring them into a relationship with God. Jesus himself emphasized this aspect: "For God so loved the world that He gave His only begotten Son, that whoever believes in Him shall not perish, but have eternal life" (John 3:16 NAS). When a Philippian jailor, about to commit suicide, questioned what he should do to be saved, the apostles responded, "Believe in the Lord Jesus, and you shall be saved, you and your household" (Acts 16:31 NAS). Because salvation is solely by God's grace, the only possible response that can be offered to accept this gift is faith: "For by grace you have been saved through faith; and that not of yourselves, it is the gift of God; not as a result of works, that no one should boast" (Eph 2:8–9 NAS). Faith, or turning to Jesus Christ, is an essential element of conversion, a human response to God's work of salvation when the good news of Jesus Christ is heard.

Faith includes three elements. The first is an intellectual understanding of who Jesus is and what he has done to accomplish salvation. The basics of the gospel must be grasped. This need for people to understand the gospel is a key reason that Christians engage in communicating the good news about Jesus Christ. The second element is an emotional sense that the gospel resolves the problem of sin and meets the deepest needs of life. People must acknowledge the message of salvation as being specifically directed at their lives. The third element is a person's willful decision to trust in Jesus Christ to save him from his sins. This involves deliberately forsaking whatever one relies on to make him acceptable to God—being raised in a

Christian home, religious activities, good works to help others, the ability to figure it all out—and depending on Christ and Christ alone. All three aspects—intellectual, emotional, willful—are involved in turning to Jesus Christ in faith.

Thus, conversion consists of two activities: repentance from sin and faith in Jesus Christ. This is the proper and anticipated human response to God's work of salvation when the good news of Jesus Christ is heard. This too is part of the act of salvation at the beginning of God's powerful work to rescue sinful people.

Not only does God summon people convincingly through his call and work powerfully to impart new life through regeneration; he also works to establish a new relationship through *justification*.[6] Justification is part of the drama of salvation as seen in Paul's placing it in the midst of his description of God's mighty acts on behalf of his children (Rom 8:29–30). To grasp this reality, God must be recognized as "the Judge of all the earth" (Gen 18:25). Imagine appearing before God in a courtroom. He is the judge to whom all people must give an account of everything they have ever done. The verdict that God renders is to find sinful human beings guilty, liable to punishment and condemnation. Now imagine a new scene. God, the Judge of all the earth, declares sinful human beings not guilty but righteous instead. In what has been called the "sweet exchange," God substitutes human sin for Christ's righteousness. All sins, together with the guilt and condemnation deserved because of those sins, are transferred to Jesus Christ. When Jesus died on the cross, he bore human guilt and condemnation, paying the price for sins in the place of those who committed them. This is called the *imputation* of sin to Christ. At the same time the righteousness of Jesus Christ—who perfectly obeyed the Father in everything and never once sinned—is transferred to the account of those whom God declares not guilty. This is called the *imputation* of Christ's righteousness. Then, when he considers people, he no longer considers them guilty but righteous instead. Human sin has been exchanged for the righteousness of Jesus Christ. (See Figure 9.1.)

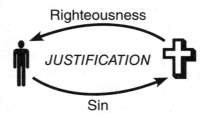

Figure 9.1: Exchange

This work of God to establish a new relationship with us is called *justification*. Go back to imagining the courtroom setting: God as the Judge justifies sinful people; that is, he bangs down his gavel and declares them not guilty but righteous instead. Paul emphasized that God demonstrates "his righteousness at the present time, so that he might be just and the justifier of the one who has faith in Jesus" (Rom 3:26 ESV). God himself is just in making this legal declaration because Jesus has truly paid the penalty for human sins, and his righteousness is truly credited to their account. God does not just pretend to deal with sin; he does not ignore the problem, nor does he brush aside sin without taking care of it. Rather, God remains just because he punishes sin (though the punishment falls on Jesus Christ), and he justifies people by declaring them not guilty but righteous instead.

Clearly, justification is a gift, not something that could ever be earned or achieved by human merits. Paul emphasized that "all have sinned and fall short of the glory of God, being justified as a gift by His grace through the redemption which is in Christ Jesus" (Rom 3:23–24 NAS). The ground or basis of justification is the salvation that Jesus Christ accomplished through his perfect life and his sacrificial death for human sins. The only response that one can offer to God is to receive this gift; that is, the only response is *faith*. God is "just and the justifier of the one who has faith in Jesus" (Rom 3:26). Thus, justification is by faith and faith alone; no one can be justified by doing good works. Again Paul emphasized this: "We maintain that a man is justified by faith apart from the works of the Law" (Rom 3:28 NAS). Faith, not good works, is the means by which people receive God's justification. He does not justify those who try hard to earn his love and forgiveness. In fact, Paul noted: "To the one who does not work, but believes in Him who justifies the ungodly, his faith is reckoned as righteousness" (Rom 4:5 NAS). God reserves his justification for the *ungodly*—for those who are far from him, who have given up attempting to make themselves better to win God over to their side. Only when they cease trying to do good works to earn God's favor can they be justified, declared not guilty but righteous instead, by faith.

Of crucial importance is what justification means for life in relation to God. Paul explained that "having been justified by faith, we have peace with God through our Lord Jesus Christ" (Rom 5:1 NAS). This peace is far more than a temporary feeling that is strengthened or weakened by the good or bad circumstances of life. Rather, it is the reality of no longer being separated from God, enemies of his because of sinful indifference and rebellion. In place of this, the new reality of peace means that people fully enjoy his forgiveness and love. They now experience a personal, intimate, living relationship with God himself! Justification is another part of the act of salvation at the beginning of God's powerful work to rescue sinful people.

Beyond all that has been described thus far, another aspect of God's work is making his former enemies the members of a new family. This work of God is called *adoption.*[7] Adoption encompasses several elements. First, Christians become "children of God" (John 1:12) who relate to him as their Father. In describing this "adoption as sons," Paul commented: "Because you are sons, God has sent forth the Spirit of His Son into our hearts, crying, 'Abba! Father!' Therefore you are no longer a slave, but a son" (Gal 4:5–7 NAS). As adopted children of God, Christ followers relate to him intimately, relying on him as Father to provide for all their needs—wise guidance for life, strength to obey him when the going gets tough, comfort when they are hurt and disturbed by life's unfair circumstances. They tell their Father that they love him, and they thank him for his work in their lives. Ever mindful not to disappoint or sadden him, they seek to please him in all that they are and do. They imitate him, reflecting his character in the world in which they live (Eph 5:1; 1 Pet 1:14–16). As his beloved children, they enjoy nothing more than being with their Father, just as he desires an intimate relationship with them.

The second element of adoption as children of God is that Christians belong to the family composed of all followers of Jesus Christ. Together they are all brothers and sisters, members of the family of God. Whatever else of note that divides or distinguishes them—race or ethnicity, skin color, language, economic or social status, gender, and so forth—these points of differences ultimately fade away in light of the commonalities that they possess in Jesus Christ: "There is one body and one Spirit, just as also you were called in one hope of your calling; one Lord, one faith, one baptism, one God and Father of all who is over all and through all and in all" (Eph 4:4–6 NAS). Indeed, far more unites them than divides them, and this is so because they have been adopted as brothers and sisters into the same family with the same Father, Lord, and Holy Spirit. Adoption is also a part of the act of salvation at the beginning of God's powerful work to rescue sinful people.

As noted above, Paul indicated that Christians are all part of "one body" (Eph. 4:4). This imagery, like that of a family, speaks of connectedness with Jesus Christ and with others. This is due to being given a new identity through *union with Christ*.[8] Paul explained in 1 Cor 12:12–13 (NAS):

> For even as the body is one and yet has many members, and all the members of the body, though they are many, are one body, so also is Christ. For by one Spirit we were all baptized into one body, whether Jews or

Greeks, whether slaves or free, and we were all made
to drink of one Spirit.

Look at this picture of the church: Jesus Christ is the head of the
body, and individual Christians compose the various members—
eyes, feet, hands, ears—of that one body. Certainly there is great
diversity, but there is only one body, the body of Christ. Membership in this body, this church, takes place through *baptism with the
Holy Spirit*. That is, Christ himself baptizes Christians with the
Spirit and places them into his body. This baptism is not a physical
reality, like baptism with water. Rather, it is a spiritual reality that
identifies people with Christ and with one another. As members of
the same body, Christians belong to him and to one another.

Paul referred to this reality as being "in Christ." This means
several key things. As already discussed, it means being chosen
by God for salvation: God chose us in Christ before the foundation of the world (Eph 1:4). It also means being given grace for
salvation according to the purpose of God, "who has saved us
and called us with a holy calling, not according to our works,
but according to His own purpose and grace which was granted
us in Christ Jesus from all eternity" (2 Tim 1:9 NAS). All this
was carried out "in Christ."

Furthermore, being "in Christ" means that Christians are
identified with the key events in the life of Jesus. So when God
considers them as being "in Christ," he counts them as having
experienced what Christ himself experienced. Specifically, they
are identified with Christ in his death, resurrection, and ascension. This means that Christians have made a decisive break
with sin and can no longer live as they lived previously. Also,
it means that they are to dedicate everything they are and do to
God, to be used to further the cause of Jesus Christ. Furthermore, it means that they exist in the realm of God's blessings
so that now and for all eternity God richly rewards and honors
them with his approval, comfort, joy, and glory. This also is part

of the act of salvation at the beginning of God's powerful work
to rescue sinful people.

The call of God. Regeneration, or the new birth. Conversion,
consisting of both repentance and faith. Justification. Adoption. Union with Christ and baptism with the Holy Spirit. All of
these elements are part of the act of salvation at the beginning
of God's powerful work to rescue sinful people. Together, they
constitute the second act in the drama of salvation.

DRAMA OF SALVATION
ACT 3: ONGOING FORWARD PROGRESS

The third dramatic act is characterized by ongoing forward
progress that begins with the initial application of salvation and
continues throughout the earthly lives of Christians. This cooperative venture between God and Christians is commonly called
sanctification: "Sanctification is a progressive work of God and
man that makes us more and more free from sin and like Christ
in our actual lives."[9] The mighty initial work of God in sinful
people—calling, regeneration, justification, and so forth—sets
in motion his ongoing power to transform new Christians, newly
enlivened from deadness and riddled with sin, into growing and
maturing Christians. And this process will continue throughout
their earthly lives.

Much of Scripture is dedicated to instructing and motivating
believers to walk progressively with God. This was certainly
true for the people of Israel living under the old covenant, to
whom were given narratives, laws, prophecies, apocalyptic
visions, and wisdom literature (the Jewish Bible, which Christians now call the Old Testament). This was oriented toward
bringing about the Israelites' increasing distinction from the
unholy paganism of surrounding cultures and greater obedience
and faithfulness to Yahweh, the one true and living God. No
wonder, then, that the psalmist prayed:

> How can a young man keep his way pure? By keeping
> it according to Your word. With all my heart I have

sought You; do not let me wander from Your commandments. Your word I have treasured in my heart,
that I may not sin against You (Ps 119: 9–11 NASB).

This word of God was accessible and intelligible for the people of Israel, as Deut 30:11–14 (NASB) states:

For this commandment which I command you today
is not too difficult for you, nor is it out of reach. It is
not in heaven, that you should say, "Who will go up to
heaven for us to get it for us and make us hear it, that
we may observe it?" Nor is it beyond the sea, that you
should say, "Who will cross the sea for us to get it for
us and make us hear it, that we may observe it?" But
the word is very near you, in your mouth and in your
heart, that you may observe it.

The ready accessibility and clarity of his word was God's gracious provision for the sanctification of his old covenant people.
Thus, the choice of obedience leading to life and blessing, or
disobedience leading to death and curse, was set before the people of God: "I have set before you life and death, the blessing
and the curse. So choose life in order that you may live, you and
your descendants, by loving the Lord your God, by obeying His
voice, and by holding fast to Him" (Deut 30:19–20 NASB).

So it is for Christians, the new covenant people of God. To
the Jewish Bible, the 39 books of the Old Testament, were added
the 27 books of the New Testament: four Gospels, a narrative of
the early church, numerous letters, and an apocalyptic vision,
so that Christian Scripture is the sufficient and clear revelation dedicated to instructing and motivating Christians to walk
progressively with God. The Old Testament contributes to the
sanctification of the new covenant people of God. For example,
the apostle Paul, after recalling four narratives depicting Israel's
sins and God's accompanying judgment and condemnation,
explained: "Now these things happened to them [the people of
Israel] as examples, and they were written as a warning to us

[Christians], on whom the ends of the ages have come" (1 Cor 10:11 HCSB).[10] The New Testament also emphasizes the importance of sanctification—"this is God's will, your sanctification" (1 Thess 4:3 HCSB)—and provides instructions about and exhortations to sanctification—"Just as you offered the parts of yourselves as slaves to moral impurity, and to greater and greater lawlessness, so now offer them as slaves to righteousness, which results in sanctification" (Rom 6:19). Moreover, the power and resources of God himself are made available through the Holy Spirit for this progressive sanctification:

> Walk by the Spirit and you will not carry out the desire of the flesh. For the flesh desires what is against the Spirit, and the Spirit desires what is against the flesh; these are opposed to each other, so that you don't do what you want. . . . But the fruit of the Spirit is love, joy, peace, patience, kindness, goodness, faith, gentleness, self-control. . . . If we live by the Spirit, we must also follow the Spirit (Gal 5:16–17,22–23,25 HCSB).

It becomes clear from this that sanctification is a cooperative venture between God who sanctifies and the believer who is being sanctified. Indeed, Paul commanded believers to "work out your own salvation with fear and trembling. For it is God who is working in you, enabling you both to will and to act for His good purpose" (Phil 2:12–13 HCSB). Corresponding to the divine initiative in sanctification is the human response in sanctification: God is the one who grants both the passionate desire and powerful dedication to pursue his will; and Christians single-mindedly devote themselves to the ways of God, wanting never to dishonor him through disobedience and/or faithlessness. As Grudem noted: "We are not saying that we have equal roles in sanctification or that we both work in the same way, but simply that we cooperate with God in ways that are appropriate to our status as God's creatures."[11] On God's part, sanctification by the Spirit (1 Thess 2:13; 1 Pet 1:2) includes his wise leading (Rom 8:1–16), purposeful discipline (Heb 12:3–13), powerful protection (1 Pet 1:5; 1 Cor 10:13), and transforming freedom (2 Cor 3:17–18), among many other resources. To this divine role in sanctification, Christians respond in two ways, passively and actively. The passive role includes yielding to the work of the Spirit: "Yield yourselves to God as men who have been brought from death to life" (Rom 6:13 RSV). So Christians respond to the command to "be filled with the Spirit" (Eph 5:18) by yielding to the Spirit's guidance in their lives. The active role includes reading, studying, memorizing, and meditating on Scripture (John 17:17); prayer "at all times in the Spirit" (Eph 6:18 HCSB; see Phil 4:6); full engagement in a local church (Heb 10:24–25; Eph 4:1–16), including worship (Eph 5:18–20; Col 3:16); deadening sinful desires (Rom 6), including avoiding sexual immorality (1 Cor 6:12–20; 1 Thess 4:3–8); and other similar disciplines. As a result of this cooperative effort between God and his people, sanctification of Christians in their totality—intellect, emotions, will, body, motivations, purposes—will progressively take place.

Indeed, the goal of sanctification can be described in terms of the original design and purpose for God's creation of human beings: to be the creatures who bear the divine image, the only creatures in the universe that God fashioned in this way. So at the time they were created, the first two people imaged God properly; like mirrors Adam and Eve reflected God in the world in which they lived. This original image, defaced because of the fall into sin, was so ravaged that it became a hideous parody of its pristine reality. Because of redemption, however, this marred and tainted image is being progressively restored through the ongoing process of sanctification: "We all, with unveiled faces, are reflecting the glory of the Lord and are being transformed into the same image from glory to glory; this is from the Lord who is the Spirit" (2 Cor 3:18 HCSB; see Eph 4:24; Col 3:10). As the next section explains, the future will bring the complete restoration of the divine image, for all who have been redeemed through Christ will fully bear his image (Rom 8:29). But during their earthly pilgrimage, Christians are designed and equipped to make ongoing progress in their renewal in the image of God.

DRAMA OF SALVATION, ACT 4: THE COMPLETION YET TO COME

Although already enacted in part, the last dramatic act for the completion of salvation awaits future divine intervention, including the return of Jesus Christ and the remaking of all of creation for a new eternity future. This fourth act must be seen in relation to the three acts that precede it. The opening act, which features the eternal choice of God, "takes place" in eternity past. This election, or God's own gracious choice of some people to experience his love and forgiveness through Jesus Christ, is the first dramatic act in salvation. The second act in this drama occurs in time when the work of Jesus Christ on behalf of sinful human beings is applied to the actual lives of specific people. At the start of their Christian lives, those who are chosen by God hear his summons, the divine call; experience regeneration; respond with repentance and faith through conversion; are justified, declared not guilty but righteous; become the children of God and members of the same family through adoption; and are identified with Christ through union with him and placed into his body, the Church, through baptism with the Holy Spirit. The third act is the ongoing drama of sanctification, the transformation from sinfulness and deadness into greater and greater conformity to the image of Christ. This ongoing progress continues throughout the Christian life but is never fully completed, awaiting the fourth act of the drama. By indicating that this final act has already been enacted in part, I mean that the first three acts are preparatory for, and find their fulfillment in, the last act. The first three acts anticipate all along the finale, and the final act is the completion of all that goes before it. Salvation is purposed, then applied, then progresses, then finds perfection.

This final work of God is commonly called *glorification*:

> Glorification is the final step in the application of redemption. It will happen when Christ returns and raises from the dead the bodies of all believers for all time who have died, and reunites them with their souls, and changes the bodies of all believers who remain alive, thereby giving all believers at the same time perfect resurrection bodies like his own.[12]

That glorification is part of the drama of salvation can be seen in Paul's placing it in his description of God's mighty acts on behalf of his children (Rom. 8:29–30). This final act of glorification involves two groups of people: Christians who have died, and those who remain alive until the time of Christ's second coming. In the case of the first group, who have been living joyfully in the immediate presence of Christ in heaven, he will reunite them with their bodies that were sloughed off at death and that are miraculously and marvelously resurrected as imperishable, splendid, strong, Spirit-dominated, and Christlike bodies (1 Cor 15:42–44,49). In the case of the second group, who are still alive when Christ returns to earth, he will immediately and instantaneously change their present bodies into new, glorified bodies with the same characteristics of the first group (1 Cor 15:51–52).

This is exactly what Christ himself promised when he came to engage in his earthly ministry in obedience to the Father's plan:

> This is the will of Him who sent me: that I should lose none of those He has given Me but should raise them up on the last day. For this is the will of My Father: that everyone who sees the Son and believes in Him may have eternal life, and I will raise him up on the last day (John 6:39–40 HCSB).

Likewise, Paul promised,

> Our citizenship is in heaven, from which we also
> eagerly wait for a Savior, the Lord Jesus Christ. He
> will transform the body of our humble condition into
> the likeness of His glorious body, by the power that
> enables Him to subject everything to Himself (Phil
> 3:20–21 HCSB).

Significantly, salvation is not limited to the human immaterial
reality, the soul or spirit. Rather, the fullness of salvation involves
the human material reality, or body. Again Paul assured Christians that God is "for the body. God raised up the Lord and will
also raise us up by His power" (1 Cor 6:13–14 HCSB). Sadly
and incorrectly, many (perhaps even most) Christians have been
taught and believe that their ultimate hope is to die in Christ so
as to live with him in heaven forever. But that is not the Christian
hope as presented in Scripture because the fullness of salvation
takes place at the return of Christ with its accompanying resurrection of the body (Titus 2:13). Indeed, even that destiny is not
the ultimate hope for the created universe in its totality because
the divine plan and promise includes the destruction of the current universal order to give way to a renewed and reconstituted
"new heavens and a new earth, where righteousness will dwell"
(2 Pet 3:13 HCSB; see Rom 8:18–25; Rev 21–22). Glorification
is the fullness of salvation. Because it is the completion yet to
come, it constitutes the future final act of God's powerful work
to rescue sinful people.

IMPLICATIONS OF THE DRAMA OF
SALVATION FOR CHRISTIAN EDUCATION

In the light of God's revealed plan of salvation, there are six
implications for Christian education.

Offering a Wide Variety of Educational Initiatives

Christian education must provide ongoing opportunities and
a wide variety of delivery systems in which the Word of God is

communicated indiscriminately to both believers and unbelievers. If, as we have seen, God is summoning his chosen people
to himself by means of his divine call through the gospel, then
Christian education has the responsibility to give every person
the opportunity to investigate the good news about Jesus Christ.
This should not be narrowly construed to mean just offering
explicit evangelistic meetings of various kinds. The notion here
is much broader than that. Especially in a society moving more
and more toward becoming post-Christian and religiously plu-
ralistic, Christian education bears the burden of educating people from completely non-Christian outlooks and philosophies
in the essentials of the Christian worldview. The basic story line
of the Bible—creation, fall, redemption, and consummation—
needs to be told honestly, creatively, passionately, relevantly,
clearly, winsomely, and urgently to any and all who will listen. Replacing the old "attractional" paradigm—which says
that Christian education is responsible for providing instruction
within the four walls of a church though outsiders are invited—
is paramount today. Certainly, the church as a local reality gathers together regularly, and part of what goes on in the church
building is Christian education. But the church also gathers to
scatter, and in its missional "sendedness"[13] it takes its education
with it into homes, businesses, schools, art galleries, offices,
corner hangouts, block parties, social gatherings, and the like.
Christian education outside of the walls of the church results
from the centrifugal force of the church's missional identity.

Emphasizing the Word of God and the Spirit of God

This may seem obvious, but one common theme in the doctrine of salvation is the absolutely essential importance of the
Word of God and the Spirit of God. Without the two working in
conjunction, regeneration does not occur, truthful revelation to be
trusted and obeyed is missing, and divine power for sanctification
is absent. Again, though it may seem obvious, by "Word of God"
is meant the entire Bible—both the Old Testament and the New

Testament. Accordingly, Christian education must be centered on communicating the Word of God in the power of the Spirit of God. This was Paul's point when he first communicated the gospel among the people of Corinth (1 Cor 2:1–5 HCSB):

> When I came to you, brothers, announcing the testimony of God to you, I did not come with brilliance of speech or wisdom. For I determined to know nothing among you except Jesus Christ and Him crucified. And I was with you in weakness, in fear, and in much trembling. My speech and my proclamation were not with persuasive words of wisdom, but with a demonstration of the Spirit and power, so that your faith might not be based on men's wisdom but on God's power.

The simple and straightforward rendering of the good news of Jesus Christ, eschewing human cleverness and rhetorical brilliance, was Paul's purpose at the outset. But even when the Corinthian church was more established and Paul turned to communicating "God's hidden wisdom in a mystery"—"What no eye has seen and no ear has heard, and what has never come into a man's heart, is what God has prepared for those who love Him"—to "the mature," the apostle still communicated this divine revelation "by the Spirit" (1 Cor. 2:6–16 HCSB). Certainly, this is "not a wisdom of this age, or of the rulers of this age" (v. 6); it does not come *from* the wise and powerful of this world, nor is it revealed *to* them. Rather, this wonderful divine wisdom is revealed "by the Spirit" (v. 13), for he alone—that is, unlike the wise and powerful of this world—knows the deep mysteries of the Godhead. Furthermore, by the Spirit we "know what has been freely given to us by God" (v. 12), and it is "not in words taught by human wisdom, but in those taught by the Spirit" (v. 13) that this divine revelation is communicated—a reference to the inspiration of Scripture by the Holy Spirit. So whether the focus is the proclamation of the initial message of the gospel of Jesus Christ or the communication of wise biblical instruction for Christian growth and advancement, Paul's reliance was on the Word of God and the Spirit of God.

Therefore, this must be the point of confidence and the focus of Christian education as well: communication of the Word of God in the power of the Spirit of God. One wonders, given the penchant of some educators to attempt to impress and mesmerize their audiences with enhanced communicative methods, if the medium gets in the way of the message and renders it mute and impotent. This is not to denounce the careful study and consideration of the most creative and clear methods of communicating Scripture. Indeed, teachers of Scripture should never be monotonous and boring! Some Christian educators trip up on this point, then attempt to excuse their lack of preparation with the smug assertion that they don't want to get in the way of the Spirit of God by relying on human ingenuity. But such poor preparation or lack of creativity does not represent reliance on the Spirit; instead, it shows a failure on the part of the educators themselves who may or may not rescue human ineffectiveness for their own good purposes. This is not a denouncement of creative Christian education, but it is a warning against reliance on humanly wise creative methods that (often unwittingly) end up distracting from the divine revelation of the Word of God and also end up substituting human ingenuity for the work of the Spirit of God.

Practically speaking, how does Christian education do what is being proposed? Certainly the key here is the Christian educators themselves. They must let the Word and Spirit of God transform their own lives so they first live the truth themselves before they engage in communicating it to others. So in one sense transformed educators embody or "flesh out" the message they bring. An important question Christian educators may ask themselves is "Does the Word of God work in my life?" If so, educators can draw on their personal appropriation of the Word as illustrations and encouragement for others, knowing and communicating an appropriate confidence that the Word can work in the lives of their audience. This presupposes, of course, that Christian educators engage in interpretive integrity, discovering and grasping the meaning of the Word as it is intended to be understood. Such interpretive integrity eschews proof texting, wrenching verses out of their literary-historical-cultural context, flattening out intentional biblical tensions (such as Paul's teaching on justification versus James's teaching on justification), stringing together passages that are not genuinely related, and committing other such hermeneutical errors. Further, this assumes that Christian educators approach their task responsibly with conscious, prayerful reliance on the Spirit of God for help in both the process of interpreting the Word and the designing of messages or lessons to communicate that Word. Finally, Christian educators who know their audiences well are able to identify points of entry into their lives and target their teachings, admonitions, warnings, exhortations, and words of comfort and hope in a powerful manner.

Expecting Spirit-Borne Educational Surprises

This reliance on the work of the Holy Spirit that we have been emphasizing is also a reason to pause to consider the unpredictability of Christian education. A natural part of any educational process is the setting of goals and targeting of objectives, followed by the development of a program to accomplish those goals and reach those objectives. This is all well and good, and a responsible Christian education ministry works diligently and intentionally along these lines. However, it must also reckon with the words of Jesus in John 3:8 (NAS): "The wind blows where it wishes and you hear the sound of it, but do not know where it comes from and where it is going; so is everyone who is born of the Spirit." Both the new birth and subsequent life in the Spirit are quite mysterious; indeed, no one can grasp and control the Holy Spirit and the fruit he bears. As the Spirit of God engages in his transforming ministry in the lives of those who follow Christ, using the well-intentioned and well-designed programs and activities of Christian education, the seemingly spontaneous and unexpected fruit that follows should not be a surprise. Indeed, the educator's prayer should always be for the Spirit to do far more—in terms of both extent and depth—than could ever be anticipated and planned. Further, this reliance on the unbounded work of the Spirit should be a constant reminder that Christian education cannot take a cookie-cutter or one-size-fits-all approach. Rather, it must be tailor-made for its individual participants as it seeks to work in conjunction with the personalized attention of the Holy Spirit in them. Solid programs are essential, but Christian education should never lose sight of the fact that such programs must always be designed for people in whom the Holy Spirit is at work. Then a purposeful and programmed approach may attain unpredictable results.

Educating with a Strong Community Dynamic

Christian education also takes a community approach toward its participants. This is due especially to the reality that is created through God's work of adoption and the believer's union with Christ and baptism with the Spirit. The new reality that results from these particular acts of God in salvation is a community of Christians joined together as brothers and sisters in the family of God and as members of the body of Christ, the Church. So while Christian education works with individuals, it ministers to and with them as Christians in community. Unlike most other settings where competition is the order of the day (think of the fierce competition for good grades and high test scores that typifies academia as students lobby for admission to their schools of choice), Christian education focuses on cooperation characterized by love, patience, forbearance, and forgiveness (Eph 4:32). And Christian education is not selective, in the sense of weeding out the weak so as to privilege the strong. On the contrary, Paul explained, "We proclaim Him [Christ], warning and teaching everyone with all wisdom, so that we may present everyone mature in Christ. I labor for this, striving with His strength that works powerfully in me" (Col 1:28–29 HCSB).

Even more Christian education takes into account the community dynamic in its instructional process, relying on both formal and informal events to actualize the following exhortation: "Let the [word of Christ] richly dwell among you, teaching and admonishing one another in all wisdom, and singing psalms, hymns, and spiritual songs, with gratitude in your hearts to God" (Col 3:16 HCSB, with author's modification). That is, in a properly functioning church, all its members make a significant contribution to the constructive process of Christian education. Moreover, this community dynamic demands authenticity on the part of all church members, as they "walk the walk" and do not just "talk the talk." Indeed, there is some truth to the motto that Christian faith and life are caught rather than taught. This modeling aspect is especially emphasized for church leaders engaged in Christian education, to whom is written this instruction: "shepherd God's flock among you, not overseeing out of compulsion but freely, according to God's will; not for the money but eagerly; not lording it over those entrusted to you, but being examples to the flock" (1 Pet 5:2–3 HCSB). The following charge is directed toward those who benefit from this exemplary educational leadership: "Remember your leaders who have spoken God's word to you. As you carefully observe the outcome of their lives, imitate their faith" (Heb 13:7 HCSB). The presupposition in all this discussion is the strong community dynamic as a constitutive component of Christian education.

Facilitating a Holistic Response

Beyond communicating clearly and accurately the truth of God's revelation in Scripture (content), Christian education must also motivate its participants to respond rightly and decisively to the truth presented. This proper response involves rightly affirming the truth (*orthodoxy*), rightly feeling the truth (*orthopatheia*), and rightly practicing the truth (*orthopraxis*)—the classic Christian education triad of head, heart, and hand (Figure 9.2 on next page). To put it differently, Christian education is directed toward the intellect, the emotions or affections, the will or volition, the body, the motivation and purposing, and so forth.

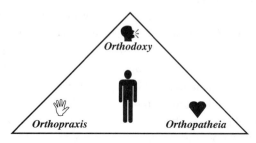

Figure 9.2: Holistic Response Triad

This was underscored in the discussion about repentance and faith, which are multidimensional human responses to God's work. Various aspects—intellectual, emotional, willful—are involved in repentance from sin and faith in Christ, both in their initial expression at conversion as well as in their ongoing expression in sanctification. With regard to repentance, for example, it is simply not adequate for people to admit mentally that they have sinned. It is one thing for them to agree intellectually that they are sinners because the Bible indicates that to be the case, but it is quite another thing to be incapable of admitting any specific errors on their part in broken relationships, in family difficulties, in failed jobs. Likewise, it is not enough to feel sorry for sins. Some people are sorry for their failures, but in reality they merely regret that their problems were exposed so that they got caught. Intellectual understanding, emotional sorrow, and a willful decision to turn away from sin are the three elements needed for proper repentance to take place.

So it is with faith. All three aspects—intellectual, emotional, willful—are involved in trusting Christ. It is simply not adequate to be able to recount the facts about Jesus. Many people can intellectually recite plenty of things about Jesus, but those facts make no difference at all in their lives. Likewise, it is not enough to get emotionally worked up about Jesus—especially when facing deep problems that seem impossible to handle. Intellectual understanding, emotional approval, and a willful decision to trust in Jesus Christ for salvation are the three elements needed for saving faith to take place. Therefore, Christian education must be directed toward encouraging proper responses to God's powerful work in people's lives; thus, it seeks to inculcate genuine repentance and faith in their multidimensionality. Practically speaking, this implication is incorporated into the educational process when different types of objectives—cognitive, affective, volitional, behavioral—are targeted in developing a lesson plan. As a result of this educational activity, students will think differently about various things, feel differently in this sense, choose this rather than that, and act responsibly in obedience/trust/praise/thanksgiving. Thus, teaching for a holistic response incorporates a multidimensional approach and is a mark of mature Christian education.

Aiming toward an Eschatological Goal and Blessing

This multidimensional approach was also underscored in the discussion about sanctification, which is progressively directed at Christians in their totality—intellect, emotions, will, body, motivations, purposes, and so forth. As noted, the goal of this process of sanctification is the restoration of sinners to bear fully the image of God, an image that was defaced by sin. This provides Christian education with its goal in terms of what it should purpose to accomplish in terms of its participants. From the time of the initial application of salvation throughout the earthly lives of all believers, Christian education is the ongoing process that is directed toward and facilitates their renewal in the divine image. Specifically, this educational process includes

- Preaching, teaching, other activities of worship, other large group meetings, Sunday school classes, home fel-

lowship groups, Bible studies, accountability groups, and
other situations
- Mentoring or discipling in small groups or regular indi-
vidual appointments, whether formal or informal
- Leadership and teachers training
- Equipping Christians to identify, develop, and engage in
the exercise of their spiritual gifts
- Intensive educational opportunities through periodic
retreats
- Participation in seminars and conferences

The constant goal through all these different means of Christian
education is to facilitate greater and greater conformity to the
image of Jesus Christ so that Christians are enabled to reflect
him in the world in which they live. Thus, a vital task incumbent on Christian educators is that they themselves know what
Christlikeness is like!

At the same time Christian education acknowledges that ultimate transformation, resulting in perfect conformity to the image
of Christ, is an eschatological blessing. That is, it is a reality that
awaits completion in the age to come, when Jesus Christ himself
will come for the second time. Accordingly, there is a built-in failure and frustration in relation to the educational goal that Christian education establishes for itself in accordance with Scripture:
It seeks to attain the unattainable. All Christians who participate in
the Christian educational process—even the most well-designed
and Spirit-empowered program—will fall short of the ultimate
goal of that process. Try as they might, they will never achieve
the goal because the goal that is set—and set rightly, in conformity with biblical instruction—is one that can never be achieved
by Christians during their earthly pilgrimages. Now, in most
educational systems, unattainable goals are recast and brought
more in line with realistic expectations.[14] But this option is not
available to Christian education because such tampering with the
aim would contradict biblical exhortations like that of Jesus: "Be

perfect as your heavenly Father is perfect" (Matt 5:48 NAS). So the goal is established by divine prerogative and incorporated into the Christian education process out of obedience. Therefore, nothing short of full restoration of the fallen divine image will suffice as a target. But this full conformity to the image of Christ is an eschatological blessing, a reality that is not attainable now (though its realization is begun now) but that awaits the return of Jesus Christ when it will be attainable in full.

REFLECTION QUESTIONS

1. How connected are your ideas of evangelism and education? How about in your congregation?
2. What educational opportunities are present in your congregation? Are you a single or multiple format education ministry?
3. How does your congregation provide educational initiatives to individuals of different spiritual and life needs? For example, new Christians, new members, young Christians, mature Christians, those entering leadership?
4. Can you give examples of how the educational ministry contributes toward the building of Christian community and elicits a holistic response from individuals?
5. In terms of the holistic response (*orthodoxy, orthopraxis,* and *orthopatheia*), in terms of your congregation, rank them in priority. How does your congregation prioritize the three? How well are these three integrated into an approach to Christian living?

---

1   Some of this material is adapted from my earlier writing, *Jesusology: Understand What You Believe about Jesus and Why* (Nashville: B&H, 2005), 110–12.
2   Paul stated elsewhere that God "has saved us and called us with a holy calling, not according to our works, but according to His own purpose and grace which was granted us in Christ Jesus from all eternity" (2 Tim 1:9 NAS).

3 W. Grudem, *Systematic Theology: An Introduction to Biblical Doctrine*
   (Grand Rapids: Zondervan, 1994), 693.
4 Most likely, Jesus was referring to a prophecy that had been given to
   God's people centuries prior to his earthly ministry: "Then I will sprinkle clean water on you, and you will be clean; I will cleanse you from
   all your filthiness and from all your idols. Moreover, I will give you a
   new heart and put a new spirit within you; and I will remove the heart
   of stone from your flesh and give you a heart of flesh. I will put My
   Spirit within you and cause you to walk in My statutes, and you will
   be careful to observe My ordinances" (Ezek 36:25–27 NAS). That is
   why, later in his conversation with Nicodemus, Jesus expressed surprise
   that this "teacher of Israel" did not understand his words about the new
   birth (John 3:10). Nicodemus should have been familiar with Ezekiel's
   prophecy and related it to what Jesus was saying about being born again
   of water and the Spirit, two key images in that prophecy. See Allison,
   Jesusology, 127–29.
5 See ibid., 112–17.
6 See ibid, 130–33.
7 See ibid, 133–34.
8 See ibid, 135–38.
9 Grudem, *Systematic Theology*, 746.
10 The four Old Testament narratives Paul referenced are (in his order)
   Exod 32:1–14; Num 25:1–9; 21:4–9; 16:41–50.
11 Grudem, *Systematic Theology*, 753.
12 Ibid., 828.
13 Though certainly not a new concept, the term *missional* is challenging
   the term *mission* or *missions* as better expressing the church's reality.
   Taking its cue from John 20:21, in which Jesus told his disciples, "As
   the Father has sent Me, I also send you" (HCSB), proponents of "missional" focus on this as an essential attribute of the church, constituting
   its very identity. Just as the Father sent the Son into the world, so the Son
   sends his church into the world. Thus, the church is not so much about
   "mission" or "missions," in the sense of organizing, promoting, and sup-
   porting certain activities. Rather, the church's identity is a missional one,
   and that is true first and foremost of the church as a corporate entity and
   only secondarily of the individual members of the church. The church is
   missional, then, in the sense of having a corporate identity of sendedness
   into the world, and the church expresses this not only in communicating
   the gospel of Jesus Christ (though this is certainly the key element in its
   missional identity), but in whatever the church engages so as to further
   the kingdom of God in the world, including feeding the poor, tutoring
   students, caring for senior citizens, championing environmental steward-
   ship, planting churches, cleaning up the neighborhood, becoming patrons
   of the arts, and so forth.
14 For example, no high school superintendent would ever set as a goal
   to have all the students in all the high schools under his jurisdiction
   achieve a perfect 36 on the ACT exam and a perfect 1600 on the SAT
   test.

CHAPTER 10

Ecclesiology and Christian Education

James Riley Estep Jr.

O
ur concept of church is in a constant state of refinement throughout our Christian lives. As children we said these lyrics with the appropriate hand motions: "This is the church, this is the steeple, open the doors, and see all the people," which incorrectly identifies the church as the place where people worship. Some time later we gain the insight that the people comprise the church, not the building or its steeple. At some point we begin to understand the church as God's community of the saved, his people who as such live distinctively from the world. Evangelical ecclesiology presents a range of models from traditionally liturgical Anglican or Episcopal churches to charismatically oriented ministries meeting in storefronts and from Rick Warren's emphasis on the purpose of the church to the most recent emergent and emerging church movements.[1] This chapter will endeavor to draw a basic sketch of the church as the community of the people of God, a community that is trinitarian, visible yet invisible, missional, worshipping, institutional, exclusive-inclusive, and eschatological. From this portrait educational implications will be drawn.

THE CHURCH AS GOD'S COMMUNITY

The Greek word for church in the New Testament is *ekklesia* and can refer to: (1) individual house churches (Rom 16:5), (2) all the churches in a particular region (Gal 1:22), all churches in general (1 Cor 14:34), the church in general (Matt 16:18), and the church in heaven (Heb 12:23). Thus, the term *church* may refer to a local church, the universal Church, or the heavenly church. Noteworthy is the fact that the New Testament does not use the term *church* to refer to a building—which is not surprising since the early church did not meet in special buildings—or to a denomination like the Presbyterian Church—again, this should not surprise us—or to a church worship service on Sunday mornings from 11:00 a.m. to 12:00 p.m.

The church finds its antecedents in the Old Testament community of faith. Israel of the Old Testament and the church of the New Testament share the distinction of being God's people. God's faith community begins with his people, Israel, starting with the call of Abram (God later renamed him Abraham) and his family (Gen 12:1–3; 15:1–6). Eventually, the nation of Israel was his people, beginning with the Mosaic covenant.[2] Later insights into God's relationship with Israel in the Old Testament bear out this covenantal relationship between God and his people.[3] However, God likewise promised an even broader covenant, one that would fulfill the promise to Abraham: "All peoples on earth will be blessed through you" (Gen 12:3). In Jeremiah 31:31 God promised a new covenant in which salvation would be extended to all the peoples and nations, which is seen in the church of the New Testament.[4]

JESUS AND THE CHURCH

In the teachings of Jesus, the transition from the nation of Israel to the church as God's people is foreseen, emphasizing the inclusion of the Gentiles into God's people (see the parable of the vineyard; Matt 21:33–46). Jesus explained this parable with the cryptic conclusion, "Therefore I tell you that the kingdom of God will be taken away from you and given to a people who will produce its fruits" (Matt 21:43). Other parables likewise convey the idea of kingdom growth through including others, such as the parables of the seeds, tares, mustard seed, and leaven (Matt 13:3–9,24–33), as well as parables about the recovery of the lost sheep, the lost coin, and the lost or prodigal son (Luke 15).[5]

The most direct reference to the church in the teaching of Jesus is in his response to Peter's confession, "You are the Christ, the Son of the living God" (Matt 16:16). Jesus replies,

> "I tell you that you are Peter, and on this rock I will build my church [*ekklesia*], and the gates of Hades will not overcome it. I will give you the keys of the kingdom of heaven; whatever you bind on earth will be bound in heaven, and whatever you loose on earth will be loosed in heaven" (Matt 16:18–19).

In this passage Jesus identifies the future community of God as the church and associates it with (1) the confession of Christ as the Son of God, (2) power for withstanding and overcoming attacks against it, (3) the kingdom of God, and (4) the gospel that brings the forgiveness of sins. Peter himself would later describe the church with the following expressions:

> But you are a chosen people, a royal priesthood, a holy nation, a people belonging to God, that you may declare the praises of him who called you out of darkness into his wonderful light. Once you were not a people, but now you are the people of God; once you had not received mercy, but now you have received mercy (1 Pet 2:9–10; see Rom 11:30–32).

Peter wrote this not of Israel but of the church. In short, Jesus' ministry *was* the transition from Israel as the people of God to the church as the people of God.

THE CHURCH AS TRINITARIAN COMMUNITY

As God's people the Church reflects the triune nature of God (see chapter 5). Paul wrote, "For through him [Christ] we both have access to the Father by one Spirit" (Eph 2:18). The Church is not just any assembly or gathering of individuals but the people and community of the triune God. This section will address the Church as a trinitarian community of faith.

Community of the Father

The Church is the community of God the Father. The New Testament frequently refers to the church of God[6] or the churches of God.[7] Using Old Testament imagery and citations, Paul described the church as "the temple of the living God" (twice in 2 Cor 6:16a), explaining,

> As God has said, "I will live with them and walk among them, and I will be their God, and they will be my people."
> "Therefore, come out from them and be separate,"
>   says the Lord,
> "Touch no unclean thing,
>   and I will receive you."
> "I will be a Father to you,
>   and you will be my sons and daughters,"
>   says the Lord Almighty (2 Cor 6:16b–18).

As "the temple of the living God," the Church is the people of God privileged to have the Father living among them. God is their Father, and they are called his "sons and daughters." This family intimacy and identity has important ramifications for the church as the Father's children. It is to be a holy, counter-cultural reality that intentionally distinguishes itself from the world in which it lives, rejecting the prevailing non-Christian worldviews, values, pleasures, purposes, and goals. To love and long for these trivial pursuits would be to betray the God who has welcomed the Church as the community of the Father.

Community of Christ

The foundation of the Church is Jesus Christ (1 Cor 3:11; 1 Pet 2:4–8), and this is our confession (Matt 16:16–18).

Perhaps the most familiar metaphor for the Church is "the body
of Christ" (1 Cor 12:12–27; Eph 4:12; Col 1:18), with Christ's
headship of the body further emphasizing his presence in the
community (Eph 1:22–23; Col 1:18,24; 3:15). Specifically, the
headship of Christ over the Church indicates the following: (1)
Christ's incomprehensible, sacrificial love for the Church, which
compelled him to die so he could cleanse it and render it holy
and blameless (Eph 5:25–27); (2) Christ's authority to set the
Church's agenda and direct the Church to accomplish his will
(Eph 1:22); (3) the church's need to submit willingly and whole-
heartedly to Christ's design for it (Eph 5:24). Further, as members of the body of Christ, believers: (1) belong to Christ and
owe him their ultimate allegiance (1 Cor 6:15–17); (2) experience church unity as well as work diligently to maintain it (1 Cor
12:12–13; Eph 4:3–6); (3) enjoy loving fellowship as members
of one another (Rom 12:5); and (4) contribute to one another's
growth and maturity in Christ (1 Cor 12–14). This metaphor of
the church as the body of Christ and Christ as the head of the
church is indeed rich in significance and implications!

Another familiar metaphor presents Christ as the groom or
husband to his Church as an awaiting virgin and bride (Eph
5:22–32; 2 Cor 11:2; Rev 19:7; 21:9). This metaphor emphasizes
not only Christ's headship as the groom but also the relationship
he shares with his Church and the character of the Church. Specifically, the Church as Christ's virgin-bride indicates: (1) living
in anticipation of the groom's arrival, the return of Christ (Rev
19:7; see Matt 25:1–13); (2) the purity of the bride, as a radiant church, without stain or wrinkle or any other blemish, but
holy and blameless" (Eph 5:27); and (3) a solitary commitment
to Christ alone as his only bride (2 Cor 11:2).

Christ and the Lord's Supper. Communion is one of the most
ancient Christian practices. While its antecedent is the Passover
meal (see Exod 12:1–30), its symbolism in the New Testament
as the body and blood of Jesus Christ is distinctively Christian.
It was initiated by Jesus himself in these terms[8] and was prac-

ticed regularly by the early church (Acts 2:42,48; 20:7; 27:35), according to Jesus' institution and apostolic instruction (1 Cor 11:17–34).

Four dominant views of the nature of the Lord's Supper, specifically the presence of Christ in it, are present in the contemporary church: (1) The Roman Catholic tradition teaches transubstantiation, maintaining that Christ is physically present in the elements in a literal sense. The eucharistic bread is transubstantiated, or changed, into the body of Christ, while the cup of wine is transubstantiated into the blood of Christ. Because the Eucharist is a sacrament—indeed, the highest of the sacraments—participation in it is necessary for salvation. (2) Consubstantiation is the teaching of the Lutheran tradition and maintains that Christ is physically present "in, with, and through" the elements of the Lord's Supper, which is the last will and testament of Jesus Christ. Jesus Christ was the testator who died and bequeathed an inheritance to his heirs. Christians are the heirs of Christ and the beneficiaries of his death, and the inheritance is the promise of the forgiveness of sin. (3) The Reformed tradition maintains that Communion offers several benefits, including spiritual nourishment that furthers the Church's sanctification, and the experience of unity with fellow members of Christ's body. The signs of the Lord's Supper—the bread and wine—are indeed symbols, but they are not empty symbols; they convey what they symbolize. Thus, Christ is not present physically with the elements, but he is present spiritually to bless. Finally, (4) in accordance with Christ's command to celebrate the Lord's Supper "in remembrance" of him, various traditions teach that Communion is a memorial. Most Baptist, Free Church, Mennonite, Stone-Campbell, and Bible Church adherents maintain that Communion is a remembrance of the sacrifice of Christ and that Christ is present through the individual and collective memory of the body of Christ as it partakes of Christ's body (1 Cor 10:16).

While the contemporary church is divided about the Lord's Supper, several significant points of agreement also unite it. All the traditions maintain that Communion: (1) was established by Jesus; (2) requires regular observance and participation (Matt 26:29); (3) proclaims Jesus' death (1 Cor 11:26); (4) expresses the unity of church members (1 Cor 10:16–17); (5) offers numerous spiritual benefits to the church and its members; and (6) is the continuing rite or celebration of the Christian faith.

Christ and Baptism. If the Lord's Supper is the ongoing ordinance of the church, then Christian baptism is the initial ordinance. Finding its antecedents in the baptism of John,[9] Christian baptism is distinctive from it, being instituted by Christ himself in the Great Commission (Matt 28:18–20).[10] Christian baptism was first practiced on the day of Pentecost, the day of the church's birth and of the Spirit's descent (Acts 2:38,41).

Christian baptism identifies the participants with Christ, into whose name they are baptized (Matt 28:19; Acts 2:38; Gal 3:27). Historically, there have been five major traditions regarding the nature of baptism: (1) The Roman Catholic tradition regards baptism as a sacrament, a means of saving grace. In the case of infants, who are the proper recipients of baptism, original sin is removed, and baptized infants are regenerated or born again. In the case of adults who are baptized following a period of catechesis, original sin is removed, all actual sins that have been committed are forgiven, and after baptism they are regenerated. Recipients of Catholic baptism receive grace simply by having the rite administered to them. (2) The Lutheran tradition maintains baptism, which is water united with the Word of God, is the new birth that "gives forgiveness of sins, redeems from death and the devil, and gives eternal salvation."[11] Because of the promissory nature of baptism, faith is an essential element of Christian baptism. (3) In the Reformed tradition, baptism is regarded both as a sign of regeneration and union with Christ and as a sign and seal of the covenant of grace. Because the covenant community consists of both believers and their children, baptism is

administered to these children as an indication of their membership in the church. This does not ensure their salvation however,
which is God's gift of forgiveness and justification that must be
received by faith at a later time. (4) Anabaptists and contemporary Baptist traditions regard baptism as a symbol or token of
salvation. It is not administered to infants since it is reserved for
those who can give a credible profession of faith in Jesus Christ.
Moreover, the proper mode of baptism is immersion, or plung-
ing under water. Finally, (5) members of the Stone-Campbell
tradition regard baptism as the occasion of salvation but not the
means of it. Clearly, in addition to differences about the nature
of baptism, the Christian community is also divided as to the
recipients (infant baptism or believer's baptism) as well as the
mode (sprinkling, pouring, or immersion).

In spite of these distinctive differences, several significant
points of agreement about baptism unite most theological traditions. First, Christian baptism is "into" the name of the Triune
God: the Father, the Son, and the Holy Spirit (Matt 28:18–20).
Second, baptism is efficacious; it accomplishes something.
While the various traditions comprising evangelical Christianity may differ on the nature of its efficacy, they concur that
baptism is efficacious, which indicates that it is a meaningful
act. Third, baptism is also symbolic, an activity that identifies
us with Christ's death and resurrection. Paul said, "Or don't
you know that all of us who were baptized into Christ Jesus
were baptized into his death? We were therefore buried with
him through baptism into death in order that, just as Christ was
raised from the dead and through the glory of the Father, we
too may live a new life" (Rom 6:3–4). Fourth, baptism is an
act of faith. Whether that faith is expressed by the candidates
being baptized, by their sponsors, or by the church that baptized, baptism is considered to be an act of faith. Finally, while
there is indeed only one baptism (Eph 4:5), the implications
of receiving baptism are life changing. The previous passage
quoted from Romans 6 emphasizes the "new life" in Christ that

is symbolized in our baptism. The rest of the chapter continues with this theme: "In the same way, count yourselves dead to sin but alive to God in Christ Jesus. Therefore do not let sin reign in your mortal body so that you obey its evil desires" (Rom 6:11–12).

Community of the Spirit

The church is likewise a community of the Holy Spirit. Scripture describes the church as the "fellowship of the Spirit" (2 Cor 13:14; Phil 2:1), paralleling the same ideas of fellowship of the Father (1 John 1:3) and the Son (1 John 1:3; 1 Cor 1:9). Moreover, the Church is called "the temple of God" in which the Holy Spirit dwells (1 Cor 3:16–17). In the book of Acts, some mistakenly regard Peter and Paul as the key figures in Luke's narrative of the early church, when in fact the Holy Spirit is the principal figure in the narrative.

The Holy Spirit directs activity in the church in several ways. At Pentecost the Spirit gave birth to the church (Acts 1–2). Through Spirit baptism (1 Cor 12:13), each individual Christian is incorporated into the church. The gift (*dorea*, not *charismata*) of the Spirit[12] signifies and seals salvation, and the unity of the Spirit (Eph 4:3) enables the church to cohere and work together.

The Holy Spirit is not simply present in the church; he is actively ministering in it. The Spirit's ministry is most frequently described as "filling,"[13] which is the most general description of occasions when the Spirit's presence is made evident. Perhaps the most obvious ministry of the Spirit is seen in the *charismata* or gifts, which include teaching, leading, faith, mercy, prophecy, speaking in tongues, healings, helps, and many others. While lists of the *charismata* vary in Scripture,[14] the purpose of spiritual gifts is the edification of the congregation (1 Cor 14:1–5). The Holy Spirit is responsible for the sovereign distribution of these gifts to each member of the Church (1 Cor 12:11).

THE CHURCH AS VISIBLE AND
INVISIBLE COMMUNITY

The Church is a visible and invisible community (Figure 10.1). The invisible Church emphasizes the union of Christ and his assembly, sometimes referred to as the mystical or spiritual Church, whereas the visible church is the local congregation and universal Church. Paul's letters to churches begin with an address to individual congregations, "To the church of God in Corinth" (1 Cor 1:2a), or congregations in a particular geographic region, "To the church of God in Corinth, together with all the saints throughout Achaia" (2 Cor 1:2). Perhaps the best early portrait of the universal Church is seen in Acts 15 when multiple leaders from at least the Antioch church and the Jerusalem church (and possibly other Christian communities) are gathered together, forming an actual physical gathering of congregations. Finally, the invisible Church is referenced by metaphors reflecting the spiritual dimension of the Church, such as the body of Christ or household of God, which present an ideal image of the spiritual community.

Visible Local   Visible Universal   Invisible Spiritual

Figure 10.1

THE CHURCH AS COMMUNITY OF THE WORD

The Church is the community of the Word of God, grounded upon the authoritative revelation of God in Scripture. A key biblical metaphor emphasizes this aspect of the Church as the purveyor of God's truth. In 1 Tim 3:15 Paul described the household of God as the "church of the living God, the pillar and foundation of the truth." As the community of the Word, the Church supports and sustains the truth of God, articulating it and defending it against attack. This household metaphor is also used in Eph 2:19, which emphasizes the household's foundation to be Christ himself. Furthermore, the command to Christians to "speak the truth in love" (Eph 4:13) occurs in the context of helping the Church to avoid shipwreck and to grow in maturity in Christ. Indeed, one of the major themes of the Pastoral Epistles (1 and 2 Timothy and Titus) is sound doctrine, again emphasizing that the Church is the community of the Word.[15]

THE CHURCH AS MISSIONAL COMMUNITY

Luke opens the book of Acts with the affirmation that the ministry of the Church is a continuation of Christ's ministry to the world. "In my former book [Luke's Gospel], Theophilus, I wrote about all that Jesus *began* to do and to teach" (Acts 1:1, emphasis added). In other words, the Church engages in the mission of God. The Church must not only *be* a community of faith in the Triune God, it must also *do* the ministry that God has called it to accomplish. This was Jesus' point as he challenged his disciples after his resurrection. Appearing before them, he commissioned them with the following: "As the Father sent me, so I send you" (John 20:21). The sending of the Son by the Father becomes the paradigm for the Son's sending the Church. Thus, the mission of God with regard to Jesus Christ is the template for the Son's mission for the Church.

The Threefold Mission to the World

The Church's ministry to the world may be seen in three modes of operation: evangelism of the unsaved, witness of a new community to the world, and engagement in mission and sociocultural concerns (Figure 10.2).[16] First, the Church is a community of disciples sent into the world to *evangelize*. This mode stresses the urgency of proclamation of the gospel to all peoples of the world. Such a mode for the Church stresses God's sovereignty, Christ's sole role in salvation, the passionate love of Christians for others, and the accompanying concern that others embrace salvation in Christ. This builds a sense of urgency to our evangelistic mission. The mission of the Church is to convert and save the lost (Rom 15:14–21; see Matt 28:16–20). This dimension of the Church's mission would be represented by intentional, equipped endeavors to share the gospel locally, cross-culturally, and globally through contact missions programs.

Second, those who are saved become disciples of Jesus Christ and form a distinctive community, the Church. In this sense the Church may be seen as a community of visible witnesses to the world. The world sees the Church as a distinct community; the Church should make it a positive distinction. Underlying Paul's concern with the Corinthian church was their deficient, immoral example to the Corinthian community (1 Cor 5:1–8), and he discouraged lawsuits between Christians in part because of its negative witness to an unsaved judge (1 Cor 6:1–6). In this dimension of its mission, the Church should provide an authentic, personal, and communal Christian witness to the world, engaging them through persuasion, challenge, and eventually conversion into the faith community. The Church should also endeavor to inspire individuals, challenge them to affirm the faith, and lead them toward transformation (Acts 2:14–40; 4:1–12; John 13–15). This may be accomplished by a congregation that provides ministry opportunities to the community. Though not purely evangelistic, these opportunities would allow the community to gain a positive encounter with authentic people of faith in situations such as support groups, family activities, or religious holiday events like Easter or Christmas.

A final mode in which the church may conduct its mission is as a community of healing and reconciliation. "Let us not become weary in doing good, . . . as we have opportunity, let us do good to all people, especially to those who belong to the family of believers" (Gal 6:9a,10). On five occasions Paul urged the church on Crete to do good (Titus 2:7,14; 3:1,8,14). Such congregations would emphasize the mission of the Church as an agent of "doing good" in the world. This dimension of the mission calls the church to engage in ministry beyond its own walls, and beyond the purpose of evangelism, toward serving the needs of humanity. This may entail such ministries as providing services to the poor and indigent, as well as promoting just and fair practices in society.

Disciples Sent into the World — Witness to World — Reconciling and Healing a Broken World

Figure 10.2: Three Images of the Church's Mission

All three of the images of the church's mission have the common thread of the Church as an agent for reconciling the world to God through evangelism, witness, and service. "Therefore, we are ambassadors for Christ, as though God were making an appeal through us; we beg you on behalf of Christ, be reconciled to God" (2 Cor 5:20).

THE CHURCH AS A WORSHIPPING COMMUNITY

At the core of the Church is its worship of the triune God.[17] The corporate worship of God is a time when the Church actually becomes an assembly and his people come together (Heb 10:25; 1 Cor 14:26) with him as the focus of their worship (Pss 29:2–16; 96:8; 1 Chr 16:29; Isa 6:2; Rev 4:6–8; 5:9). God alone is worthy of worship, and hence our worship of him is an expected response to his holiness, majesty, goodness, and glory.

Worship in the Scriptures consists of several elements. Music, both instrumental and noninstrumental, was used by both choirs and congregants to express their intense praise and thanksgiving to God.[18] Some form of message was delivered, either through teaching or preaching[19] and especially instruction in the Scriptures (Neh 8:1–9; 1 Tim 4:13). Worship also called the faithful to prayer, both individually and corporately.[20] Additionally, the early Christian community valued giving as part of their worship (Acts 2:42–47; 2 Cor 8–9). Likewise, faithful instruction and admonition was part of the church's worship: "Let the word of Christ dwell in you richly as you teach and admonish one another with all wisdom, and as you sing psalms, hymns and spiritual songs with gratitude in your hearts to God" (Col 3:16). Finally, the church celebrated the ordinances of baptism and the Lord's Supper.

One overarching principle of corporate worship is that "God is not a God of disorder but of peace. . . . But everything should be done in a fitting and orderly way" (1 Cor 14:33a,40). As a body of believers with a concern for orderly conduct, the church is also an institution with a structure to support its identity and mission.

THE CHURCH AS AN INSTITUTIONAL COMMUNITY

All matters of church governance begin with Christ as the spiritual head of the body and then structure the actual operational governance through a variety of means. Three models seem to be prevalent in evangelical Christianity (Figure 10.3). The hierarchical model—such as Anglican/Episcopalian churches and Methodist churches—places a superstructure above the local congregation, typically dividing a denomination into geographic regions with a pyramid of leaders placed in authority over them. In this model, authority is typically held by those in the superstructure, and congregations receive instruction and direction handed down from the denominational leadership. In some cases the congregation is regarded as a support for the hierarchical structure. The assemblies model— such as Presbyterian churches and Reformed churches—is a

second type of church government. While local church officers serve their own congregations, they also exercise some
type of authority above the local church level. For example, the
General Assembly of the Presbyterian Church USA functions
as a hierarchical authoritative body above individual member
churches. In some cases the assemblies model holds the local
congregation to be the primary authority but adds to it a collective sense of church governance over the denomination or
tradition, all in support of the local congregation. A final model
for church governance maintains that there is no authoritative
structure above the local church level, so the local church is
independent. The local congregation is responsible to itself,
owning its own property, calling its own officers, choosing its
own leaders, and making its own decisions through regular
congregational business meetings. Independent churches may
belong to a broader theological tradition, but this tradition does
not contribute any additional structure to the governance of the
local churches. Furthermore, these may operate paracongrega-
tional ministry agencies (as do the other two models) for the
support of evangelism, missions, and the like, but the support
of such agencies is purely voluntary.

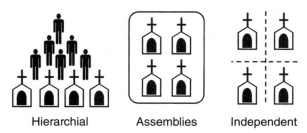

Hierarchial   Assemblies   Independent

Figure 10.3: Models of Church Governance

Regardless of which model is adopted by one's theological
tradition, one common affirmation is the headship of Christ
over the church: "He is the head of the body, the church; he is
the beginning and the firstborn from among the dead, so that in

everything he might have the supremacy" (Col 1:18). Christ as head of the church has five implications for the church.[21]

1. Christ is Lord and Savior of the church.
2. Christ's words to the church are his authority in the church.
3. Christ grants the church its mission through his authority.
4. Christ calls individuals to fulfill specific functions in the church.
5. Christ places the leadership of the church in the local congregation.

The New Testament identifies two basic leadership positions or offices in the local congregation. The first is that of elders or overseers (Gk. *presbuteroi* and *episkopoi*, respectively),[22] also called pastors or pastor-teachers (Eph 4:11). The functions of elders are leading or ruling (1 Tim 5:17; Titus 1:7), shepherding (Acts 20:28; 1 Pet 5:2), teaching or educating (Eph 4:12–13; 1 Tim 3:2), praying for the healing of the sick (Jas 5:14–16), and being involved in the exercise of church discipline (Titus 1:9). Because of the high importance and weighty responsibilities of elders, Paul established qualifications for those desiring to serve (1 Tim 3:1–7; Titus 1:5–9; see 1 Pet 5:1–4).

A second position is that of deacons or servants (Gk. *diakonoi*). Deacons are mentioned after elders in Phil 1:1 and 1 Tim 3:8–12. Some recognize the selection of seven individuals from the Jerusalem congregation in Acts 6:1–6 as the first deacons. Like elders, deacons must meet certain specific qualifications (1 Tim 3:8–12), among them passing a test of their ability to serve. It is this role of service for Jesus Christ in the local church that deacons are called to exercise (see Rom 16:1–2). Thus, deacons may serve in men's and women's ministries, youth and children's ministries, bereavement events, financial committees, and so on.

THE CHURCH AS AN EXCLUSIVE-
INCLUSIVE COMMUNITY

The church is simultaneously exclusive and inclusive. Scripture is explicit in its claim that salvation is through Jesus Christ alone. "Salvation is found in no one else, for there is no other name under heaven given to men by which we must be saved" (Acts 4:12). Scripture offers no other alternative; Christ Jesus alone is the Savior of humanity. Paul cautions the Galatian church that there is no other gospel, no alternative salvation. "If anybody is preaching to you a gospel other than what you accepted, let him be eternally condemned!" (Gal 1:9b). As such, the Church is an exclusive community, one that is limited in membership to those who acknowledge Christ as Savior and Lord. "And the Lord added to their number daily those who were being saved" (Acts 2:47b). In a world of tolerance, relativism, and pluralism, Christianity makes a claim of exclusivity; that is, salvation is found in Jesus Christ alone.

At the same time salvation is not limited by ethnicity, nationality, geography, language, gender, socioeconomic status, or age; as such, it is an inclusive community of all those who acknowledge Christ. The Church is God's new society, and though still in the world it is to be distinct from it.[23] Its newness is not a matter of age or date of origin but resides in its capacity to establish a new social norm, one that is unified. Jesus' prayer for his disciples was, "I have given them the glory that you gave me, that they may be one as we are one" (John 17:22). On the day of Pentecost, the inauguration of the Church, the Old Testament prophecy Peter quoted states, "I will pour out my Spirit on all people," including young and old, male and female, slave and free (Acts 2:1–18; citing Joel 2:28–32). This unity that Jesus desires among his followers is further explained by the apostle Paul: "There is neither Jew nor Greek, slave nor free, male nor female, for you are all one in Christ Jesus" (Gal 3:28; see Col 3:11–12). The Church is not to mimic the sociocultural divisions of the world in which it exists but rather present to the world a new kind of community—one without division. Additionally, the Church is an intergenerational community, placing value on the young and the old. As E. Clowney wrote, "The way in which the people of God are joined together by this assembly and presence produces their distinctive fellowship."[24]

THE CHURCH AS AN ESCHATOLOGICAL COMMUNITY

In addition to seeking to understand the Church in the present age, we may also wonder about the future of the Church. Eschatology can provide an answer to this question. While eschatology is a broad and divisive subject among Christians today, this section will simply endeavor to identify the place of the Church in the four main eschatological systems (amillennial, postmillennial, historic premillennial, and dispensational premillennial) so as to understand better the place of the Church in God's ultimate plans.

In eschatology the Church's relationship to the millennial kingdom (Rev 20:1–6) is a central focus. Key elements associated with this millennium period include the binding of Satan (Rev 20:1–3), faithfulness to Christ (v. 4), resurrection (vv. 4–6), judgment, and reigning with Christ (v. 6). Furthermore, the millennium is a precursor to the judgment of the dead (Rev 20:11–15), the new Jerusalem (Rev 21:10–27), and the new heavens and new earth (Rev 21:21:1–8), which is the eternal state of the whole universe. One's understanding of the millennial kingdom's relation to the Church is rather critical for a complete understanding of the nature of the Church.

The Church as Millennial Kingdom

Amillennialism and postmillennialism identify the millennial kingdom with the period of the Church's existence, in whole or in part. Amillennialism (Figure 10.4), literally "no

millennium," maintains that the millennium corresponds figuratively to the Church age. The millennium and the Church are
equated as God's kingdom. This view is held by G. Beale, W.
Hendrickson, and A. Hokema.

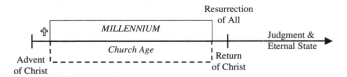

Figure 10.4: Amillennialism

Postmillennialism (Figure 10.5) regards the millennium to
be the latter part of the Church age. As a result of the preaching
of the gospel and the conversion of more and more people to
Jesus Christ, Christianity will spread increasingly throughout
the world. This will issue in a golden age of peace and pros-
perity—the millennium. Thus, the Church is a key instrument
in the coming and expansion of the millennium throughout the
earth. J. J. Davis is a proponent of this view.

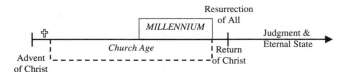

Figure 10:5: Postmillennialism

In both of these views, the Church and the millennium are
in whole or in part equated. The millennial reign of Christ in
this view is understood to be either his reign over the Church
(amillennialism) or the last peaceful and prosperous part of the
Church age (postmillennialism).

The Church as the Precursor to the Millennial Kingdom

The latter two views of eschatology regard the Church and millennial kingdom as distinct from each other, with the Church as a predecessor of the millennium. Historic or traditional premillennialism (Figure 10.6) maintains that the Church age will end with the return of Christ, which then ushers in the literal thousand-year reign of Christ. Prior to Christ's second coming, a period of great tribulation, lasting seven years, will come upon the earth and will involve great persecution of the Church. Such scholars as C. Blomberg, G. Osborne, R. Mounce, M. Erikson, W. Grudem, and G. E. Ladd hold this view.

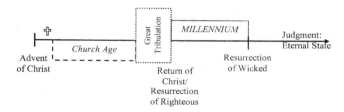

Figure 10:6: Traditional Premillennialism

A later development of premillennialism is dispensational premillennialism (Figure 10.7). First presented in the late nineteenth century, it has become a popular view of eschatology. D. Bock, H. Bateman, and G. Johnson advocate this view. The main distinction between dispensational and historic or traditional

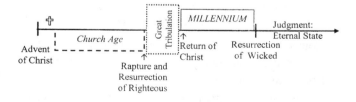

Figure 10:7: Dispensational Premillennialism

premillennialism is the Church's relationship to the seven-year tribulation. In the dispensational scheme the Church is exempted from this time of distress; thus, immediately prior to the tribulation, Christ comes for his Church and, by means of the rapture, removes it from the earth. With the Church living with Christ in heaven, the Antichrist gains political and social control of the world. Seven years later Christ returns with the Church, defeats the Antichrist, and establishes a literal thousand-year reign on the earth.[25]

Hence, as an eschatological community, the Church is either equated with the millennial kingdom or is a precursor to the establishment of the millennial kingdom. In any case, the Church is God's community awaiting the return of Christ; it is an eschatological community. How does the Church await Christ's return? In Titus 2:11–15 Paul wrote,

> For the grace of God that brings salvation has appeared to all men. It teaches us to say "No" to ungodliness and worldly passions, and to live self-controlled, upright and godly lives in this present age, while we wait for the blessed hope—the glorious appearing of our great God and Savior, Jesus Christ, who gave himself for us to redeem us from all wickedness and to purify for himself a people that are his very own, eager to do what is good. These, then, are the things you should teach. Encourage and rebuke with all authority. Do not let anyone despise you.

EDUCATIONAL IMPLICATIONS OF THE CHURCH

What is the place of Christian education in the church? How is it related to the community of the faithful? While some regard Christian education to be simply a program, such as Sunday school, or a set of programs, such as a ministry department or specialized pastoral role, some regard Christian education to have a broader role within the community.

> I worry about the idea that religious education is some special activity separated from the total life of the church. When that happens, it makes it appear that what the church does in its worship is something different from what it does in its education. I would contend that everything the church is and does is "religious education." Put more strongly, the church does not "do" religious education at all. Rather, the church *is* a form of education that is religious.[26]

The Church, as described previously, is God's means of maturing Christians.

If this broader role is accepted, the previously mentioned limitations frequently placed on Christian education are removed, and it is seen as a comprehensive ministry in the congregation. Such a model is frequently articulated by Christian educators based on E.V. Hill's model for the church, as represented in Figure 10.8.

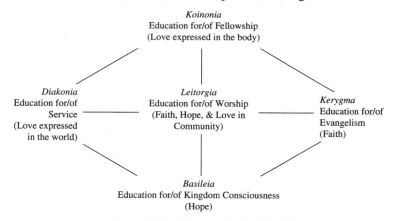

Koinonia
Education for/of Fellowship
(Love expressed in the body)

Diakonia
Education for/of
Service
(Love expressed
in the world)

Leitorgia
Education for/of Worship
(Faith, Hope, & Love in
Community)

Kerygma
Education for/of
Evangelism
(Faith)

Basileia
Education for/of Kingdom Consciousness
(Hope)

Figure 10.8: Education in the Church[27]

As one may observe, worship is the central concern of the Christian congregation, and other elements of the church's life are fellowship, evangelism, service, and a focus on social-community concerns. However, in this model, where is teaching? Is it really absent? Is it unimportant? Not at all. Teaching is in each category, and it informs the content of each of these five areas and how they interrelate.[28] Robert Pazmino comments on the possibility of 10 connections between these elements, requiring

> teachers to foster a vital connection for Christians through the explicit curriculum or content of Christian education. . . . These links also provide a means by which to assess the educational diet of any particular community and to discern particulars of the explicit, implicit, and null curricula that need attention.[29]

This would further integrate the ministry of Christian education with the body life of the church, wherein Christian education is inseparable from the congregation.

Another way of understanding Christian education in the church is represented in Figure 10.9. While in agreement with the previous model, it would add the dimension of Christian education on the z-axis. If the previous model is regarded as two-dimensional, on an x-y axis, then Christian education would be on the z-axis, adding a third dimension to it. Christian education would be in support of all the ministries of the church, as well as in a directing role for each.

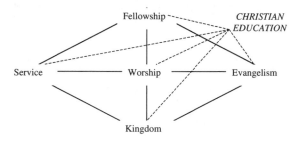

Figure 10.9: Christian Education and Church Life

Thus, Christian education is the overarching paradigm for the congregation's ministry. It is not only the lines connecting the various elements of the congregation's life; it is also the ministry that provides the necessary attention to each element of the congregation's life (worship, fellowship, evangelism, service, and kingdom). As such, education is seen as an integrated part of the congregation's life, occurring through participation with the community's life and as a distinct ministry, providing intentional instruction in the faith. For example, a congregation's evangelism ministry may need to equip individuals to present the gospel in an effective manner. The Christian education ministry could either provide educational insights into the training process as well as expertise in producing educational materials, or it could choose to integrate such equipping into existing educational ventures, such as new members classes, leadership development programs, or an Adult Bible Fellowship (ABF).

Education for Becoming the Church

The Church is indeed a distinctive community, one that is in the world, but qualitatively different from it in terms of identity, mission, relationships, and exclusive-inclusive character. Individuals do not simply become Christian in character instantaneously. Paul acknowledged the distinction between immature (carnal) and mature (spiritual) Christians in the church at Corinth (1 Cor 2:6–3:3). One does not automatically acquire Christian maturity upon accepting Christ as Savior and becoming part of the body of Christ. Likewise, Christians in relation to one another in the community of the Church do not necessarily assume a Christian posture as a corporate body, the Church. It is a process of growth in Christ, becoming Christlike individually and the church corporately. As such, education in the Church is in part a process of socialization, whereby the community's character is incorporated into the individual members comprising it. However, it is also a community that provides direct intentional instruction in the faith as a means of becoming the Church.

Dykstra commented, "People are formed in faith as Christian in Christian community, and our word for that is church."[30] He stated further that if faith is the participation with God and the things of God, then we must portray "the church as context of participation."[31] For example, an individual may experience the transcendence of God while participating in worship, but he also encounters the immanence of God in the relationships experienced in small groups. "Christian education must instill the identity, values, vocation, practices . . . [and] the culture of the congregation into the individual Christian and the individual Christian affirming the priority of the corporate body and gleaning their individual identity from the corporate body."[32] As indicated previously, Christian education is not a matter of a program or ministry but the immersion of the individual into the total body life of the Christian community, engaging not only in Christian education proper but all aspects of the congregation's life. Peter Hodgson, referring to Calvin's *Institutes* (4.1.5), commented, "The church as teacher . . . is the function of the school, that is, of education as institutionalized activity, and the church is a kind of school, the school of the Holy Spirit."[33]

More specifically, four aspects of the church provide educational opportunities for the individual Christian:

- *Transmitting Theological Heritage:* Instruction in the content of the faith; for example, Scripture, theology, and the history of the congregation and denomination/tradition.
- *Imitating a Faithful Heritage:* Continued observance of the distinctive practices of the congregation; for example, the ordinances and rituals of the church.
- *Participating in the Ministry:* Commitment to fulfilling the mission of the congregation as well as serving in the institutional structure of the congregation; for example, the ministries and missions of the church.

- *Partaking in the Life of the Spirit:* Involvement in the spiritual practices of the congregation; for example, spiritual disciplines and congregational observances.

In short, we become the Church as we grow toward Christ-likeness, both personally and corporately, through the engagement of the individual with the community of the Church.

Affirmation of Tradition and Heritage

While there is one true Church, the invisible Church, there are many churches, the visible church. The spiritual image of the Church as a unified community of the saved is the ideal to which the church should aspire. In reality, as members of the visible church, we recognize that the universal Church is indeed divided. Our individual congregations may be members of a denomination, a broader theological tradition, or an ecumenical structure; nonetheless, the present reality of the church is one of division. As Christians, we not only find our spiritual identity in the images depicting the invisible Church but also in the individual congregation in which we worship, study, and serve.

Christian education should seek to explore this reality. Christians should know their congregation's heritage, as well as the heritage of the denomination and tradition. Christians would benefit by knowing their relative location on the theological and historical landscape to which they belong. While some may identify the church as just the local congregation because this is the scope of their experience, they should gain a glimpse into what the invisible Church must be like—a greater fellowship—as their understanding of the church broadens to their denomination or tradition. People can comprehend the vastness of the Church universal when they realize that the sun never sets on it since it is a global fellowship of believers. The faith community is no longer limited to the local congregation, for it includes other congregations as well as parachurch organizations in support of the local congregation, such as

seminaries, publishers, missionaries, and educational agencies
around the world.

Equipping to Lead and Serve

Education in the church must also provide for the training of
its leadership. A commitment to an equipped leadership is not
simply due to institutional necessity but reflects the theological
convictions of the church as an institution and individuals as
called by God to serve in the congregation. The qualifications
for elders and deacons are based on the assumption that the
church has produced such mature individuals to fill these positions. For example, these individuals are obviously people of
exemplary moral character and knowledge of the truth, so they
can teach God's Word in the congregation and in the family and
so they can defend God's truth against heresy as they represent
the church with integrity (1 Tim 3:1–13; Titus 1:5–9). Education in the church should endeavor to generate such individuals
for leadership roles as needed by the congregation.

Leaders are neither made nor born; they are summoned,
called by God. Leaders of such qualities as described above
require a specified endeavor to equip them. While they may
learn Scripture and theology in the classroom, a long process of
discipleship and mentoring should also be used to build Christian character and provide time for spiritual maturity. This is the
reason a "recent convert" cannot be considered for leadership
(1 Tim 3:6a). Equipping leaders to serve in the church takes a
long-term commitment so members can mature spiritually and
develop sound theology. Only then should they be recognized
as servants who can provide evidence of a call to serve in a specific capacity with practical orientation to the area of service.

Diversity in Education

The early church was a diverse community. Jews, Gentiles,
men, women, freemen, slaves, old, young—all were part of
God's new community. To assume that the formation of such

a union was automatic and without challenges would be a mistake. The earliest conflicts in the church were over ethnicity, as seen in the oversight of the Grecian widows in Acts 6:1–7, the Jerusalem counsel of Acts 15 when the spiritual status of Gentile believers was determined, and other conflicts reflected in the epistles. For example, Paul reminded the Roman congregation, "Accept one another, then, just as Christ accepted you, in order to bring praise to God" (Rom 15:7). The world offers only tolerance, but the Christian community is one of acceptance, recognizing one another's differences while valuing their presence as brothers and sisters in Christ. It is not a unity based on social necessity or legal pressure but on the spiritual reality of a common salvation in Christ and a valuing of the unique contribution each culture can make to the life and ministry of the church. This requires Christians who are instructed in the basic theological convictions of the faith in regard to salvation and the church and who also have specific training in building relationships and cultural sensitivity. Methods of instruction that draw from differences in a constructive manner, such as discussion and decision making, provide community-building opportunities for the church.

Perhaps the most obvious implication of the inclusive diversity of the church is intergenerational education. The intergenerational nature of the faith community was addressed in chapter 3, but now it is more fully expressed in understanding the community of the church.[34] The church is for all generations, for people from cradle to grave. The positive benefit of diversity in the church is indeed seen in the intergenerational nature of the congregation. Paul addressed this in Titus 2:1–8:

> You must teach what is in accord with sound doctrine. Teach the older men to be temperate, worthy of respect, self-controlled, and sound in faith, in love and in endurance.

Likewise, teach the older women to be reverent in the way they live, not to be slanderers or addicted to much wine, but to teach what is good. Then they can train the younger women to love their husbands and children, to be self-controlled and pure, to be busy at home, to be kind, and to be subject to their husbands, so that no one will malign the word of God.

Similarly, encourage the young men to be self-controlled. In everything set them an example by doing what is good. In your teaching show integrity, seriousness and soundness of speech that cannot be condemned, so that those who oppose you may be ashamed because they have nothing bad to say about us.[35]

Congregations that engage in intergenerational experiences and education benefit principally in two ways. First, younger generations benefit from the life experience, wisdom, leadership, maturity, and spirituality of the older generation. The older generations have the ability to provide guidance and direction to the next generation. Second, older generations benefit from the energy, enthusiasm, idealism, volunteerism, and resourcefulness of younger generations. This also builds cohesion between the generations presently comprising the church.

Eschatology and Education

Since eschatology shapes the church's self-perception, it also influences how education may be done in the church. Education in part is designed to prepare individuals and communities for the future. The flow of history's direction in part dictates the direction education takes in the church. For those who see the Church as the millennial kingdom (amillennialism and postmillennialism), education would be *for* the millennium. Education would be for the purpose of Christians identifying themselves as citizens of the kingdom, the reign of God; and for postmillennialism it would add the dimension of ushering in the millennium, that is, social justice and global mission. Since Christians would be part of the millennium, education would emphasize counterculture as the church endeavors to serve as an embassy for God in the world.

When the church is viewed as a precursor to the millennial kingdom (historic and dispensational premillennialism), education would be *in preparation for* the millennium. The millennium and the Church are two different periods of time, linked but not equated, so education that reflects such eschatological views would emphasize awaiting the return of Christ and being prepared for his return. While to some extent all these eschatological educational implications could be shared by anyone holding to any of the four eschatological views, they differ in emphases. One common element to all of them is that they would ultimately contend that Christians should focus on eternity. "Set your minds on things above, not only earthly things. For you died, and your life is now hidden with Christ in God. *When Christ, who is your life, appears, then you also will appear with him in glory*" (Col 3:2–4, emphasis added). Hence, education should always include an emphasis on the future, with application in the present, as we develop a patient waiting on the inevitable return of Christ for his people, the Church.

REFLECTION QUESTIONS

1. How are new believers acculturated into your congregation? How are they introduced to the culture of the faith community?
2. In what ways is your congregation inclusive? How does it endeavor to embody seamlessness in terms of ethnicity, gender, or age?
3. How does your congregation's education ministry endeavor to fulfill the threefold dimensions of the Church's mission?
4. How well does your congregation provide for the equipping and training of leaders for service?

1   See J. R. Wilson, "Practicing Church," in *The Community of the Word: Toward an Evangelical Ecclesiology*, ed. M. Husbands and D. J. Treier (Downers Grove, IL: InterVarsity, 2005), 63–70.

2   Exod 19:4–6; 35:1; Lev 20:8; Deut 4:20; 7:6; 10:4,34.

3   Pss 23:1; 74:1; 78:52; 80:1; 95:7; 100:3; Jer 3:20; Isa 54:5–7; 58:6–7; 62:4; Ezek 16:15; Hos 2:7; 6:8; Amos 3:2; 5:15,24.

4   Isa 42:6; 49:6; Jer 31:31–34; Ezek 36:26–27. See discussion in A. F. Johnson and R. E. Webber, *What Christians Believe: A Biblical and Historical Summary* (Grand Rapids: Zondervan Academic, 1989), 326–28.

5   Johnson and Webber, *What Christians Believe,* 330.

6   1 Cor 1:2; 10:32; 15:9; 2 Cor 1:1; Gal 1:13; 1 Tim 3:15.

7   1 Thess 2:14; 1 Cor 11:16.

8   Matt 26:17–46; Mark 14:12–26; Luke 22:7–38.

9   Matt 3:7; 21:25; Mark 1:4; 11:30; Luke 3:3; 7:29; Acts 1:22.

10 Acts 10:37; 13:24; 18:25; 19:3–4.

11 M. Luther, *Smaller Catechism*, 2.

12 Luke 11:13; John 3:34; Acts 2:38; 8:20; 10:45; 11:17.

13 Luke 1:15,41,67; 4:1; Acts 2:4; 4:8,31; 6:3,5; 7:55; 9:17; 11:24; 13:52; Eph 5:18.

14 1 Pet 4:10; 1 Cor 1:7; 12:4,9,30; Rom 12:6; Eph 4:11.

15 1 Tim 1:3; 2:7; 3:9,15–16; 4:6; 6:3,20; 2 Tim 1:13–14; 2:15–18; 3:8; 4:3–4; Titus 1:13; 2:1.

16 D. Senior, "Correlating Images of Church and Images of Mission in the New Testament," *Missiology* 23.1 (1995): 3–16.

17 D. Peterson, *Engaging with God: A Biblical Theology of Worship* (Downers Grove, IL: InterVarsity, 2002).

18   Exod 15:1–18; Pss 92:1,4; 95:1; 149:1–4; 150:3–5; Matt 26:30; 1 Cor 14:26; Eph 5:19.

19 1 Chr 16:9,23; Pss 95:1; 96:2–3; 1 Cor 14:1–5,26–32; 1 Pet 2:9.

20 Ps 66:18; Jer 5:25; Matt 6:9,14–16; Phil 4:6; 1 Thess 5:25; 1 Tim 2:1–4; Jas 5:16.

21 See L. Berkhof, "The Governance of the Church," in *Readings in Christian Theology, Volume 3: The New Life*, ed. M. J. Erickson (Grand Rapids: Baker, 1979), 320–23.

22 The terms *elder* and *overseer/bishop* in the New Testament denote the same office. See Acts 20:17,28; 1 Tim 3:1; 4:14; 5:17,19; Titus 1:5,7; 1 Pet 5:12.

23 See D. S. Dockery, "A Theology for the Church," *Midwestern Journal of Theology* 1.1–2 (2003): 13.

24 E. Clowney, "Toward a Biblical Doctrine of the Church," in *Readings in Christian Theology, Volume 3: The New Life,* 24.

25 It should be noted that in some forms of dispensational eschatology the rapture occurs prior to, during, or immediately after the reign of the Antichrist.

26 S. Hauerwas, "The Gesture of a Truthful Story," in *Theological Perspectives on Christian Formation*, ed. J. Astley, L. J. Francis, and C. Cowder (Grand Rapids: Eerdmans, 1996), 97.

27 See Hill, "A Congregation's Response."

28 R. W. Pazmino, *God Our Teacher* (Grand Rapids: Baker, 2001), 114–15.

29 R. W. Pazmino, *Principles and Practices of Christian Education* (Grand Rapids: Baker, 1992), 94–95.

30 C. R. Dykstra, "No Longer Strangers: The Church and Its Educational Ministry," in *Theological Perspectives on Christian Formation*, ed. Jeff Astley (Grand Rapids: Eerdmans, 1997), 106.

31 Ibid., 109–13.

32 F. B. Veverka, "Congregational Education: Shaping the Culture of the Local Church," *Religious Education* 92.1 (1997): 77–90.

33 P. C. Hodgson, *God's Wisdom: Toward a Theology of Education* (Louisville: Westminster John Knox, 1999), 33.

34 See A. G. Harkness, "Intergenerational Education for an Intergenerational Church?" *Religious Education* 93.4 (1998): 431–47.

35 The psalmists also spoke of passing on their beliefs to the next generation; see Pss 48:13; 71:18; 78:4.

CHAPTER 11

Toward a Theologically Informed
Approach to Education

James Riley Estep Jr.

*I*f someone were to observe a Sunday school class at
your church, or perhaps a midweek Bible study, or a
classroom at a Christian school, would the observer see
anything distinctively Christian about it? Would the Christian
distinctive be so self-evident that even an unbeliever would
detect a qualitative difference in the education? If education in
the church is to be qualitatively different, it must be based on
educational principles that reflect Christian theological beliefs.
Our theology must be incarnated in our approach to education.

This chapter endeavors to provide a basic framework of
theologically informed educational principles, so it is by no
means a complete and systematic theory of education, which
would have to involve the integration of social science theories such as learning or developmental theories. Rather, I utilize the seven common elements of every approach to education (identified in chapter 1) and address each element from
the theological perspective presented in this book. It will cut
horizontally across the text to provide a brief sketch of educational principles that are collectively informed by the individual doctrines discussed in the previous chapters. The seven
essential elements of education are: (1) the purpose and objectives of education, (2) the role of the teacher, (3) the role of the

student, (4) the relationship between the teacher and the student, (5) the curriculum content, (6) the learning environment and methods, and (7) the means of evaluation. In discussing these elements, I hope to give the reader a basic but comprehensive expression of the Christian distinctive of education in the form of theologically informed principles for the Christian educator.

THE PURPOSE AND OBJECTIVES

As with anything Christian, education's ultimate purpose is to bring glory to God. Education that glorifies God is God centered, viewing every subject and decision with him ultimately in mind. Because God is as he is described in the Scriptures, he is worthy and able to be the center of our approach to education. This is made possible because God has revealed himself to us through his creation but more specifically through his Word, the Bible. While some approaches to education marginalize or excuse God from them, Christian education's purpose is to glorify him in every element of its approach to education. How does it do this?

Education that glorifies God is one that transforms individuals into mature followers of Jesus Christ. The objectives of Christian education reflect this God-centeredness in terms of how it endeavors to transform. Christian education is not primarily about content, teaching methods, audiovisual technology, or facilities; it is about people! Hence, the objectives of Christian education are centered not on teaching but on the life characteristics it endeavors to promote in the Christian's life. Its prime objective is to see the members of the body in the church—both on the individual and cooperate levels—mature in their relationship with God. To this end three sets of objectives are essential to Christian education.

First, Christians must consistently approach all of life with a Christian worldview. Worldview is the ultimate expression of

Christian thought. It is built on the foundation of our study of Scripture, the formation of doctrine, the development of theology, and ultimately addresses the philosophical issues of reality, truth, ethics, and aesthetics that produce a Christian perspective on all of life. This is possible because of the nature of God's special revelation, Scripture. As such, worldview serves as a framework through which all of life is viewed. Without a Christian worldview, it is virtually impossible to expect Christians to live as Christians should. Since the formation of a Christian worldview begins with a thorough knowledge of Scripture as God's Word, it requires a content-centered approach to curriculum. If Christians are to think as Christians should, then Christian education must be designed so as to promote the formation of Christian worldview among all those in the church as a foundation for the Christian life in relationship to God. Education that glorifies God is one that transforms individuals into mature followers of Jesus Christ. "Do not conform any longer to the pattern of this world, but be transformed by the renewing of your mind. Then you will be able to test and approve what God's will is — his good, pleasing and perfect will" (Rom 12:2). Educational goals that reflect this objective may be expressed as follows:

- Mature Christians have a thorough knowledge of Scripture.
- Mature Christians comprehend essential Christian doctrines.
- Mature Christians value Scripture and theology in their lives.
- Mature Christians are able to study Scripture for themselves.
- Mature Christians are able to think theologically about life decisions.

Goals such as these, and others that reflect the particulars of our congregations, further express the Christian worldview objective, making it more lucid and measurable.

Second, Christians must develop piety and character consistent with their faith. Spiritual maturity is more than just piety, as noted in chapter 9, but it must include piety and character while conforming our lives to the example of Jesus Christ. If our relationship with God is to be personal, an experienced relationship, then Christians must have piety and character. Without piety and character, Christianity becomes overly intellectual, a mental assent to Bible content, theology, and worldview. For Christian education to achieve this objective, it must move beyond the classroom and into the lives of the individual Christian. The curriculum would have to be more student centered, perhaps even designed with the individual Christian in mind. While education of this kind would require the use of Scripture, it would not be principally for content mastery, as in the first objective, but more for personal reflection, practicing the spiritual disciplines, meditation, and devotional application. Educational goals that reflect this objective may be expressed as follows:

- Mature Christians practice a regular pattern of devotion.
- Mature Christians exhibit a loving relationship toward God, fellow Christians, and the community.
- Mature Christians affirm their commitment to Christ.
- Mature Christians exhibit a high level of theologically informed moral reasoning.
- Mature Christians maintain a consistent Christian witness.

Measuring goals in the affective domain of learning is difficult to say the least, and they are less quantifiable than cognitive. But they are measurable through qualitative means, as explained later in this chapter. These goals require an approach to education that includes mentoring, discipling, and the practice of spiritual disciplines.

Third, Christians must serve as the church. Christians do not serve *in* the church but *as* the church. We *are* the church.

When this is instilled in the minds and on hearts of Christians, their participation in ministry becomes a natural expression of their relationship with God. However, knowing about serving and having the desire to serve are not enough; the congregation must provide opportunities and equip Christians to serve. If Christians are to serve as Christians should, a process-centered approach to instruction is required. Like learning to ride a bike, Christians need to be instructed on the process of doing evangelism, musical performance, teaching, and even leading as a Christian. Educational goals that reflect this objective may be expressed as follows:

- Mature Christians commit themselves to a ministry in the church.
- Mature Christians develop their talents for Christian service.
- Mature Christians value ministry participation as a means of spiritual formation.
- Mature Christians demonstrate a Christian motive and rationale for serving as the church.
- Mature Christians participate in training and equipping for service provided by the congregation.

For Christian education to achieve this objective, it must have a long-term commitment to the equipping of believers, which includes recruitment, orientation, training, and continual equipping of other Christians to serve in ministry as the church. How is all of this achievable? No single curriculum or approach to education is able to address all the objectives sufficiently. What is required is a multidimensional approach to education in the church, all the dimensions of which are theologically informed principles. Figure 11.1 on the next page is an adaptation of Figure 9.2. It illustrates the relationship between Christian education and the spiritual maturity of Christians.

The key to the holistic approach is to recognize that each form of education must be centered on the ultimate purpose of education, bringing glory to God. If the objectives are mistaken for the purpose, it would be disastrous for the Christian and the congregation. For example, if a church overemphasizes piety and character, education results in experiential fluff, warm feeling, devoid of substance. If the church overemphasizes service, we may

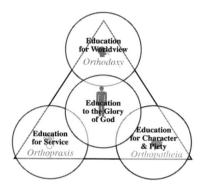

Figure 11.1: Holistic Response Model

see Christians experience spiritual burnout because they have been overextended in service projects. Even an overemphasis on worldview, which focuses exclusively on the intellectual study of Scripture and theology, produces a dry orthodoxy and could result in legalism. If the church keeps God in the center of education and his glory as its purpose, the other objectives are kept in balance. This leads to a holistic approach to spiritual formation in Christian education.[1] Christian education wants Christians to think like Christ, value like Christ, and serve as Christ has called us to serve. By the intentional alignment of the remaining educational elements toward the achievement of these objectives, Christian education glorifies God and matures the faithful, individually and corporately.

THE ROLE OF THE TEACHER

What does it mean to be a Christian teacher? Obviously, a teacher is one who teaches since the title is defined by the action. However, what it means to be a teacher in the church is multidimensional. Some seek to define an effective teacher as a gifted scholar, a competent methodologist, a spiritual guide, or one who focuses on the role of a teacher in relation to the objectives of Christian education. To all of these we would say yes. There is more to being a teacher than just teaching.

Essentially, the Christian teacher has five roles. *First, the teacher is an instrument of God.* Those who teach in the church must approach the task with humility since their authority, message, position, and call to serve all come from God. As an instrument of God, teachers realize that they are *not* God but are called by him to fulfill a ministry in the church. This should shape the teacher's disposition as one whose life exemplifies humble submission to God as well as to the ministry of instruction to which he or she has been called.

Serving as an instrument of God should likewise call the teacher to higher and ever increasing expectations of one's service. Teachers are to strive toward excellence in all they do, not to gain acclaim or accomplishment but to glorify God through their service. Paul admonished the Christian community at Colossi, "And whatever you do, whether in word or deed, do it all in the name of the Lord Jesus, giving thanks to God the Father through him" (Col 3:17), and again, "Whatever you do, work at it with all your heart, as working for the Lord, not for men, since you know that you will receive an inheritance from the Lord as a reward. It is the Lord Christ you are serving" (vv. 23–24). Christian teachers are held to a higher standard because of a higher calling (Jas 3:1), so they seek opportunities for continued improvement and development and endeavor always to represent God in all that they do and say in the classroom and in the community.

Second, the teacher must be a diligent student of the Word. This is a practical necessity, but it is primarily because Scripture is the revealed and inspired Word of God. The Scriptures describe Ezra as one who "had devoted himself to the study and observance of the Law of the Lord, and to teaching its decrees and laws in Israel" (Ezra 7:10). Before he taught God's Word, he studied and lived it. Typically, effective teachers have been good students and are recognized as those who know the Word, not only in a formal sense but in a personal sense as well. Regardless of the teachers' instructional context or which learning objective they endeavor to address, a thorough knowledge of Scripture is foundational to their effectiveness. Congregations must commit to a well-resourced program of equipping teachers to be students of Scripture that does not simply relying on weekend workshops or the occasional guest speaker to equip adequately a teacher to teach Scripture in any capacity. Teacher development requires not only basic orientation and training but mentoring by a more experienced teacher, assessment with feedback, Bible study resources (in the church's library or Web site), and opportunities for Bible instruction, not just training in teaching methods. Teachers who do not know Scripture or who serve in a congregation lacking in opportunities for teacher development may eventually become intimidated or disenchanted with the call to teach.

Third, the teacher must assume the role of a mentor. The role of a teacher extends beyond the classroom. Teachers assume the role of the one with greater maturity in the learning relationship. Teachers must be experienced Christians who experienced conversion many years earlier and also have a Christian lifestyle that demonstrates a maturing relationship with Christ. Teachers serve as examples to their students, teaching not only with their words but with their lives. Christian teachers assume the role of being faithful role models and mentors of their students faith. This requires them to know the students beyond the confines of a classroom or group setting, demonstrating a willingness to become personally engaged with students one-on-one in a discipling relationship. Praying for students, giving attention during times of spiritual or personal need, and spending time over coffee just sharing about life and faith are part of fulfilling this ministry role of a teacher.

Fourth, the teacher must be a servant leader in the church. Given the nature of the church, teachers automatically assume the mantle of leadership. Most Christian education occurs in the context of the local congregation, and those who assume the role of teacher in the church likewise assume the role of servant leader. Teachers are perceived as leaders by those they teach, and in many respects their instruction is recognized as the official voice of the church since their ministry is part of the infrastructure of the church. In fact, 1 Tim 3:2 (see Titus 1:9–11) requires that congregational leaders be "able to teach" as part of fulfilling their leadership responsibilities. As servant leaders, teachers understand that their instruction is to be used in the service of the congregation, God's people. They understand their teaching is in the service of the class and congregations. Teachers must be faithful to the theology of their congregation, and as servant leaders they must use their position to uphold the beliefs, practices, and direction of the congregation. Teachers do this best when they understand their place in the ministry of the church. As servant leaders teachers must also realize that their influence goes beyond the walls of the classroom or group setting. Teachers are not only servants but leaders.

Finally, the teacher must be a learning specialist, knowing the students and the curriculum. A Christian teacher, as one called by God and authorized by the congregation to be a biblical instructor and mentor, also assumes the responsibility of teaching well. To this end teachers must have an intimate knowledge of their students' faith and lives as well as the curriculum they use to instruct them. Teachers who do not assume this role inevitably approach teaching as a stale and routine method of generic information dissemination without taking into account the specific needs of their students or the nature of the instructional materials. As learning specialists they endeavor to know their students (as would a mentor) and make the appropriate use of Scripture (students of God's Word) to address their lives and spiritual needs. Teachers who assume this role intentionally spend time with other teachers, sharing ideas and seeking new materials and methodologies for classroom use, rather than settling for whatever the congregation may provide as a basic curriculum.

THE ROLE OF THE STUDENT

Christian educators first and foremost understand that their students are more than what developmental theories can determine. Developmental*ism*, as an approach to comprehending human nature or speculating about spirituality, is insufficient for Christian educators. We understand the essential nature and identity of students to be as those who are God's image bearers. Students are made in God's image. They are valuable to God regardless of their spiritual status (lost, immature, or mature). With this core understanding of the student's human nature, what can teachers reasonably expect from students? What role should students understand themselves to assume as part of the learning environment? The students' role is directly tied to the learning objective being addressed by the teacher since with each of the three basic learning objectives the students assume a new role in the learning process. If we reflect on Figure 11.1, each objective places on the student an assumed role in the learning environment.

- *Education for Worldview:* The Student as Learner—the Teacher as Knowledgeable Instructor
- *Education for Character and Piety:* The Student as Disciple—the Teacher as Pastoral Mentor
- *Education for Service:* The Student as Apprentice—the Teacher as Trainer-Coach

Of course, the principle aim of a Christian's life is to glorify God, and hence that becomes the central expectation and role of a student. How is this done by a student in an educational setting? A student moves toward having an increasingly God-centered life in three main ways: (1) diligently studying God's Word; (2) being a faithful disciple of Jesus Christ; and

(3) becoming an equipped servant of the kingdom. All three of these are explained more fully below.

First, the student is a learner, shaping the Christian mind. Students must assume the role of learners, those who are responsible for committing their minds to knowing God's Word so as to develop a Christian mind-set. In this instance the teacher is an instructor to the students. In order to fulfill this role, students must develop four learning qualities. (1) Students must be *attentive* learners, hearing the instructions of their teachers and demonstrating a willingness to listen and learn. It is difficult to learn of one is unwilling to listen. (2) Students must be *respondent* learners, who not only listen but engage with the instructor in posing questions and in desiring to comprehend what is being taught. It is difficult for students to learn if they do not raise critical questions and seek clarification. (3) Students must eventually become *participatory* learners. As learners increase in their knowledge and comprehension, it is possible for them to engage in an informed dialogue with one another. While the teacher is still involved with the instructional process, students should mature to the point that they are capable of teaching one another through intelligent dialogue. Students cannot learn if they do not eventually become active participants in a learning community. (4) Students must ultimately become *self-directed* learners, possibly becoming teachers themselves. As students mature intellectually, they develop the traits of self-directed, lifelong learners who are no longer directly dependent on the guidance of an instructor. They cannot be learners if they don't develop the disposition and skills to search for answers independently. In short, the role of students as learners is in itself a fluid one since it changes as students intellectually develop from dependence on the instructor to an interdependence with each other. Ultimately, independent learners become teachers themselves.

Second, the student is a disciple, shaping the Christian heart. As students endeavor to pattern their lives to what God has revealed in Scripture, they transform their lives into the image of Jesus Christ. This is a lifelong, cumulative effect of assuming the role of a disciple, one who orients his heart toward God. In this case the teacher assumes the role of a mentor, one who provides guidance in matters related to the integration of faith into life. Rather than the sage on the stage, the teacher becomes the guide at the side. As a disciple studies Scripture, every stage of his life is addressed. For example, as one reads Eph 5:21–6:10 throughout his life, different messages surface and find new applications to life. As a child, "Children obey your parents in the Lord, for this is right" (6:1) becomes a highlighted theme. As one grows older and marries, "Wives, be subject to your own husbands" (5:22) or "Husbands, love your wives" (5:25) is quite applicable. Still later, when one becomes a parent, "Fathers, do not provoke your children to anger" (6:4) becomes a resounding admonition. On each occasion Scripture's content does not change, but its applicability addresses our faith needs at every stage of life. This devotional use of Scripture, or engaging in personal theological reflection, is associated with being a disciple. Students must assume the role of a disciple to make use of the Scriptures to transform their lives.

Third, the student is an apprentice, shaping the Christian servant. To be a wholly devoted follower of Christ, the student must assume responsibility for participating in the ministry of the congregation. Without this role students will lack the spiritual satisfaction of serving others as the church. In this case teachers assume the role of trainer-coach, and the student becomes their apprentice. Learning to serve in the church requires more than a classroom orientation and instruction effectively to engage in ministry. Learning to evangelize requires that one be taken on an evangelistic call by someone who is proficient at evangelism. Learning to be a teacher requires that one observe and be observed by an experienced, competent teacher. Serving as a leader in the congregation should be preceded by a period as an apprentice with a mature and capable congregational leader.

If a student is unwilling to assume the role of apprentice, it may indicate an unteachable spirit, one that does not see the necessity or value of being trained by an experienced person. Students assume the role of apprentice when they recognize the need for instruction beyond the classroom in order to participate in congregational ministry.

What keeps these roles in balance? Just as the objectives they reflect are held in balance by a God-centered life, the desire of the student to be a Christian who lives a God-centered life keeps these roles in balance. These three roles—learner, disciple, and apprentice—are all centered on becoming a more complete and fulfilled Christian. If this purpose can be kept in focus, the roles will be kept in balance with each other.

THE RELATIONSHIP BETWEEN THE TEACHER AND THE STUDENT

How do students and teachers interact? From a Christian perspective, relationships are a reflection of the trinitarian God in whose image we were created. Hence, the teacher-student relationship is not simply a means of enhancing educational effectiveness but a necessity of participating in a God-centered education. As previously mentioned, the teacher may assume a different role with a student, such as being a knowledgeable instructor, pastoral mentor, or trainer-coach, each with a different relational dynamic. However, our theological foundations provide four basic principles that shape the relationship shared by teachers and students in any circumstance.

First, the teacher-student relationship is one of respect. Regardless of the student's spiritual or social status, or the student's race, gender, or ethnicity, he is made in God's image; and since this is true, he must be treated with respect. R. Habermas identified three "practical dimensions" of the *imago Dei* in the teacher-student relationship: (1) It facilitates a "transformed attitude" toward others. (2) It requires "transformed behaviors" as to how a student treats others. (3) It engenders a "greater appreciation for diversity" among all of humanity.² Because of these dimensions, students must be treated fairly and indiscriminately and given equal opportunities to succeed. They must never be shunned or intentionally embarrassed but should always be shown respect from the Christian teacher.

Second, the teacher-student relationship is primarily spiritual. If the Holy Spirit has any role in Christian education, particularly in the area of teaching and learning, then the relationship shared by the teacher and student must be a spiritual one. The spiritual facet of the teacher-student relationship is the primary dimension of any Christian relationship. Regardless of how many other ways we may relate to another Christian, the primary relationship is one of spiritual siblings in Christ. Before believers become students of a certain teacher, they are that teacher's brothers and sisters in Christ. The primacy of being spiritual siblings with students causes the teacher not only to respect students further as Christians—members of Christ's body—but also to recognize their mutual dependence on Christ for their salvation and continued transformation. It reminds the Christian teacher that intellectual achievement as a learner, moral excellence as a disciple, and practical competence as an apprentice are secondary to the student's relationship with God. We are brothers and sisters in Christ regardless of anything else that may enter into the relationship.

Third, the teacher-student relationship is a formative one. Teachers understand that, while they and their students are colearners and spiritual siblings in Christ, teachers are more advanced than the students. In the teacher-student relationship the teacher is the leader, and the student is the follower. It is the teacher's task to lead the student into a more mature relationship with God, one which teachers presumably already possess, which means that the relationship is a formative one. Teachers must on occasion assess the degree of spiritual maturity in the student and seek to aid in the spiritual formation process. In many instances the teacher must believe in the student more than the student believes in himself or herself. Teachers assume the responsibility of building a relationship with students as a means of advancing the students intellect, disposition, and competencies in the service of God, and of conforming their lives to God's Word.

Fourth, the teacher-student relationship is ecclesiastical. Since most of Christian education is done in the context of a congregation or a church-related institution, the relationship between the teacher and the student is one that exists in an ecclesiastical context. This refers to the context of the Christian community wherever it may be assembled, not to a building. The relationship shared by the student is also one of comembers of Christ's body, the Church. Teachers and their students are among the people of God, so both are called to be servants—not *in* the church but *as* the church. Both students and teachers are endeavoring to mature in all dimensions of their spiritual lives to become able-bodied servants *as* the Church. As the Church their relationships have a common identity and context in which they learn, live, and labor. Hence, teachers and students are to be churchmen and churchwomen. They do not simply seek to serve one another, nor to advance an institutional agenda, but to advance God's mission—something beyond all of them that requires the joint commitment of both teachers and students.

THE CURRICULUM CONTENT

When one sees the word *curriculum,* it often conjures up the image of a packet of materials purchased from a publishing company, such as a 13-week week curriculum for a Sunday school class or a book with a leader's guide for a small group. While these images are partially accurate, they do not do the term justice. *Curriculum* comes from the Latin *currere*, which literally means "to run" and indicates the course of one's studies or the direction of one's race in life, such as in preparing a *curriculum vita*. Curriculum is the manifestation of education, as Figure 11.2 on the next page depicts.[3]

The Visible Part of the Curriculum

- The teaching-learning situation in the local church
- The experiences of learners under church guidance
- Printed resources and helps
- Other learning aids

The Root System of the Curriculum

- Theology
- Social science theories
- Curriculum theory
- Curriculum design

Figure 11.2: Curriculum and Education

D. C. Wyckoff explained curriculum as "the plan and program by which the church seeks to fulfill its educational imperative," including programs, theory, design, content, and materials.[4] It is the capstone of education in the church, the ideal expression of everything educational. In fact, the journal *Educational Leadership* is almost exclusively about curriculum development. So what is Christian curriculum?

Christian curriculum must advance the transformative objective of Christian education since it is tied to the God-centered purpose and transformative learning objectives previously mentioned. There are six principles for curriculum content.

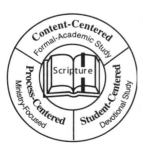

Figure 11.3: Scripture-Centered Content

The first principle is that Scripture is the essential focus of the content. As the Word of God, it contributes to the various functions of fulfilling the objectives of Christian education. Christian curriculum provides its users significant engagement in Scripture on every level of instruction (see Figure 11.3).

While each objective may make a different use of it, Scripture is nonetheless the central content of a Christian curriculum. The content-centered approach is aimed at making students master the actual content of Scripture and theology and further develop their theological reasoning abilities. A student-centered approach would aim students toward making use of Scripture devotionally or as a source for theological reflection. Even the process-centered approach toward education, designed primarily to equip students with ministry skills, would make use of Scripture to explain the rationale, motive, and "oughtness" of Christian ministry. It would be difficult to assess any curriculum as being "Christian" if it in fact omitted Scripture.

The second principle is that curriculum content must engage Scripture in an ever-increasing depth of study. The continuous study of Scripture on the same level or depth is insufficient to advance Christian maturity. This is not simply a pragmatic necessity but one reflected in the biblical foundations of education and in our concept of human salvation and sanctification. Educational theorists have developed taxonomies for knowing (cognitive learning domain),[5] valuing (affective learning domain),[6] and doing (psychomotor or behavioral learning domain)[7] that demonstrate an ever-increasing depth of learning, requiring a curriculum to facilitate the development of such depth (see Figure 11.4). Peter wrote, "Like newborn babies, crave pure spiritual milk, so that by it you may grow up in your salvation, now that you have tasted that the Lord is good" (1 Pet 2:2–3). Scripture frequently uses the metaphor of milk versus solid food or meat, often condemning the lack of growth in a congregation (1 Cor 3:2; Heb 5:12–13). But what if a congregation is guilty of not providing anything but milk? Would this not stifle Christian growth? Education programs that offer the same level of instruction in a variety of formats are not providing an ecology for growth since people could involve themselves in every avenue of instruction offered by the congregation yet never be fed in such a way as to grow spiritually.

Cognitive Taxonomy (Bloom)	Affective Taxonomy (Krathwohl, Bloom, Masia)	Psychomotor Taxonomy (Simpson)
I. Knowledge • Of specifics • Ways and means of dealing with specifics • Universals and abstractions in a field **II. Comprehension** • Translation • Interpretation • Extrapolation **III. Application** **IV. Analysis** • Elements • Relationships • Organizational Principles **V. Synthesis** • Production of a unique communication • Production of a plan, or proposed set of operations • derivation of a set of abstract relationships **VI. Evaluation** • Judgments in terms of internal criteria • Judgments in terms of external criteria	**I. Receiving (Attending)** • Awareness • Willing to receive • controlled or selected attention **II. Responding** • Acquiescence in responding • Willingness to respond • Satisfaction in response **III. Valuing** • Acceptance of a value • Preference for a value • Commitment **IV. Organization** • Conceptualization of a value • Organization of a value system **V. Characterization by a Value or Value Complex** • General set • Characterization	**I. Perception** • Sensory stimulation • Cue selection • Translation **II. Set** • Mental • Physical • Emotional **III. Guided Response** • Imitation • Trial and error **IV. Mechanism** (habitual) **V. Complex Overt Response** • Resolution of uncertainty • Automatic performance	

Figure 11.4: Learning Taxonomies

The third principle is that curriculum content must be owned by the congregation and/or institution. Curriculum is not something that can simply be purchased. When taken seriously, curriculum is the expression of the congregation's educational ministry and even culture. M. Harris described the church as God's curriculum for transforming lives into God's people.[8] When one grasps the truth that the church is the people of God, the development of a curriculum uniquely and specifically designed for a congregation becomes even more pressing. While congregations may share a common theological understanding of the nature of the church (see chapter 10), each one is inimitable in its individual character or path in adhering to the pattern described in Scripture; hence, no canned curriculum can suffice for the congregations. Within each congregation, a team (whether it be a committee, board, or task force) must be responsible for identifying learning objectives and assessing how well the congregation's curriculum content adheres to those objectives so as to give ownership of the teaching ministry to the congregation.

The fourth principle is that curriculum content must aid the student in building a relationship with Jesus Christ. Curriculum also possesses an often neglected personal dimension. While it is easy to regard curriculum content as nothing more than the selected topics of study being taught in sequence at an increasing depth, Christian curriculum ultimately aids at building a relationship with Jesus Christ. Relationships are between people, not things. The curriculum in many respects is aimed at introducing Jesus to the students and building a relationship with him throughout their lives. Thus, regardless of the subject matter, the curriculum must point individuals to Jesus Christ and help them establish a more lasting and meaningful relationship with him. While this principle is perhaps most readily applicable to the affective learning domain—personal piety and character—it is likewise necessary for the other domains. This can be done in several ways, such as referring to Jesus as a "who" and not a "what," drawing examples from the life of

Christ as it relates to the session's content, closing the class with a brief discussion on how the day's lesson aided their relationship with Jesus, and most obviously by studying the life of Jesus and Christology.

The fifth principle is that curriculum content is in part reliant on the work of the Holy Spirit. No matter how gifted the teacher, no matter how elaborate the facilities, no matter how sophisticated the instructional methodologies—none of these can replace the work of the Holy Spirit in the learning process. The Holy Spirit is at work in the life of the teacher as well as the student, so he has an integral part in the teaching-learning process. The selection, preparation, lesson planning, and presentation of the curriculum materials are thus in part reliant on the ever-present leading of the Holy Spirit in the life and ministry of the teacher—not to mention the work of the Holy Spirit in enlightening students about application (1 Cor 2:10–16). For this reason teachers should not only stay in tune with the lives of their students but also with their own spiritual lives. Furthermore, they should pray for the Holy Spirit's leading in their lesson preparation and be open to his influence in their teaching ministry.

Finally, the sixth principle is that curriculum content must be future focused. As Christians, we not only have a heritage and a history but a future as well—an eschatological perspective. Christian curriculum, and particularly its content, should not only strive to root the Christian individual and congregation in the historical heritage of our faith, including the biblical pattern for the Christian life, but it should also recognize the need to prepare Christians for the future. Christians must be prepared to address new questions and challenges to their faith, so the curriculum content must prepare them to know the essentials of the faith and to think theologically about life, culture, and spiritual issues. Curriculum would require Christians to study eschatology and to become familiar with the implications of adhering to a particular eschatological viewpoint. Such implications may include content on evangelism and world missions, seeking social justice and reform, personal piety in terms of relationships between Christians in their communities, and the impact of the congregation on its culture. Such a curriculum calls the Christian to view world history as *his*-story, asking where God is involved in contemporary world events and practicing theological reflection on history. Curriculum content should be formulated in anticipation of the future and what believers need to thrive in their spiritual lives.

The Place of the Scriptures in Scope and Sequence

In terms of curriculum, scope refers to the parameters of the curriculum, its limitations, while sequence refers to the specific order in which content will be addressed. A question unique to Christian educators is the relationship of the Bible to other subjects within the scope and sequence of the curriculum. This applies to every educational situation but most specifically to formal educational settings, such as a Christian school or institution of higher education (college, university, or seminary).[9] What is the Scripture's "place" in the scope and sequence?

The first possible response is that the Bible is part of the curriculum; it is one topic of study among others with all topics being treated equally (Figure 11.5a). This may be similar to some public schools or higher education institutions that offer "Bible as literature" or "religion" courses. In this instance the Bible is an interesting topic of study, but it is not given any special or unique attention more than any other topic.

The second option is that the Bible could be considered the whole curriculum, using the Bible to the omission and intentional exclusion of other topics (Figure 11.5b). This may be typical of Sunday schools, small groups, or a Bible institute curriculum. In this instance the Bible is regarded so highly that it leaves no room for the study of other subjects, even to the point of excluding them from the curriculum.

A third option is to integrate the Bible into every subject of study so that it is not an independent field of study. For example, biblical or theological insights may be included as one studies history, geography, literature, biology, and so forth; but the Bible would not receive separate attention (Figure 11.5c). At one time a noted Christian school curriculum publisher did not produce a Bible study module but included the Bible and other Christian materials in all their other curriculum materials, such as studying creation in science, biblical literary forms in English, and Christian missionary work in world history.

While all these potential places of the Bible in the scope and sequence of the curriculum have merit, for many evangelicals they are simply insufficient, particularly for institutions of Christian higher education. A preferred place of the Bible is as the interpreter of subjects *and* as the subject for interpretation (Figure 11.5d). In this curriculum Scripture is given due attention as an independent field of study, as in the first two options mentioned previously, and Scripture (along with theology) provides the proper perspective for the interpretation of the other fields of study, as would be the case in the third option.

This fourth option has all the strengths of the former three

Figure 11.5a-d: Bible in the Curriculum

while minimizing their innate weaknesses. It provides for the scriptural focus of Christian education's curriculum while providing due attention to other fields of study but from a biblical perspective.

THE LEARNING ENVIRONMENT
AND METHODS

Oftentimes, when one thinks of Christian education, class-room settings and instructional methods immediately come to mind. However, these items directly flow from the learning objectives and the curriculum design (see Figure 11.6). On a purely practical level, the "best" learning environment and instructional methodology is the one that most effectively and readily achieves the desired learning objective.

Figure 11.6: Objectives, Environments, and Methods

For example, is classroom lecture a poor teaching method? If the objective is the transfer of Bible content, lecture in a classroom setting is the preferred method. If the objective is building relationships with other Christians, lecture in a class-room setting is among the least preferred methods of instruction since building relationships favors a less formal environment and a method that facilitates dialogue between participants. The learning environment and the instructional methods are inter-related since one can detract from or contribute to the other's effectiveness. Excellent settings do not ensure learning without excellent instruction, nor do excellent settings make up for poor instruction. The best learning occurs when the learning environment and the instructional methodology coalesce into an optimal setting for learning. G. C. Newton commented when writing about the Holy Spirit and learning:

> Learning experiences such as Moses by the burning bush, Jews in the tabernacle or the temple, Jesus and his disciples at the Sea of Galilee, the early disciples in the upper room, Paul and Silas in the jail at Philippi,

or Paul and the philosophers in the midst of the Are-
opagus illustrate the importance of environment
related to the learning of truth. Both the teacher and
the learner cooperate with the Holy Spirit by strategi-
cally designing the physical and aesthetic aspects of a
learning environment to allow the Holy Spirit freedom
to accomplish his purposes.[10]

If the learning environment and instructional methods are
to facilitate spiritual formation so as to mature the individual
Christian (and the congregation) into Christlikeness, several
basic principles need to be considered regarding both. The overarching principle is that the educational priorities are the learning objectives and the students, not the learning settings and
methods. Once again, since the appropriateness of learning settings and methods are contingent on the learning objectives and
the learner, Christian educators *first* have to ask, "What learning
objectives are we trying to achieve with what set of students?"
and *then* ask, "What setting and methods are most conducive to
accomplishing these objectives?" With this in mind, three general principles can be made regarding learning environments
and instructional methodologies. While these principles may
seem to be purely practical, they are in fact derived from our
understanding of the church as the people of God, the context
of Christian education, and our understanding of human beings
as students.

*The first principle is that a congregation must have multi-
dimensional programs to achieve balance in spiritual maturity.*
Christian education is more than Sunday school. It is also more
than small groups, or just training, or just a church library, or
just discipleship, or just mentoring. Christian education that
is one-dimensional in its approach to programming on many
occasions undermines the effectiveness of the ministry. The
only way in which a single educational program could appropriately address all three objectives is in two instances. (1) The

objectives are minimized so as to allow one education program to address all three. For example, a congregation may only use small groups, but in order to use them exclusively as its education program, it minimizes its goals under the worldview objective, in effect lowering its expectations of cognitive learning. In this situation the small-group ministry may seemingly address all three objectives. (2) The single educational program in effect has three different kinds of curriculum functioning in it, so that it really has three educational programs under one label. For example, a congregation may have only the Sunday school as an education program, but if it had some elective classes that are content based, others that are more experientially based, and still other Sunday school classes focused on equipping individuals to serve, then the one education program would be addressing the three general learning objectives of the Christian education ministry. In effect, three different programs exist. The point is simply that congregations should not limit their educational programming to any single, exclusive ministry; rather, they should develop alternative educational programs to address more fully the learning objectives.

The second principle is that a congregation must have multilevel educational programs to ensure continued growth toward spiritual maturity. How does this differ from the above mentioned point? Just as a congregation should have more than one educational program, each program must progressively delve deeper into the learning objectives if continual maturation in Christ is to occur. As previously mentioned in reference to curriculum, the congregation's education program should progressively build toward more advanced levels of learning, moving through the learning taxonomies. This requires congregations intentionally to develop programs designed for some and not for others. D. Willard once commented, "I'm waiting to find a Sunday school that actually has prerequisites," calling for the need of multilevel educational programs in the congregation.[11] How deep would your congregation promote spiritual growth?

What ceilings are present in your educational programming? These questions are not just about how many opportunities for education you provide but about how they differ in terms of expectations of the teacher, the curriculum, and the students' role and participation.

The third principle is that a congregation must have multiple learning environments to support the learning objectives and students. Because of the multidimensional and multilevel education program, a variety of learning environments and instructional methodologies will naturally be employed to address the needs of these programs. For example, in terms of learning settings, classrooms may be regarded as more suitable for cognitive outcomes, whereas a small-group setting, such as a home, may be more suited for developing relationships in the affective domain, and "in the field" may be more advantageous for ministry training. Any learning environment, whether it is a classroom, home, or school, is a microcosm of the church. It is not an appendage or a separate entity; it must reflect the character of the church as the people of God.

Similarly, instructional methodologies vary depending on the learning objective. Without listing teaching methods, which is all too common in Christian education texts, D. Lambert provided one cautionary note:

> What is the absolute worst teaching strategy in the world? Lecture? Osmosis? Memorization? Exams with 100 multiple-choice questions? Long essay questions? Anarchy? The answer is . . . none of the above. The world's worst teaching method is the one you always use, no matter what it is or how well you do it. . . . If you don't know what your favorite teaching method is, ask your students—they'll know.[12]

Any instructional method, whether lecture, discussion, or self-study, must be used to promote the spiritual formation of the student. The key issue of method selection is one of "fit." Does the method fit the learning objective, the students (in terms of life need, developmental level, commitment), and the teacher's capability to use it. If these three basic criteria are met, then instruction should be effective and beneficial to all involved.

THE MEANS OF EVALUATION

Evaluation is in fact a simple matter if you have something to evaluate! If the Christian educator has: (1) a concrete understanding of the purpose and objectives of Christian education, (2) an expectation of the roles and relationships between the teacher and the learner, (3) the specific learning goals of the curriculum, and (4) a solid grasp of how each program in the congregation is designed to facilitate the accomplishment of all this, then evaluation becomes a simple matter of asking: "Are we doing it?" "How well are we doing it?" "Where are the occasions for commendations and the necessity of change?" Once again, evaluation is predicated on what you already have in place; and if it is there, evaluation is a simple matter. Christian educators must evaluate everything previously mentioned in this chapter if they are going to gain a comprehensive portrait of the ministry's achievement.

Many times the idea of evaluating Christian education in the church is met with resistance on two fronts. A theological reaction is, Is evaluation Christian? A practical reaction is, How can one evaluate a church ministry? Evaluation is not only a practical necessity for advancement of Christian education in the church (what some may call a necessary evil), but it is also a theological necessity for the people of God.[13]

Is Evaluation Christian?

If we evaluate Christian education, are we not ultimately judging those who volunteer to serve in programs and those who wrote curriculum? Evaluation is by no means contradictory to the injunction of Jesus, "Do not judge, or you too will be judged" (Matt 7:1). In fact, Jesus clarified his own statement in the following verse, voicing concern about an *unfair* and *unilateral* critical attitude: "For in the same way you judge others, you will be judged, and with the measure you use, it will be measured to you" (v. 2). In another instance Scripture calls Christians to evaluate and assess individuals' character and worthiness to serve as leaders.[14]

Christian educators can evaluate without being judgmental. This can be done by grounding our evaluation in our theology. Four theologically informed criteria can readily guide us in assessing Christian education in the church, whether it is a program, learning, or personnel: (1) Does it bring glory to God? (2) does it edify the body? (3) Is it compatible biblically and theologically with distinctively expressed Christian beliefs? Finally, (4) does it encourage and aid in the personal development of the individual? With such an approach, evaluation can be a very Christian activity, one beneficial to the individual participant.

In short, when evaluation is approached in a Christian manner, it is not a judgmental sentencing of individuals, curricula, programs, or ministries. Rather, if it is approached in a spirit of collaboration, and follows carefully determined, theologically informed criteria, it contributes to the spiritual maturing of the individual, the ministry, and the congregation.

How Can One Evaluate a Church Ministry?

As previously mentioned, with each of the items in this list of essential educational components is an implicit criterion. Such criteria may be stated in terms of the following questions: How well does the Christian education ministry

- fulfill its purpose of glorifying God?
- transform individuals into the likeness of Christ?
- fulfill its learning objectives (cognitive, affective, and behavioral)? What are the students learning?
- staff its programs with effective teachers? Are our teachers capable?

- promote positive relationships between teachers and students?
- focus its curriculum on Scripture?
- develop a multidimensional or multilevel program?
- utilize diverse instructional methodologies?

With such questions Christian educators can assess the relative strengths and weaknesses of their ministry, curriculum, programs, and personnel.[15] How can such an evaluation occur? From where does the information come? Should we rely on personal experience, anecdotal insights, and subjective feelings? While these are not to be excluded from assessment, a more systematic and formal method of evaluation would be beneficial to consider. Three general principles of evaluation help guide Christian educators in conducting reasonable and insightful evaluations.

First, listen to multiple voices in evaluation. Evaluation occurs on many levels: self-evaluation, subordinate evaluation, peer evaluation, and superior evaluation. No single voice provides the complete picture, but each voice is important. For example, if a teacher thinks he is incapable of doing his job well—even if his students love him, peers admire him, and superiors appreciate him—his self-evaluation must be taken seriously. In this instance sharing with the teacher the comments and evaluations of others may provide invaluable encouragement to the teacher. Hence, it is important to have more than one voice in evaluation and to listen to each voice with care.

Second, use both quantitative and qualitative means of evaluation. Quantitative assumes the evaluation is somehow numerical since quantities are given in terms of numbers. Qualitative assumes evaluation is to some extent verbal since it is given in terms of words. Using one or the other may provide good feedback, but using both provides a more comprehensive picture of what is occurring. For example, what if you give a survey (numerical data) that asks, "On a scale of 1 to 5, how intellectually challenging is this Sunday school class?" What does it means when the class responds with a 1.7? While the number should give a signal for follow-up, that is virtually all it does. By itself it cannot explain why this class gave such a low response. Christian educators may want to follow up the quantitative survey with a qualitative instrument, such as a focus group or interview that asks, "In what ways is the class intellectually challenging? How is it not? What would you change to improve its intellectual challenge?" This kind of information would enable Christian educators to gain a more thorough, accurate, and helpful picture of the classroom than just relying on one or the other set of insights.

Third, evaluation is not beneficial without follow-up as a pastor. Evaluation is worthless without rendering a decision based on it. Evaluation calls for either commendation, change, or at least affirmation. Without follow-up, evaluation is a meaningless exercise. However, as a minister, the Christian educator must follow up with a pastoral approach, especially when addressing individuals with less than desirable evaluations. For example, R. Wicks commented about evaluating an individual's performance in the congregation as an opportunity for spiritual growth:

> To grow spiritually, feedback from others is essential. We often back away from this process because we are frightened of what we might hear. Our anxiety is an indication once again that we have centered ourselves on something or someone less than God. It is a sign that we have set ourselves up to filter out the positive and emphasize the negative—to hear praise as a whisper and negative comments as thunder.[16]

Approaching evaluation from a Christian perspective that is conducted in a pastoral manner makes evaluation of Christian education an avenue for improving both the program and the people involved in it.

CONCLUSION

Christian education is an applied theological discipline. It is not systematic theology, but as a practical ministry of the church it is indeed theological at its core. As Christian educators, it may appear that we live in two worlds, one theological and one practical. However, through this book, and this chapter in particular, we have endeavored to demonstrate that these two worlds are not as distant and distinct as once thought. We are not called to be Christians and educators but Christian educators. Our field is not Christian and education; it is Christian education. By engaging the theological beliefs of the church as we develop our education ministry, we ensure that it will be a *Christian* education.

REFLECTION QUESTIONS

1. How well documented is your church's ministry of education? Where does it spell out its approach to the teaching ministry?
2. What implications does this theory have for teacher/sponsor training? How would you communicate this to them?
3. What implications does this theory have for how you administrate Christian education? How does your administration ensure that education is indeed Christian in your congregation?
4. Who is responsible for developing your congregation's approach to education? What routines or procedures should be developed to review continually your congregation's philosophy of education?

ENDNOTES

1   W. R. Yount, *Called to Teach: An Introduction to the Ministry of Teaching* (Nashville: B&H, 1999), 253–56.
2   R. T. Habermas, "Practical Dimensions of the Imago Dei," *Christian Education Journal* 13.2 (1993): 90–91.
3   Adapted from H. P. Colson and R. M. Rigdon, *Understanding Your Church's Curriculum* (Nashville: Broadman, 1969), 40–41.

4   D. C. Wyckoff, *Theory and Design of CE Curriculum* (Philadelphia: Westminster, 1961), 27–28.

5   B. S. Bloom, *Taxonomy of Educational Objectives: Book 1—Cognitive Domain* (White Plains, NY: Longman, 1956).

6   D. R. Krathwohl, B. S. Bloom, and B. B. Masia, *Taxonomy of Educational Objectives: Book 2—Affective Domain* (White Plains, NY: Longman, 1964).

7   E. J. Simpson, *The Classification of Educational Objectives, Psychomotor Domain* (Champaign-Urbana, IL: University of Illinois, 1966).

8   M. Harris, *Fashion Me a People: Curriculum in the Church* (Louisville, KY: Westminster/John Knox, 1989).

9   See J. R. Estep Jr., "The Church and College in Culture: A Paradigm for Faith-Learning in the Bible College Curriculum," *Stone-Campbell Journal* (Fall 1999): 191–208.

10 G. C. Newton, "Holy Spirit," in *Evangelical Dictionary of Christian Education*, ed. M. Anthony (Grand Rapids: Baker, 2001): 341.

11 D. Willard, Plenary Address, North American Professors of Christian Education annual meeting (Orlando, FL), October 2004.

12 D. Lambert, *Teaching That Makes a Difference* (Grand Rapids: Zondervan, 2004), 137.

13 See J. R. Estep Jr., "Conducting Performance Reviews," in *Management Essentials for Christian Ministries,* ed. M. Anthony and J. Estep Jr. (Nashville: B&H, 2005), 389–90, for a comprehensive discussion of the theology of assessment.

14 Luke 7:43; 1 Cor 5:12; 1 Tim 3:1–13; Titus 1:5–9; 1 Pet 5:1–4.

15 See Estep, "Conducting Performance Reviews," 387–410, and M. Simpson, "Evaluating the Effectiveness of Programs," in *Management Essentials for Christian Ministries*, 411–26.

16 R. J. Wicks, "Spirituality and Ministry," *The Princeton Theological Bulletin* 12 (1991): 24.

Conclusion:
The Christian Educator
and Theology

James Riley Estep Jr.

F or the last few decades, Christian education has been a
discipline with an identity crisis. Left unresolved, this
identity crisis has caused Christian education to stall
as a movement. As mentioned in chapter 2, numerous recognized authorities in the Christian education community, such
as Melchert, Westerhoff, Ward, and Hull, have raised the question of the exact nature, function, and direction of education
in the church. Even more recently, the North American Professors of Christian Education (NAPCE), the largest association
of evangelical Christian educators in the world, engaged in a
healthy exchange of ideas regarding the trajectory of Christian
education. One reason for engaging in the discussion was the
fragmentation of Christian education into what is now a con-
glomeration of more specialized educational ministries, such
as children or youth ministry, adult discipleship, family life, or
Christian spiritual formation. In fact, NAPCE even discussed
renaming the association in light of such debates, but after several deliberations and polls of its membership, no consensus on
a new name could be reached. Contemporary Christian education exists in a fluid state, lacking definitive direction or substance.

Christian education is at this moment in a period of definition, or perhaps redefinition, as it seeks a new identity and rele-

vant direction for the twenty-first century. As in any identity crisis, contemporary Christian educators have appealed to various elements to find an answer or indication that may resolve the crisis. Their search for identity indicators seems to have found insight from four elements: theory, task, target, and theology. While each of these four qualifiers provides its own direction for Christian educators, they are not inherently contradictory. Christian educators have chosen on occasion to grant primacy to one element over the others in determining the nature and direction of Christian education. This chapter will endeavor to demonstrate how these elements can be combined, with an emphasis on theology, to provide identity for Christian education.

WHAT IS CHRISTIAN EDUCATION?

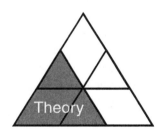

Christian Education as Theory

Essentially, education is an application of social science theories regarding learning, development, and behavior, so it is a social science. Some Christian educators have argued that immersing Christian education into a social science *framework* will provide a suitable identity for education. For example, J. M. Lee advocated that Christian education is like any other education, so it should draw direction and identity from the social sciences upon which he based his approach.[1] While his approach has found limited acceptance in the Christian education community, it nonetheless demonstrates one way in which educators could endeavor to define Christian education in terms of its theoretical bases—for example, developmental theories, learning theories, even the history of Christian education as part of education's basic context.

Christian Education as Task

What is the primary *function* of Christian education? What activity is principally associated with Christian education? Some Christian educators seek to define Christian education by its essential task: the teaching

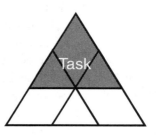

ministry. In this instance it is the *function* of Christian education that provides its identity. Just as the task of preaching often defines the identity of the senior pastor, so also the Christian educator's identity may be identified with the act of teaching. This approach is reflected in the titles of many books and courses in higher education that emphasize teaching as the principal task of the Christian educator. For example, both W. R. Yount's exceptional book *The Teaching Ministry of the Church*[2] and the typical Christian education course required of all ministry majors entitled "Creative Bible Teaching" emphasize the primacy of teaching in understanding the nature of education ministry. While it does not exclude the other elements, primacy is given to the function of teaching as a means of finding identity.

Christian Education as Target

What is the *focus* of Christian education? Many contemporary ministers of education place their *focus* on Christian or spiritual formation. They believe that we have Christian education to provide an

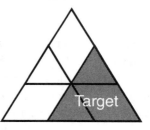

ecology wherein Christians can mature into full Christlikeness through the educational process. This approach to education is readily seen in the plethora of spiritual formation programs in many Christian colleges and seminaries. Many of these conceive of Christian education as the means of facilitating the spiritual formation process. An example of this focus is J. Wilhoit's insightful *Spiritual Formation as if the Church Mattered.*[3]

Hence, Christian educators have sought to identify Christian education through its theoretical frameworks, its task of teaching, and its target of facilitating spiritual formation in believers. In fact, since these are not mutually exclusive, their interplay in the literature of Christian education is quite prevalent—for example, how developmental theories inform the process of spiritual formation, how teaching must be for the purpose of facilitating spiritual formation, or how learning theories relate to teaching methodologies. The interrelatedness of theories, teaching, and formation is virtually self-evident. However, not one of these by itself, or even all three combined, would be sufficient in providing direction for a *distinctively* Christian education. Any variety of approaches to education would utilize theoretical frameworks and exemplify teaching as its principle task, and any religious group would advocate the advancement of spirituality or an individual-corporate transformation. Only when these elements are integrated *with* a theological core are they sufficient for identifying Christian education. Therefore, theology is *the* essential element for an education that is Christian.

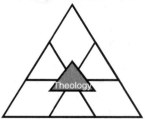

Theology as the Foundation of Christian Education

What is the core essential for Christian education? It is a theological *foundation* that can both inform and unite the theory, task, and target dimensions of Christian education's identity. Yes, for Christian education to be "educational," it requires the theories, teaching task, and target; but for Christian education to be "Christian," it requires a theological determinant with a profound influence in the life and ministry of the Christian educator.

The theories, task, and target may interact and inform one another to some extent, but theology is ultimately the core determinant of Christian education that informs all of them. For example, theology explains what is Christian about spiritual formation, as opposed to the spiritualities of other religions; it also provides the content for the task of teaching since it is what we teach. Theology likewise interacts with theories to remind the Christian educator that people are God's image bearers, not simply the sum of their developmental parts. As such, Christian education is a theological discipline that draws insight from social science theory to develop an approach toward facilitating spiritual formation through teaching.

WHAT ABOUT THE CHRISTIAN EDUCATOR?

Christian education is not a disembodied entity that exists apart from men and women called to serve as Christian educators. What does this model of Christian education call us to be? How does all this impact our understanding of the role of the Christian  educator? First, Christian educators must be not only students of theology but *theologians* as well. When Christian educators fail to study theology continually, they endanger their ministries by losing their theological moorings and placing their foundations in something other than the Word of God. Being students of theology enables Christian educators to think theologically about the theoretical foundations, the content of their teaching, and the theological necessity of being a pastor to those maturing in their faith. We must also seek to answer educational questions with more than "educational" answers but respond with our theological voice loudly and clearly heard. Theology and Christian educators must be constant allies in ministry.

Christian educators are *theoreticians* in that they develop a theologically informed approach to the education ministry. Christian educators must think integratively, uniting theology and the social sciences into a seamless approach to education in the church. Without the social sciences, education may be Christian but not necessarily educational. Christian educators must make appropriate use of developmental, learning, and organizational theories so as to enhance the education ministry's effectiveness. Christian educators engage in practical theology, developing a tangible system of education implications from their theological beliefs, informed by the social science theories that are part of the education community.

Christian educators are *teachers*. Whether Christian educators teach Scripture, doctrine, ethics, church history, or even practical Christian living, all of it is ultimately defined within a theological context. Our principle task or expression of our pastoral call is to teach. Just as we give theology and the social sciences their due attention, we must also be attentive to the task of teaching. Sacrilege is not limited to the theology we espouse, for it may likewise be the result of teaching sacred truth in an inappropriate or ineffective manner. For example, a church may embrace an evangelical understanding of salvation and voice a strong commitment to evangelism. But if it intentionally or unwittingly uses an ineffective method of outreach (such as aggressive confrontation), is it not compromising its beliefs through its practices? Using appropriate teaching methods is more than just a practical concern and more than a matter of creativity or entertainment. It takes into consideration the preservation and presentation of the truth of Scripture. We must be the teachers of the church as we also teach others to teach.

Christian educators are also *trainers*. There is more to Christian education than teaching and more to being a teacher than teaching. Teaching that is "Christian" is concerned with the transformation of the Christian into a Christlike citizen of the kingdom of God. Christian education aims to engage in spiritual formation as the process leading toward becoming a mature follower of Jesus Christ. While this process can be engaged in the classroom and through teaching, it is also engaged through one-on-one interaction, mentoring, accountability, and spiritual guidance. Thus, Christian educators are those who train others in the life of the Spirit, leading them to a more complete and full spirituality. As trainers of others, Christian educators assume responsibility for the spiritual life of those they instruct and provide a more comprehensive ecology for spiritual growth. If we perceive ourselves as just theologians, theoreticians, and teachers, then we miss the human element of dealing with real people in real life situations. The role of trainer calls us to active engagement within the ministry of spiritual formation.

Christian education is a multifaceted discipline, with theology at its center, informing every aspect of the ministry. The role of Christian educators is likewise multifaceted, but the theologian informs all the other roles. Above all, theology reminds us that regardless of the form of Christian education ministry in which we serve, we are called by God into his service as pastors of the church, servants of his kingdom, and students of his Word.

---

1 See J. M. Lee's trilogy on the subject, *The Shape of Religious Instruction* (1971), *The Flow of Religious Instruction* (1973), and *The Content of Religious Instruction* (1985), all published by Religious Education Press (Birmingham, AL).
2 W. R. Yount, *Teaching Ministry of the Church*, 2nd ed. (Nashville: B&H, 2008).
3 J. Wilhoit, *Spiritual Formation as if the Church Mattered* (Grand Rapids: Baker, 2008).

Selected Bibliography

Allison, Gregg R. *Getting Deep: Understand What You Believe about God and Why.* Nashville: B&H, 2001.

_____. *Jesusology: Understand What You Believe about Jesus and Why.* Nashville: B&H, 2005.

_____. "The Protestant Doctrine of the Perspicuity of Scripture: A Reformulation on the Basis of Biblical Teaching." Ph.D. diss., Trinity Evangelical Divinity School, Illinois, 1995.

Anthony, Michael J., ed. *Evangelical Dictionary of Christian Education.* Grand Rapids: Baker, 2001.

Anthony, Michael J., and Warren S. Benson. *Exploring the History and Philosophy of Christian Education.* Grand Rapids: Kregel, 2003.

Astley, Jeff, ed. *Theological Perspectives on Christian Formation.* Grand Rapids: Eerdmans, 1996.

Berkhof, Louis. *Systematic Theology.* Grand Rapids: Eerdmans, 1968.

Burgess, Harold W. *An Invitation to Religious Education.* Birmingham, AL: Religious Education Press, 1975.

_____. *Models of Religious Education.* Wheaton, IL: Victor, 1996.

Boys, Mary C. *Educating in Faith.* New York: Harper & Row, 1989.

Clark, Robert E., ed. *Christian Education: Foundations for the Future.* Chicago: Moody, 1991.

Crenshaw, James A. *Education in Ancient Israel.* New York: Doubleday, 1998.

Cully, Iris V., and Kendig Brubaker Cully, eds. *Harper's Encyclopedia of Religious Education.* San Francisco: Harper & Row, 1990.

Downs, Perry G. *Teaching for Spiritual Growth.* Grand Rapids: Zondervan, 1994.

Elias, John L. *Psychology and Religious Education.* Malabar, FL: Robert E. Krieger, 1990.

Eldridge, Daryl, ed. *The Teaching Ministry of the Church.* Nashville: B&H, 1995.

Elwell, Walter A., ed. *The Evangelical Dictionary of Theology.* Grand Rapids: Baker, 1984.

Erickson, Millard J. *Christian Theology.* Grand Rapids: Baker, 1983.

_____. *God in Three Persons: A Contemporary Interpretation of the Trinity.* Grand Rapids: Baker, 1995.

Estep, James Riley, Jr. "Philosophers, Scribes, Rhetors . . . and Paul? The Educational Background of the New Testament." *Christian Education Journal*, Series 3, 2.1 (2005): 30–47.

Estep, James Riley, Jr., ed. *CE: The Heritage of Christian Education.* Joplin, MO: College Press, 2003.

Estes, Daniel, J. *Hear My Son: Teaching and Learning in Proverbs.* Downers Grove, IL: InterVarsity, 1997.

Ferré, Nels F. S. *A Theology for Christian Education.* Philadelphia: Westminster, 1967.

Gibbs, Eugene, ed. *Reader in Christian Education: Foundations and Basic Perspectives.* Grand Rapids: Baker, 1992.

Griggs, Donald L. "The Bible: From Neglected Book to Primary Text." *Religious Education* 85.2 (1990): 246–54.

Grudem, Wayne. *Systematic Theology: An Introduction to Biblical Doctrine.* Grand Rapids: Zondervan, 1994.

Habermas, Ronald T. "Practical Dimensions of the Imago Dei." *Christian Education Journal,* 13.2 (1993): 83–92.

Harkness, Allan G. "Intergenerational Education for an Intergenerational Church?" *Religious Education* 93.4 (1998): 431–47.

Harris, Maria. *Fashion Me a People: Curriculum in the Church.* Louisville, KY: Westminster/John Knox, 1989.

Hodge, Charles. *Systematic Theology.* Grand Rapids: Eerdmans, 1995.

Hodgson, Peter C. *God's Wisdom: Toward a Theology of Education.* Louisville, KY: Westminster/John Knox, 1999.

Hull, John M. "What Is Theology of Education?" *Scottish Journal of Theology* 30 (1977): 20–31.

Husbands, Mark, and Daniel J. Treier, eds. *The Community of the Word: Toward an Evangelical Ecclesiology.* Downers Grove, IL: InterVarsity, 2005.

Johnson, Alan F., and Robert E. Webber. *What Christians Believe: A Biblical and Historical Summary.* Grand Rapids: Zondervan Academic, 1989.

Knight, George R. *Philosophy and Education.* 3rd edition. Berrien Springs, MI: Andrews University Press, 1998.

————. "The Scriptures Were Written for Our Instruction." *Journal of the Evangelical Theological Society,* 39.1 (1996): 31–42.

Lambert, Dan. *Teaching that Makes a Difference.* Grand Rapids: Zondervan, 2004.

LeBar, Lois. *Education That Is Christian.* Old Tappan, NJ: Fleming H. Revell, 1981.

Lee, James Michael. *The Content of Religious Instruction.* Birmingham, AL: Religious Education Press, 1985.

———— *The Flow of Religious Instruction.* Birmingham, AL: Religious Education Press, 1973.

———— *The Shape of Religious Instruction.* Birmingham, AL: Religious Education Press, 1971.

Macquarrie, John. *Principles of Christian Theology.* New York: Charles Scribner's Sons, 1977.

Melchert, Charles F. *Wise Teaching: Biblical Wisdom and Educational Ministry.* Harrisburg, PA: Trinity Press International, 1998.

Miller, Randolph Crump, ed. *Theologies of Religious Education.* Birmingham, AL: Religious Education Press, 1995.

Morgan, Donn. *The Making of the Sage: Biblical Wisdom and Contemporary Culture.* Harrisburg, PA: Trinity Press International, 2002.

Newell, Edward J. *Education Has Nothing to Do with Theology: James Michael Lee's Social Science Religious Instruction.* Princeton Theological Monograph Series 61. Eugene, OR: Pickwick, 2006.

Osborne, Grant. *The Hermeneutical Spiral: A Comprehensive Introduction to Biblical Interpretation,* rev. and exp. ed. Downers Grove, IL: IVP Academic, 2006.

Pazmino, Robert W. *By What Authority Do We Teach?* Grand Rapids: Baker, 1994.

_____. *God Our Teacher.* Grand Rapids: Baker, 2001.

_____. *Principles and Practices of Christian Education.* Grand Rapids: Baker, 1992.

Plantinga, Cornelius Jr. *Not the Way It's Supposed to Be: A Breviary of Sin.* Grand Rapids: Eerdmans, 1995.

Plueddemann, James E. "Do We Teach the Bible or Do We Teach Students?" *Christian Education Journal,* 10.1 (1994): 73–81.

Richards, Lawrence O., and Gary Bredfeldt. *Creative Bible Teaching,* rev. and exp. ed. Chicago: Moody, 1998.

Santrock, John W. *Educational Psychology* (Illinois Edition). Boston: McGraw-Hill, 1990.

Seymour, Jack L. "The Clue to Christian Religious Education: Uniting Theology and Education." *Religious Education* 99.3 (2004): 272–86.

Stonehouse, Catherine. *Joining Children on the Spiritual Journey.* Grand Rapids: Baker, 1998.

Tyler, Ronald L. "First Corinthians 4:6 and Hellenistic Pedagogy." *Catholic Bible Quarterly* 60.1 (1998): 97–103.

Warfield, Benjamin B. *Studies in Theology.* Edinburgh: The Banner of Truth, 1932.

Westerhoff, John. "Discipline in Crisis." *Religious Education* 74.1 (1969): 7–15.

Wilhoit, James C. *Spiritual Formation as if the Church Mattered.* Grand Rapids: Baker, 2008.

Wright, H. Norman. "Theology as the Basis for Christian Education." *Bibliotheca Sacra* 119.510 (1971): 142–47.

Wyckoff, D. Campbell. "Theology and Education in the Twentieth Century," *Christian Education Journal* 15.3 (1995): 12–26.

_____. *Theory and Design of CE Curriculum.* Philadelphia: Westminster, 1961.

Yount, William R. *Called to Teach: An Introduction to the Ministry of Teaching.* Nashville: B&H, 1999.

_____. *Created to Learn.* Nashville: B&H, 1996.

_____. *Teaching Ministry of the Church.* 2nd ed. Nashville: B&H, 2008.

Zuck, Roy B. *Teaching as Jesus Taught.* Grand Rapids: Baker, 1995.

_____. *Teaching as Paul Taught.* Grand Rapids: Baker, 1998.

Name Index

Subject Index

Scripture Index

A Theology for Christian Education